Labour Migration and Trafficking in Southeas

CW00495861

Since the signing of the UN Trafficking Protocol, anti-trafficking laws, policies and other initiatives have been implemented at the local, national and regional levels. These activities have received little scholarly attention. This volume aims to begin to fill this gap by documenting the micro-processes through which an anti-trafficking framework has been translated, implemented and resisted in mainland and island Southeast Asia. The detailed ethnographic accounts in this collection examine the everyday practices of the diverse range of actors involved in trafficking-like practices and in anti-trafficking initiatives. In demonstrating how the anti-trafficking framework has become influential – and even over-determining – in some border sites and yet remains mostly irrelevant in others, the chapters in this collection explore the complex connections between labour migration, migrant smuggling and human trafficking.

Michele Ford is Associate Professor of Indonesian Studies at the University of Sydney, where she teaches and researches about social activism and human rights in Southeast Asia.

Lenore Lyons is an Honorary Professor in the Department of Indonesian Studies at the University of Sydney.

Willem van Schendel is Professor in the Department of Anthropology and Sociology at the University of Amsterdam.

Routledge Contemporary Southeast Asia Series

Labour Migration and Human Trafficking in Southeast Asia

Critical perspectives

**Edited by
Michele Ford, Lenore Lyons and
Willem van Schendel**

Routledge
Taylor & Francis Group

LONDON AND NEW YORK

First published 2012
by Routledge
2 Park Square, Milton Park, Abingdon, Oxfordshire OX14 4RN

Simultaneously published in the USA and Canada
by Routledge
711 Third Avenue, New York, NY 10017
First issued in paperback 2014
Routledge is an imprint of the Taylor & Francis Group, an informa business

British Library Cataloguing in Publication Data
A catalogue record for this book is available from the British Library

Library of Congress Cataloging-in-Publication Data
A catalog record for this book has been requested

ISBN 978–0–415–66563–6 (hbk)
ISBN 978–1–138–81585–8 (pbk)
ISBN 978–0–203–12153–5 (ebk)
Typeset in Times New Roman
by Swales & Willis Ltd, Exeter, Devon

Contents

Illustrations

Figures

Table

Contributors

Michael Eilenberg is Assistant Professor at the Section for Anthropology and Ethnography at Aarhus University. His research is based on repeat field visits to Indonesia and Malaysia from 2002 and deals with the particular social and political dynamics taking place along the Indonesian–Malaysian border on the island of Borneo. His book based on this research, *At the Edge of States* (KITLV Press 2011), deals with the dynamics of state formation in Southeast Asian borderlands. His recent articles have appeared in *Asia Pacific Viewpoint, South East Asia Research, Review of Indonesian and Malaysian Affairs* and *Modern Asian Studies*.

Nicholas Farrelly is a Southeast Asia specialist in the College of Asia and the Pacific at the Australian National University. He earned master's and doctoral degrees at Balliol College, Oxford, where he was a Rhodes scholar. His doctoral research focused on the borderlands where China, India and Burma meet. Over the past decade Nicholas has also undertaken regular field research along the Burma–Thailand border. His research has been published in *Critical Asian Studies, Contemporary South Asia* and *Asian Studies Review*, among other academic journals. In 2006 he co-founded New Mandala, a prominent website on Southeast Asian politics and societies.

Michele Ford is Associate Professor in the Department of Indonesian Studies at the University of Sydney. Her research focuses on the Indonesian labour movement and organized labour's responses to temporary labour migration in East and Southeast Asia. She is the author of *Workers and Intellectuals: NGOs, Trade Unions and the Indonesian Labour Movement* (NUS/Hawaii/KITLV 2009) and co-editor of *Women and Work in Indonesia* (Routledge 2008); *Women and Labour Organizing in Asia: Diversity, Autonomy and Activism* (Routledge 2008); *Indonesia Beyond the Water's Edge: Managing an Archipelagic State* (ISEAS 2009); and *Men and Masculinities in Southeast Asia* (Routledge 2012).

Lenore Lyons is Honorary Professor with the Department of Indonesian Studies at the University of Sydney. She is the author of *A State of Ambivalence: The Feminist Movement in Singapore* (Brill Academic Publishers 2004) and co-editor of *Men and Masculinities in Southeast Asia* (Routledge 2012) with

Michele Ford. She recently completed a major study of citizenship, identity and sovereignty in the Riau Islands of Indonesia with Michele Ford, and a study of civil society activism in relation to the labour and human rights of female domestic workers in Singapore and Indonesia. Her work has appeared in a number of edited collections as well as journals including *Women's Studies Quarterly*, *International Feminist Journal of Politics*, *Critical Asian Studies*, *Asian Studies Review*, *Asia Pacific Viewpoint* and *Citizenship Studies*.

Sverre Molland teaches Development Studies in the Geography Department at the Australian National University. Dr Molland's research focuses on development aid and mobility in relation to discourses of prostitution, labour migration and human trafficking in Mainland Southeast Asia. He has carried out fieldwork in Laos and Thailand, where he has previously worked as a development consultant and project advisor for a UN-initiated anti-trafficking programme. His current research explores attempts to monitor supply chains and the emergent policy focus on 'safe migration' in the Asia-Pacific. His recent publications include *The Perfect Business? Anti-trafficking and the Sex Trade along the Mekong* (University of Hawai'i Press in press).

Wayne Palmer is a PhD candidate in the Department of Indonesian Studies at the University of Sydney. His research focuses on how Indonesian Government officials manage illegality in the state migration programme. Wayne won the University Medal for an Honours thesis on public–private partnerships between the Indonesian consulate and migrant worker employment agencies in Hong Kong and is a recipient of the Prime Minister's Australia Asia Endeavour Award. He is co-editor with Michele Ford of a special edition of *Inside Indonesia*, entitled 'Leaving Indonesia' (2010).

Larissa Sandy is a Vice Chancellor's Postdoctoral Fellow with the Law School at Flinders University. She conducted her doctoral research with sex workers in Cambodia and was a research analyst at the Australian Institute of Criminology on the Trafficking in Persons Project. She is author of the forthcoming book, *Women and Sex Work in Cambodia* (Routledge). Her research interests include sex work in the Asia-Pacific region, women's agency, sex work regulations, labour migration and forced migration, debt bondage and contract labour, and gender and sexuality.

Willem van Schendel is Professor of Modern Asian History at the University of Amsterdam and Senior Research Fellow at the International Institute of Social History. He is the author of numerous articles, chapters and books, including: *Global Blue: Indigo and Espionage in Colonial Bengal* (University Press, Dhaka 2006, with Pierre-Paul Darrac); *The Bengal Borderland: Beyond State and Nation in South Asia* (Anthem Press 2005); *Illicit Flows and Criminal Things: States, Borders, and the Other Side of Globalization* (Bloomington: Indiana University Press 2005, ed., with Itty Abraham); and *The Chittagong Hill Tracts: Living in a Borderland* (White Lotus 2000, with Wolfgang Mey and Aditya Kumar Dewan).

Jorge Tigno has been with the Faculty of Political Science at the University of the Philippines in Diliman since 1989. He has conducted research and published on elections and political parties and strengthening Philippine democratic institutions; changing migrant identities; the nexus between human trafficking and human security; the impacts of overseas Filipino labour migration on local communities in the Philippines; and the politics of multiculturalism in Asia. His most recent edited work is entitled *State, Politics and Nationalism Beyond Borders: Changing Dynamics in Filipino Overseas Migration* published by the Philippine Social Science Council in 2009.

Zhang Juan is a Postdoctoral Fellow at the Asia Research Institute of the National University of Singapore. Dr Zhang's research interests are borders and boundary-making, contemporary Chinese subjectivity, and everyday practices in post-socialist conditions. Her doctoral research reflected on the ways in which memory politics, individual practices, flexible strategies and post-socialist governmentality are intertwined in the local business world in post-reform China. She has published on Chinese nationalism, transnationalism, as well as migrant social spaces in Singapore.

Acknowledgements

Initial versions of the majority of the papers in this volume were commissioned for presentation at a workshop 'Labour Migration and Trafficking: Policy Making at the Border' in Kuala Lumpur, Malaysia, in 2009. The workshop, which was co-convened by the editors, was initiated as part of an Australian Research Council International Linkage Project (LX0882882) and supported financially by the Australia Netherlands Research Collaboration (ANRC), the Centre for Asia-Pacific Social Transformation Studies (CAPSTRANS) at the University of Wollongong, Asian Studies in Amsterdam (ASiA) at the University of Amsterdam and the Institute for Ethnic Studies (KITA) at the University Kebangsaan Malaysia. We would particularly like to thank Professor Shamsul AB of KITA and his staff, particularly Dr Ong Puay Liu, who ensured that the workshop was a great success.

The papers presented at the workshop challenged the current preoccupation with the influence of international agencies and non-governmental organizations on state policy and practice in efforts to address human trafficking. In demonstrating how the anti-trafficking framework has become influential in some border sites and yet remains mostly irrelevant in others, the workshop participants examined the intersections between state agents and other kinds of political authority in Southeast Asia's multiple borderlands. Workshop participants were chosen to ensure a wide representation of countries in mainland and insular Southeast Asia, as well as border sites in South Asia, Australia and the Pacific. Papers were presented by Rochelle Ball, Michael Eilenberg, Michele Ford and Lenore Lyons, Nurul Ilmi Idrus, Azizah Kassim, Amarjit Kaur, Gum Khong and Julia Marip (from the Kachin Women's Association Thailand), Ma Khin Mar Mar Kyi, Sverre Molland, Zarina Othman, Wayne Palmer, Marie Segrave, Malini Sur, Willem van Schendel, Sallie Yea and Zhang Juan. Paper givers were provided with feedback from expert discussants: Itty Abraham, Shapan Adnan, Luciana Campello Ribeiro de Almeida, Ruhanas Harun, Barak Kalir, Kamal Sadiq, Riwanto Tirtosudarmo and Diana Wong.

A policy roundtable was held in the last session of the workshop. The roundtable brought together Australian, Dutch and Southeast Asian policy-makers and NGO representatives. It provided an opportunity to discuss some of the key challenges they currently face in managing the complex issues associated with temporary labour migration flows. Speakers were present for the entire workshop and had the opportunity to contribute to the ongoing debate and discussion as it evolved over the three days. The roundtable speakers were Alex Ong, Malaysian Coordinator of the Indonesian NGO Migrant Care; Marjan Wijers, an independent scholar from the Netherlands who has had a long-term role in NGO activism and research on gender and anti-trafficking issues in Europe; Fareeha Ibrahim, a former UN consultant working on gender and development; and Rebecca Napier-Moore, from the Global Alliance Against Trafficking in Women.

Coordinating a large international collaborative project and publication such as this has necessitated a considerable degree of administrative support. A special note of thanks goes to Margaret Hanlon at the University of Wollongong who provided administrative and research assistance to the project over a three-year period, and to Helen McMartin of the ANRC. We would also like to thank Nicola Piper and Xiang Biao for their feedback on the manuscript; Robert Cribb for the production of our maps; Henri Ismail from Poros Photos for permission to use the cover image (which shows a migrant worker deported from Malaysia in the holding centre in Tanjung Pinang); and Kumiko Kawashima for her work on the index. Michele Ford would like to thank her students, Wayne and Luciana, for their enthusiasm for this project. Lenore Lyons would like to thank colleagues at the University of Wollongong, the University of Western Australia, and the University of Sydney where she was based at different times throughout its duration. Willem van Schendel would like to thank his colleagues at the University of Amsterdam, the International Institute of Social History and the International Institute of Asian Studies.

Michele Ford, University of Sydney
Lenore Lyons, University of Sydney
Willem van Schendel, University of Amsterdam
June 2011

Labour migration and human trafficking

An introduction

Michele Ford, Lenore Lyons and
Willem van Schendel

All over the world human trafficking has become a hot issue. As a result, billions of dollars are being spent on counter-trafficking initiatives. But are they necessary and do they work? We still know little about the scale and incidence of human trafficking and have little evidence that counter-trafficking programmes are effective (Chuang 2006a: 157). In fact, what critical research shows is that these projects are being used to justify state intervention in the lives of migrants and citizens with the aim of 'protecting' the state from illegal migration, terrorism and organized crime (Turnbull 1999; Chapkis 2003; GAATW 2007; Grewcock 2007; Nieuwenhuys and Pecoud 2007). There is even evidence to suggest that rather than reducing the incidence of trafficking, counter-trafficking initiatives and laws can in fact lead to its increase (Grewcock 2003; Fergus 2005; Kempadoo *et al*. 2005; Marshall and Thatun 2005).

Anti-trafficking initiatives grew exponentially since the United Nations passed the UN Protocol to Prevent, Suppress and Punish Trafficking in Persons, Especially Women and Children (hereafter the UN Trafficking Protocol) in 2000.[1] This book contributes to the growing critique of the anti-trafficking agenda by exploring the ways in which the UN Trafficking Protocol has been taken up by policy-makers, non-governmental organizations and international agencies in Southeast Asia. This region is recognized internationally as a 'hotspot' for human trafficking, but there have been few attempts to critically evaluate the vast numbers of anti-trafficking programmes and projects or counter-trafficking laws and regulations in operation in the region. Instead, much of the literature has focused on documenting the role that international agencies and NGOs have played in counter-trafficking programmes; the development of anti-trafficking laws and policies; or empirical studies of human trafficking cases and/or trends.[2] In order to address this gap, the authors in this collection focus their attention at the local level and pay careful, systematic attention to the ways that anti-trafficking initiatives have been taken up and translated by different stakeholders at different scales. As these cases show, anti-trafficking initiatives include rescue and repatriation programmes for 'victims'; education programmes about the dangerous habits of smugglers and traffickers; development programmes aimed at improving economic livelihoods in 'hotspots'; and international and bilateral policing efforts aimed at securing borders and arresting people smugglers and traffickers. Associated with the rise of a strong discourse of transnational crime prevention, these initiatives have been accompanied by numerous anti-trafficking laws and protocols passed at local, national and regional levels.

The analyses in this volume reveal the contestations that have occurred over the meaning of 'human trafficking' and the challenges that policy-makers, regulators and activists face in their attempts to implement the recommendations outlined in the Trafficking Protocol. Examining the ways in which law-makers respond to a range of internal and external pressures, the chapters draw our attention to the ways in which international counter-trafficking policy agendas are translated and enacted locally, and to the (unintended) consequences that the involvement of international aid agencies and donors has had on the lives of migrant workers. In doing so, this volume aims to fill a significant lacuna in our understanding of the processes through which the anti-trafficking framework has been translated, implemented and resisted in mainland and island Southeast Asia.[3]

The global anti-trafficking effort

Since the signing of the Trafficking Protocol in 2000, there has been intense interest in combating what many commentators have described as this 'most heinous of crimes'. This interest has given rise to a global anti-trafficking effort involving a diversity of organizations, networks and agencies which vary in size, scale, influence and ideology – a network that includes national police and immigration authorities, transnational crime prevention organizations, religious groups, feminist groups, migrant worker organizations, trade unions, human rights organizations and development aid agencies. The enormous scale of the anti-trafficking effort, as evidenced by the sheer numbers and variety of new organizations, projects and protocols that have emerged in the decade after the signing of the Trafficking Protocol, is unprecedented. As Fiona David (2009) notes, in 1998, there were only a handful of counter-trafficking projects in Southeast Asia, and Cambodia and Thailand were the only countries with laws that mentioned the word 'trafficking'. Just ten years later, nine of the ten ASEAN countries had anti-trafficking laws and there were hundreds of anti-trafficking programmes and organizations, requiring a concerted effort at national and regional coordination.

This exponential growth in regional counter-trafficking initiatives reflects the emergence of an explicit link between border control and development agendas present in the regional and bilateral programmes of many aid donors, including the United States, members of the European Union and Australia. Most influential, however, has been the United States, which has taken a particularly proactive foreign policy stance in relation to monitoring and combating human trafficking since the mid-1990s. The US launched its 'three Ps approach' – 'punish traffickers, protect victims, and prevent trafficking from occurring' – which subsequently became a central component of its initial proposal to the UN for the establishment of a trafficking protocol.[4] The US' interest in drafting the Protocol arose in the context of its desire to establish a strong international crime control strategy. Although the Vienna Process – as the Ad-Hoc Committee meetings responsible for drafting the Protocol were known – was characterized by sharp debate by a range of state and non-state actors, the final instrument reflects many of the primary concerns contained in the initial US draft. In particular, it is primarily a law enforcement instrument tied to the specific field of transnational crime and constructed primarily to respond to crimes, enforce laws, control borders and stimulate cooperation among governments.

The US drafted its own comprehensive anti-trafficking legislation – the Trafficking Victims Protection Act of 2000 (TVPA) – just weeks before the UN Trafficking Protocol was adopted. The TVPA seeks to influence the behaviour of other states through unilateral sanctions, elevating the US to the role of 'global sheriff' (Chuang 2006b). President Clinton's administration was keen to address the problem of human trafficking and, through a series of bilateral relationships and anti-trafficking initiatives, spearheaded the drafting of both the UN Protocol and its own domestic anti-trafficking legislation. The latter, however, was directed by a Republican-controlled Congress, which held a different view of the role that the US should play in global anti-trafficking efforts (Chuang 2006b: 449). The result was that while the Clinton Administration was committed to developing an international framework, Congress sought to induce international compliance to its own 'US minimum standards' by threat of unilateral sanctions (Chuang 2006b: 449).[5]

From 2001 the Office to Monitor and Combat Trafficking in Persons located within the US State Department began publishing an annual 'Trafficking in Persons (TIP) Report'. TIP Reports divide countries into three tiers according to their efforts to comply with US minimum standards for the elimination of trafficking. Tier 1 consists of those countries that fully comply with the minimum standards outlined in the TVPA; Tier 2 consists of those that do not fully comply but are making efforts to ensure compliance; and Tier 3 of those that do not comply and are not making significant efforts to bring themselves into compliance (US Department of State 2000). In addition, countries are placed in a 'Tier 2 Watch List' if the number of trafficked persons is significant or increasing and governments fail to increase their efforts to combat trafficking. Amendments to the TVPA in December 2008 automatically saw any country on the Tier 2 Watch List for two consecutive years downgraded to Tier 3, a status that involves the threat of termination of non-humanitarian aid, non trade-related assistance and US opposition to assistance from international financial institutions (Ould 2004: 61).[6]

Critics argue that the TIP Reports have focused on trafficking for sexual exploitation rather than all forms of forced labour; that they gloss over state complicity in trafficking; and that they are vague about law enforcement details, including numbers of victims, convictions and sentencing rates (Caraway 2006: 298). Chuang (2006b: 439) even goes so far as to claim that by 'injecting US norms into the international arena, the sanctions regime risks undermining the fragile international cooperation framework created by the Palermo Protocol'. There is no doubt that the TIP Reports are having an impact on policy-making and practice in countries relegated to Tier 3 or to the Tier 2 Watch List, not all of which have been positive.[7] In some cases, the threat of sanction has been used to achieve changes to immigration law that suit the United States' security agenda rather than improving the lives of victims of trafficking (Nederstigt and Almedia 2007: 105). There is also evidence that some national governments may have stopped anti-trafficking efforts or policies designed to address various forms of exploitation at a national level 'simply because they do not conform to the criteria proposed by US diplomats on the basis of the TVPA's requirements' (GAATW 2007: 20). In other cases, government policy has been re-active rather than pro-active. For example, when Malaysian authorities introduced an Anti-Trafficking Bill many local civil society actors interpreted it as a direct response to the international shame of relegation to Tier 3 status in 2007 (Lyons and Ford 2010a).

The US State Department's directives on trafficking and prostitution have also had a negative impact on NGOs working with sex workers on a range of sexual health matters. It is widely acknowledged that some elements of the international anti-trafficking movement played a key lobbying role in the rise of an 'anti-prostitution ideology' within the US Administration under President George W. Bush. In 2003, the US Secretary of State circulated a directive to United States Agency for International Development (USAID) field officers stipulating that organizations which supported the legalization of prostitution or advocated prostitution as an employment choice would not be eligible for anti-trafficking funds (Ditmore 2005: 118).[8] NGOs working in the trafficking field were required to declare their opposition to prostitution in order to be eligible for, or maintain, USAID funding. There is increasing evidence that these funding restrictions have stigmatized and alienated sex workers and sex worker organizations; discouraged the building of coalitions between advocates (Kinney 2006); undermined the use of rights-protection programmes (GAATW 2007: 237); and led to the criminalization of commercial sex workers (Kinney 2006, Sandy in this volume).[9]

The association of trafficking with sexual exploitation also dominates the counter-trafficking agendas of other major international donors, with the result that the overwhelming majority of funds are allocated to combating what has problematically been referred to as 'sex trafficking'.[10] While most anti-trafficking programmes draw on the broad definition of trafficking contained in the UN Protocol, the majority nonetheless focus on protecting and rescuing women and girls from the commercial sex industry. This focus is apparent in much of the literature on human trafficking, which makes reference to the exploitative conditions faced by documented and irregular labour migrants working in other industries, but usually only in passing (Schloenhardt 2001b; McSherry and Cullen 2007; but see Ahmad 2005). One of the consequences of this global preoccupation with saving women and girls from prostitution is that the links – and differences – between human trafficking, smuggling and the exploitation of migrants and refugees are obscured.

This blurring of boundaries is apparent in the development of increasingly restrictive immigration laws designed to protect women and girls from human trafficking. In Nepal, for example, the moral panic associated with trafficking for sexual exploitation has resulted in many women being been refused the right to leave the country for any form of travel (Frederick 2005; Joshi 2005; Hausner and Sharma 2011). Anti-trafficking efforts are also being used to legitimize the control of undocumented migration and to justify rounding up undocumented workers. In India, for example, counter-trafficking measures have served as a front for campaigns to deport Bangla-speaking people and Muslims (Ahmad 2005). In addition, researchers claim that the 'focus on smugglers/traffickers has made ... clandestine journeys *more* expensive and *more* dangerous' for the vast majority of migrants (Sharma 2005: 92, emphasis in original). Worried about the impact that anti-trafficking initiatives were having on migrant women and concerned about the lack of attention given to programme evaluation, in 2007 the Global Alliance against Trafficking in Women called for a comprehensive review of all anti-trafficking projects and policies (GAATW 2007: 23). As the studies in this collection reveal, GAATW's call has remained largely unheeded by governments and international agencies responsible for implementing counter-trafficking laws and programmes.

Trafficking, people smuggling and the management of migration

The UN Trafficking Protocol, which is one of three optional protocols contained in the UN Convention against Transnational Organized Crime (hereafter Transnational Crime Convention), came into effect in December 2003. It defines 'trafficking in persons' as

> the recruitment, transportation, transfer, harbouring or receipt of persons, by means of the threat or use of force or other forms of coercion, of abduction, of fraud, of deception, of the abuse of power or of a position of vulnerability or of the giving or receiving of payments or benefits to achieve the consent of a person having control over another person, for the purpose of exploitation.
>
> (United Nations 2000: 32)

As this definition suggests, the Protocol identifies three separate elements: (i) an *action* (e.g. recruitment); (ii) a *means* (e.g. coercion or deception); and (iii) a *purpose* (exploitation). In defining 'victims of trafficking', consent is considered to be irrelevant once it is established that deception, force or other prohibited means have been used.

In addition to the Trafficking Protocol, the Transnational Crime Convention contains a Migrant Smuggling Protocol which refers to 'the procurement, in order to obtain, directly or indirectly, a financial or other material benefit, of the illegal entry of a person into a State Party of which the person is not a national or a permanent resident' (United Nations 2000: 41). Thus, while trafficking may occur in both legal and illegal migration streams, smuggling by definition involves the illegal movement of people across national borders. Another key difference between the two Protocols lies in the purpose for which an individual is trafficked, since smuggling is deemed not to involve exploitation of the individual at the point of destination:

> Whereas the illegal crossing of borders is the aim of smuggling, the aim of trafficking is the exploitation of one's labour. In other words, the issue of

smuggling concerns the protection of the state against illegal migrants, while the issue of trafficking concerns the protection of individual persons against violence and abuse.

(Ditmore and Wijers 2003: 80)

The crucial distinction, therefore, is the forced labour or slavery-like conditions that always characterize trafficking, which is understood to be inherently exploitative and not incidentally exploitative as is the case with smuggling (Kempadoo 2005: xii).

The location of the two Protocols within the Transnational Crime Convention assumes that there is 'a clear line between legal and illegal migration' (van den Anker and Doomernik 2006: 2). In reality, however, the boundaries between smuggling and trafficking are blurred. The groups that manage the recruitment and smuggling of migrants are frequently the same groups involved in human trafficking (Skeldon 2000). Individuals who have been smuggled may find themselves working in the same industries as persons who have been trafficked and may be subject to the same exploitative practices. Conversely, victims of trafficking may be treated as undocumented migrants if they are caught outside a trafficking context. The artificial distinctions between trafficking and smuggling also overlook the temporal dimension to migration cycles, as migrant workers who cross borders for illegal work may change jobs and face exploitation (thus moving from a situation of smuggling to trafficking) many months or years after they first crossed the border, and children and teenagers, who were by definition 'trafficked', become adult migrants. Moreover, there are some groups of migrants, such as those fleeing human rights abuses in Burma, whose legal and migration status are so complex that they are not easily categorized as economic migrants, refugees or trafficked persons (Pollack 2007, Farrelly in this volume).[11] As Wong (2005: 71) notes in her study of labour migrants in Malaysia, 'individual migrant lives constantly weave their way in and out of intersecting spheres of legality and illegality' and thus while 'trafficking' and 'smuggling' are legally different, the consequences in terms of migrants' vulnerability to exploitation are similar.

Given the blurred boundaries between human trafficking and migrant smuggling, some scholars suggest that it might be best to jettison the distinction altogether on the grounds that it leads to unnecessary confusion and focuses attention on the *means* rather than the conditions of recruitment and deployment (cf. Brock *et al.* 2000; Grewcock 2003; O'Connell Davidson and Anderson 2006). As Anderson and O'Connell Davidson (2003: 7) put it:

[I]f the primary concern is to locate, explain and combat the use of forced labour, slavery, servitude and the like, then there is no moral or analytical reason to distinguish between forced labour involving 'illegal immigrants', 'smuggled persons' or 'victims of trafficking'.

The UNODC acknowledges these blurred boundaries, but clings to a distinction based on the presence of 'coercion/deception *and* exploitation':

One difference between these two groups of persons may be the amount of money that is paid prior to departure from the country of origin. Smuggled persons usually pay the amount 'upfront' and upon entering the destination country have ended their 'contractual' arrangement with their smugglers. Trafficked persons, on the other hand, may pay a percentage or pay nothing upfront and incur a debt for the remainder of the trip. This situation creates a type of debt bondage and places them at the mercy of the traffickers and in situations in which they are easily exploited.

(UNODC 2003: 25)

These ambiguities serve an important policy purpose, enabling compromises to be made between actors with different interests and concerns.

Nation-states have a vested interest in maintaining the distinction between trafficking and human smuggling whereby trafficked persons (usually women) are viewed as vulnerable victims and those who pay to be smuggled are 'queue jumpers'. This implicit link between migration and security explains why the global response to counter-trafficking has been so strong. The result is an elision between anti-trafficking and immigration control (Kempadoo 2005: xiii) in which the spectre of human trafficking is effectively mobilized to legitimize the increasing criminalization of migrants and those who assist them (Sharma 2005: 92). This elision renders border control and anti-immigration activities more 'palatable' to the public on the grounds that it contributes to the process of helping innocent victims of trafficking (Berman 2010: 89).

The consequence of fusing migration and crime in this way is that it confines all forms of migration to the narrow and restrictive security framework.[12] The UNODC is not alone in claiming that 'trafficking is almost always a form of organized crime' involving 'extensive and highly sophisticated international crime networks' (UNODC 2010). This link is made explicit in a number of studies which claim that human trafficking is the third largest organized criminal activity, after drugs and arms trafficking (cf. Jayagupta 2009). According to this logic, human trafficking and people smuggling must necessarily be combated within a law and order paradigm, most commonly by establishing legal frameworks aimed at restricting immigration and prosecuting illegal entries (Segrave and Milivojevic 2005). This involves increasingly restrictive immigration and border control regimes, the implementation of trafficking laws, the punishment of traffickers and smugglers, the repatriation of victims and the deportation of 'illegals'. The result is an approach that establishes and reinforces a false distinction between trafficking, which is typically regarded as a problem that affects women and girls in the commercial sex industry, and other migration flows, which are understood via the lens of immigration status. This approach reinforces a tendency to see women as trafficked 'victims', irregular labour migrants as 'illegals' and documented workers as 'temporary labour migrants'.

Human rights advocates have been particularly vocal in arguing that the focus on law enforcement can lead to further violations of the human rights of migrants, most significantly because the artificial distinction between trafficked persons and undocumented migrants can exclude the latter from protection as victims of human rights violations. Gallagher (2009: 834) argues that – in a context where other human rights mechanisms have considerable limitations – the Trafficking Protocol can curb the excesses of state-driven immigration and border control regimes, because it encourages states to enact local laws that prevent the exploitative recruitment and treatment of migrant workers, provide protection and assistance to victims and prosecute offenders.[13] However, other human rights advocates point out that the Trafficking Protocol is not a human rights treaty, noting that while the provisions relating to punishing traffickers are mandatory, those relating to victim protection and assistance are left to the discretion of the state.[14]

Concerned that victim protection was receiving little attention by states preoccupied with border security, in 2002 the UN High Commissioner for Human Rights submitted 'Recommended Principles and Guidelines for Human Rights and Human Trafficking' to the UN Economic and Social Council (OHCHR 2002). These Principles and Guidelines are directed at policy-makers and stress the primacy of human rights when dealing with victims of trafficking, invoking the principles of 'non-discrimination, safety and fair treatment, access to justice, access to private actions and reparations, resident status, health and other services, repatriation and reintegration, recovery and state cooperation' for all victims of exploitation (Hopkins and Nijboer 2004: 91). This rights-based approach has the benefit of focusing on the trafficked person as a 'rights-holder' rather than a 'victim' or an 'illegal', recognizing that a migrant is entitled to protection by virtue of being human, regardless of how s/he may have entered a country (Inglis 2001; Jordan 2002; Bruch 2004). These principles retain the status of guidelines, however, and are implemented at state discretion.

Some advocates of the human rights approach argue that in addition to the Trafficking Protocol there are a range of international human rights treaties under which instances of human trafficking could be prosecuted.[15] This suite of treaties and conventions may provide a more productive basis to address the exploitation of migrant workers in a context where human rights concerns are often displaced by a focus on immigration offences or crime prevention under the Transnational Crime Convention (Hopkins and Nijboer 2004; Todres 2006). However, others are less sanguine about the benefits of relying on human rights mechanisms on the grounds that they employ a vague and imprecise definition of trafficking and typically understand trafficking to be a 'violence against women' issue. In any case, the capacity of an international human rights framework to temper state behaviour is necessarily limited because there are few mandatory conditions or mechanisms to police them (Fitzpatrick 2003).

Labour migration as trafficking

In recent years, another approach to the complex relationship between human trafficking, smuggling and migration has emerged. In the face of mounting evidence documenting the range of exploitative practices encountered by labour migrants in destination countries, a number of international development agencies and NGOs have started to employ an 'anti-trafficking framework' in their thinking and practice when dealing cases of labour exploitation faced by 'legal' migrants. The problems that many of these workers face include confinement and restricted freedom of movement; falsified and fake documents; bonded labour and debt bondage; deception; violence and abuse; poor working conditions; and non-payment of wages. Rather than dealing with these issues as cases of labour abuse using the labour laws of receiving countries, migrant rights activists – and some governments – have turned to anti-trafficking laws instead. They argue that the endemic nature of these problems, and the ease with which documented migrant workers can become undocumented, means that the vast majority of low-skilled migrant workers can quite easily be characterized as 'victims of human trafficking' using the definition contained within the UN Trafficking Protocol (cf. ASI 2003; IOM 2007).

Treating 'documented/legal' migrants as 'victims of trafficking' disrupts the categories typically used by governments to regulate temporary labour migration. While the capacity for individual states to regulate labour migration varies considerably, there is a remarkable consistency in the ways in which state authorities seek to manage temporary labour flows. Both sending and receiving countries have developed complex immigration and employment regimes to recruit and deploy labour migrants and most of these regimes assume a clear distinction between legal and illegal arrival and deployment.[16] The 'labour migration as trafficking' approach reveals the tensions in this model by calling into question the basic premises that underpin most immigration and labour regimes.

This approach has been facilitated by the massive investment in anti-trafficking initiatives by international agencies and donors since 2000. While donor aid provides the resources to pursue labour abuse cases as 'trafficking cases', the political motivation for this shift in focus comes from international pressure to ratify the Trafficking Protocol and to demonstrate compliance with the minimum standards outlined in the annual TIP Reports. In addition, trafficking and smuggling, as core elements of the UN Convention on Transnational Crime, are linked with measures to address 'global terrorism' in the heightened security environment post-9/11 and governments are encouraged to take a tough stance on irregular migration through tighter border controls (Kaur and Metcalfe 2006). In this environment, dealing with documented labour migrants under anti-trafficking laws or programmes can provide states with the means to demonstrate that not only are they are 'tough' on trafficking and smuggling, but also on terrorism.

However, the framing of labour migration as trafficking should not be cynically regarded as simply a means to deal with international pressure from the US and other donor countries. It also reflects a growing view amongst some scholars and activists that labour laws are doing little to curb demand for cheap, unprotected labour (ILO 2005: 7). For example, Roger Plant, former head of the International Labour Organization's (ILO) Special Action Programme to Combat Forced Labour, notes that trafficked persons may in fact be better protected than other groups of vulnerable migrants who work in slavery-like conditions (cited in Danailova-Trainor and Laczko 2010: 67–8). The ILO notes that although most of its members have signed one or both of its forced labour conventions:

[F]orced labour is not defined in any detail, making it difficult for law enforcement agents to identify and prosecute the offence. Second, and in consequence of this, there have been very few prosecutions for forced labour offences anywhere in the world. A vicious cycle is thereby established: no clear legislation, little or no resources for prosecutions, limited awareness or publicity, thus no pressure for clear legislation, and so on.

(ILO 2005: 2)

In the face of government inaction on labour exploitation, the ILO suggests that 'legislative and judicial action against forced labour and against human trafficking can serve the same goals and be mutually supportive' (ILO 2009: 8). This is because while the definition of forced labour places emphasis on the involuntariness of the work, the Trafficking Protocol emphasizes the means by which initial consent is obtained (i.e. force, deception, coercion, etc.).

To address this intersection between forced labour and trafficking, the ILO utilizes a 'forced labour continuum' in which it identifies three categories of labour – trafficked victims of forced labour, non-trafficked victims of forced labour and successful migrants (Andrees and van der Linden 2005). It argues that trafficked victims of forced labour are subject to the worst abuses because they often have the least freedom of movement and are the most vulnerable while non-trafficked victims of forced labour face a range of exploitative conditions, including non-payment of wages, retention of identity documents, long working hours and unacceptable working conditions. The advantage of the 'forced labour continuum' over the traditional distinction between 'victims of trafficking' and 'illegal migrants' is that it provides a means to examine the 'varying degrees to which migrants can become victim of exploitation, routes that lead into forced labour and individual strategies to escape from coercion and control' (Andrees and van der Linden 2005: 63).[17] Once the focus of attention moves away from the means by which a migrant arrives in a destination country and to the conditions of work, the emphasis shifts to developing strategies that address labour exploitation and promote the social and labour rights of migrants. This includes greater regulation of migrant labour markets (Kaur and Metcalfe 2006); opportunities for labour organizing and collective bargaining (Ford 2006b; ILO 2009); the strengthening of national labour laws; the development of regional labour protocols to address the exploitation of labour migrants (Kelly 2005); and multi-stakeholder initiatives and corporate social responsibility programmes (ILO 2009). But while these initiatives may improve working conditions, they are inadequate for dealing with the particular conditions facing commercial sex workers and informal sector workers or for addressing the role played by organized crime.[18] Moreover, because the ILO's analysis of forced labour is focused on the 'worst' forms of exploitation it remains decoupled from a broader discussion of the development of all labour relations (Lerche 2007).

Some international development agencies and international NGOs go further to argue that all migrant workers who experience exploitative labour practices are 'victims of trafficking' (Rosenberg 2003; UNODC 2003; Sugiarti *et al.* 2006).

Research that demonstrates the blurred boundaries between trafficking, smuggling and labour migration provides some of the rationale for these efforts: if economic migrants experience a range of 'trafficking-like practices', then perhaps trafficking laws (rather than labour laws) offer a solution. Rather than jettisoning the concept of 'trafficking' in favour of an approach that focuses on all instances of forced labour, such a position seeks to employ the key concepts outlined in the Protocol to determine what constitutes an exploitative employment practice in relation to migrant labour. In doing so, it seeks to widen the definition of human trafficking to include 'regular', 'documented' and/or 'lawful' migrant workers who confront a range of exploitative labour conditions during their migratory experience.[19] This approach has led to a situation in which cases of forced labour and debt bondage of documented temporary labour migrants are used as evidence of the prevalence of trafficking (cf. ASI 2003; IOM 2007). For example, Anti-Slavery International includes documented migrant domestic workers in its definition of victims of trafficking, arguing that a 'sophisticated system of debt-bondage and forced labour' characterizes the domestic work industry (Ould 2004: 62). Similarly, Human Rights Watch (2008: 40) concludes that trafficking is widespread amongst migrant domestic workers. According to Jureidini and Moukarbel (2004: 585), the majority of migrant domestic workers enter into employment contracts which are deliberately misleading and that 'such direct and indirect deception regarding contractual security . . . places workers within the category of having been trafficked'.

This framing of all forms of exploitation involving temporary labour migrants as 'trafficking' ignores the agency of migrant workers and fails to acknowledge that many migrants knowingly cross borders without 'legal' papers and choose to undertake jobs deemed illegal by both sending and host societies (cf. Idrus 2008). It also overlooks what it is that migrants themselves want out of the migration process. Anti-trafficking laws and regulations not only establish a victim's status but also determine the ways in which a victim will be treated. This usually involves removal from the situation of exploitation; a period of residency in the receiving country while evidence is collected and statements are recorded; and repatriation. In many cases, migrant workers may not want any of these things to occur – they may want to continue working for their employer (but with wages paid and/or decent working hours), they may want to leave the workplace in order to find new work and/or they may want their immigration status to be regularized. Anti-trafficking laws simply cannot provide these outcomes.

In the final instance only states can determine whether an individual act should be punished as forced labour or as trafficking. The chapters in this collection reveal that while the 'labour migration as trafficking' approach is favoured by some international NGOs, most states have been much less willing to include documented labour migrants in their anti-trafficking efforts. The financial, legal and administrative problems associated with identifying labour migrants as victims of trafficking have ensured that only the 'worst cases' of exploitation, usually cases of sexual exploitation of women and children, are being dealt with in this way (Piper 2005). This does not mean that the Trafficking Protocol is not gaining traction: in fact it has begun to shape international, national, regional and local level responses to migration flows in the region. However, the implications of this shift are yet to be revealed.

Outline of the book

Through the presentation of detailed ethnographic accounts of the everyday practices of the diverse range of actors involved in trafficking-like practices and in counter-trafficking programmes, the chapters that follow explore the extent to which the anti-trafficking framework's focus on force, deception and exploitation constrains cross-border mobility in different locations. In demonstrating how the anti-trafficking framework has become influential – even over-determining – in some locations while remaining mostly irrelevant in others, the chapters in this collection reveal the intersections between state agents and other kinds of authority, in doing so problematizing the notion of the state itself.

The chapters reveal a number of key findings about the nature of anti-trafficking efforts in Southeast Asia. One issue explored in the chapters is the role that US TIP Reports have played in shaping the development of anti-trafficking laws and policies at a national level. A number of the studies confirm the view that the TIP Reports have had an over-determining role in shaping the development of national laws and anti-trafficking programmes (Sandy, Ford and Lyons, Molland, Tigno). Other chapters, however, reveal that while the TIP Reports have influenced state policy-making, domestic political agendas have played a much more significant role (Eilenberg, Farrelly, Palmer, Zhang). These differences are significant because they demonstrate the importance of paying attention to policy and discursive shifts at both the national and local scales in order to lay bare the multiple ways in which legal regimes emerge out of contestations between state and non-state actors.

Another related theme explored in some of the chapters is the need to focus attention beyond metropole-based analyses of the state to examine the periphery of the nation and the impact of counter-trafficking programmes at specific border locations. A focus on the borderlands, rather than on the point of arrival or departure, encourages an approach that addresses the phenomenon of trafficking as a process rather than an event. It also brings into sharp relief the ways in which state-driven development agendas; inter-state relations; non-state agents of political power and authority; and the nature of the border itself shape anti-trafficking programmes and agendas. Some of the case studies explored in this collection demonstrate that counter-trafficking can be used to legitimize the need to develop the borderland (Eilenberg) or can be dismissed by other development agendas (Zhang). In other contexts, the relationship between states, and particularly histories of conflict and increasing securitization of borders (Farrelly), play a significant role in determining the nature and character of counter-trafficking initiatives. Other chapters demonstrate that states are not the only agents of political power and authority in border zones (Ford and Lyons, Molland).

Exploring the historical evolution of (counter-) trafficking discourses at national and local scales, the authors in this collection overcome the tendency to focus on fixed categories of 'trafficking victims' and 'labour migrants' and explore the nexus between trafficking, smuggling and labour migration. While scholars have long argued that the legal distinctions between human trafficking and people smuggling fail to adequately address the interconnected phenomenon of forced labour and migration, the consequences of this for policymaking on other 'categories' of migrants, including temporary labour migrants, refugees, asylum seekers and displaced persons, are rarely considered. Arguably, the most significant outcome of this collection is the sustained attention it gives to the relative positioning of human trafficking and temporary labour migration: a number of authors examine national contexts where human trafficking and labour migration have been elided, with detrimental results for labour migrants (Farrelly, Ford and Lyons, Molland, Palmer, Tigno).

A final key focus of a number of the chapters is the 'unintended consequences' of anti-trafficking legislation and programmes. Some chapters move beyond the discussion of policy development to explore the consequences of laws and guidelines on the agency of labour migrants (Tigno) and commercial sex workers (Sandy). Their conclusions raise serious questions about the links between counter-trafficking efforts and human rights abuses. At the same time, however, these unintended consequences are not always negative. Where discretion plays a role in decision-making strategies employed by state agents the outcomes may sometimes be positive. For example, state agents who are posted overseas may respond to and interpret national laws and policies much more liberally than their domestically-based colleagues, or may develop responses to individual cases that do not strictly follow prescribed protocols, thereby improving outcomes for individuals (Palmer). These studies emphasize the need to evaluate anti-trafficking laws and programmes in different locations and at different scales in order to gain a clearer picture of the impact that the UN Trafficking Protocol is having in Southeast Asia as a whole.

The first two chapters introduce the themes at the heart of this collection. Through an examination of the Philippines labour export programme, Jorge Tigno demonstrates how understandings of human trafficking are embedded in and intermeshed with narratives of personal martyrdom, sacrifice and survival that underpin Filipino accounts of the country's large migrant labour workforce. In this chapter, Tigno argues that the rhetoric that surrounds trafficking in the Philippines emphasizes the vulnerabilities and subsequent victimization of women migrants, and that such a discourse does little to assist failed migrant workers or those who find themselves in exploitative labour situations. The failure of anti-trafficking laws to assist vulnerable migrant workers is taken up by Larissa Sandy, who examines the politics surrounding the passing of national anti-trafficking legislation and its immediate and far-reaching impact on the mobility and labour rights of Cambodian sex workers. Sandy argues that the 2008 Human Trafficking Law, which is exclusively focused on women and girls involved in commercialized sexual exchange, has further compounded the stigmatization, marginalization and oppression of sex workers. Through her discussion of the dangers associated with the elision of sex work and trafficking, Sandy unpacks the debates around forced and voluntary labour and provides a robust critique of the international emphasis on criminalization, rescue and rehabilitation. Her chapter demonstrates the ways in which moralistic discourses surrounding prostitution intersect with national and international development and foreign policy agendas to produce a narrow definition of human trafficking that can have devastating effects on migrant women.

The two chapters that follow take up the theme of the tension between the international and the local, but with a focus on the activities of non-state actors. Sverre Molland begins by examining the ways in which trafficking along the Thai–Lao border is made legible and thus receptive to policy interventions by the development aid sector. Molland argues that the de-territorialized nature of trafficking presents a challenge to development aid programmes, which are always demarcated in spatial terms. The ensuing emphasis on the identification of 'hotspots' (which can then become the focus of interventions) is underpinned by a market logic that understands trafficking in terms of demand and supply and anti-trafficking efforts in terms of cause and effect. Molland's detailed ethnographic analysis demonstrates that anti-trafficking programmes thus operate according to their own discursive logic – a logic that has little to do with social reality in the borderlands. In the second of these chapters, Michele Ford and Lenore Lyons assess the impact of anti-trafficking projects on migrant labour NGOs in the Riau Islands, a trafficking 'hotspot' located on Indonesia's maritime border with Singapore and Malaysia. Ford and Lyons document the extent to which US-sponsored anti-trafficking programmes succeeded in shifting the focus and activities of both local government and NGO activists concerned with sex work and labour migration. They argue that while everyday realities in these sectors have led activists to temper the extent to which they embrace the anti-trafficking agenda, its ubiquity has left them with few other options, particularly in relation to labour migration. As a consequence, temporary labour migration became synonymous with human trafficking. While some NGOs resisted this move, others were left floundering in a context where international donor funding was essential to their survival. This chapter, like Molland's before it, reveals the mismatch between the views held by international donors/agencies and those of NGOs working on the ground in internationally designated 'hotspots'.

The chapter by Zhang Juan reveals a very different account of trafficking efforts in a border hotspot. Her study of Hekou, a town on the China–Vietnam border, points to the simultaneous absence and presence of anti-trafficking discourses at the local level. According to Zhang, the Chinese government's development priorities have ensured that local state agents are hesitant to embrace the international anti-trafficking agenda despite the clear presence of trafficking in the region. By drawing attention away from Hekou as a trafficking hotspot, local officials pay lip service to moralizing discourses that portray trafficking as an issue that affects women while keeping the border open to cross-border flows that include a substantial number of commercial sex workers. Zhang describes the ways in which these women's destination – Vietnam Street, Hekou's main commercial sex market – has become a 'not spot' in China's counter-trafficking agenda. The next chapter also explores the link between anti-trafficking laws and economic development initiatives in a border zone of high strategic importance. Michael Eilenberg's study examines the place of the global discourse of anti-trafficking in the Indonesian government's efforts to justify increased militarization along the West Kalimantan–Sarawak border. Eilenberg argues that undocumented labour migration – a legitimate livelihood strategy used by borderlanders – has increasingly been criminalized as a consequence of an increased focus on counter-trafficking as a border security strategy.

The fact that international influence is by no means uniform or uncontested is a theme taken up in Nicholas Farrelly's chapter, which examines what 'human trafficking' means for migrants who leave Burma in search of better economic opportunities in Thailand. Farrelly's account supports the views of the other authors in this collection that human trafficking and smuggling is a routinized border activity. As in the case described by Zhang, Farrelly's account reveals that anti-trafficking laws and regulations serve a range of political ends, the majority of which have little to do with stopping human trafficking and exploitative labour practices. Instead, he suggests, human trafficking laws serve to define the 'problem' of illegal migration in ways which limit assistance for Burmese migrants/refugees without threatening the supply of cheap migrant labour into Thailand's farms, factories and homes.

The final chapter in the collection extends the analysis of how states operationalize anti-trafficking laws by moving beyond the geographical borders of the nation-state. In it, Wayne Palmer provides a detailed account of the microprocesses through which Indonesian bureaucrats respond to anti-trafficking legislation at home and abroad. Palmer demonstrates how dissension over the legislation within a state bureaucracy plays out overseas, arguing that the decision by labour attachés to turn a blind eye to falsified documents and underage deployment most often reflects the exercise of discretion to maintain the distinctions they believe exist between labour exploitation and trafficking. His analysis reveals that the 'pragmatic and well-meaning' actions of these bureaucrats have the consequence of involving the Indonesian state itself in trafficking-like practices. Palmer thus brings the collection full circle to consider the question of 'who are the traffickers and who are the victims?'

The study of human trafficking is a burgeoning field of research. Despite the strong and growing scholarly interest in issues related to forced labour, migrant smuggling, temporary labour migration and human trafficking, much contemporary scholarship on the region continues to focus almost exclusively on trafficking for sexual exploitation or temporary labour migration, and has little to say about the ways in which these important empirical phenomena overlap and differ, or how they are constantly recast and dealt with by lobbyists and policymakers. The chapters in *Labour Migration and Human Trafficking* examine the nexus between mobility and forced labour and provide new insights into the ways in which governments, international agencies and NGOs in Southeast Asia are promoting and responding to the emergence of the global anti-trafficking framework.

Notes

1 Also commonly referred to as the Palermo Protocol.
2 On counter-trafficking programmes see, for example, Derks (2000), Schloenhardt (2001a), Piper (2003) and Sugiarti *et al.* (2006) and on anti-trafficking laws and policies, Emmers *et al.* (2006), McSherry and Cullen (2007) and Segrave *et al.* (2009). Empirical studies of cases and trends in the region include, Grundy-Warr *et al.* (1996), Darwin *et al.* (2003), Surtees (2003), Piper (2005), Lee (2007) and Asis (2008).
3 This introduction draws on Ford and Lyons (2012) and Lyons and Ford (2009, 2010a).
4 The US and Argentinean governments made a commitment to submit initial proposals of the trafficking protocol, which they subsequently did by the end of November 1998.
5 The debates about 'forced' versus 'voluntary' prostitution/sex work that took place between 'abolitionists' and 'regulationists' which influenced the drafting of the UN Protocol also shaped the drafting of the TVPA (Doezema 2005; Chuang 2006b).
6 The US was included in the TIP Report for the first time in 2010.
7 A number of scholars have also questioned the objectives of the TVPA, pointing to US reluctance to use sanctions against non-compliant states when they are key economic partners or important security allies (Kempadoo 2005; Kapstein 2006). A July 2006 report by the US Government Accountability Office also concluded that the TIP Reports have 'limited credibility' and do not 'consistently influence anti trafficking programs' (cited in GAATW 2007: 235).
8 Similarly, the United States Leadership Against HIV-AIDS, Tuberculosis and Malaria Act of 2003 (known as the Global AIDS Act) required that any international organization working to curb HIV-AIDS must 'have a policy explicitly opposing prostitution and sex trafficking' if it wished to receive such funding (Weitzer 2007). Otherwise eligible organizations were deemed ineligible to receive US Government HIV or anti-trafficking funds if they did not expressly adopt the US Government's policy on eradicating prostitution. US funding restrictions applied to all recipient countries, irrespective of the legal status of sex work in the country.
9 Anti-trafficking efforts have also had a negative impact on migrant sex worker health (McMahon 2005). See Lyons and Ford (2010b) for details of the devastating effect that these programmes can have on NGO activities designed to assist women with HIV and other STDs in Indonesia.
10 The term 'sex trafficking' sets up a false distinction between sex workers and other migrant workers by suggesting that workers in the commercial sex industry are qualitatively different from all other types of workers who face exploitative labour practices. By privileging (and fetishizing) sexual acts, it also overlooks the enormous diversity of experiences of migrant sex workers, some of whom engage in forced sex.
11 This blurring between refugees and labour migrants is surprisingly underexplored in the literature on labour migration in Southeast Asia, which is predominantly focused on documented temporary labour migrants. For an overview of the issues, see Ford (2007).
12 Kapur (2005) goes so far as to suggest that framing the Trafficking Protocol within a convention on organized crime reflects a preoccupation with illegal immigration rather than the human rights of migrants.
13 Frequently referred to as the 'Three Ps Approach'– prevention, protection, prosecution.
14 Joan Fitzpatrick (2003: 1152) describes these as 'relatively modest obligations, written either in precatory [desirable] language or stating no more than what states would already be obliged to do under general legal principles'.
15 These include the Universal Declaration on Human Rights; the International Covenant on Civil and Political Rights (ICCPR); the International Covenant on Economic, Social and Cultural Rights (ICESCR); the Convention on the Elimination of All Forms of Racial Discrimination; the Convention on the Elimination of All Forms of Discrimination

Against Women (CEDAW); the Convention Against Torture and Other Cruel, Inhuman or Degrading Treatment (CAT); and the Convention on the Rights of the Child (CRC).

16 Nonetheless, most states exercise restraint and selectivity in addressing irregular labour migration, and their repertoire of responses varies according to socio-economic and political realities (Ahmad 2008). In some cases it may suit the interests of both states and employers to have access to a large irregular workforce (Cunningham and Heyman 2004; Ford 2006a), while in others, strict regulation of all migration flows is intimately tied to public debates about 'law and order' and 'border security'.

17 The concept of 'forced labour' has received relatively little attention within the scholarly literature on human trafficking and/or labour migration in contemporary Southeast Asia. The ILO's stance on forced labour is much more widely critiqued in studies of labour exploitation in South Asia (cf. Lerche 2007; Rogaly 2008).

18 This is of particular concern in relation to trafficking for forced labour which is deemed illegal (e.g. commercial sex work) or informal. Elizabeth Bruch notes that 'The biggest obstacle to the effective use of the labor framework to address human trafficking, however, is the continuing disagreement among states and activists as to the nature and legality of prostitution and other sex work' (Bruch 2004: 27).

19 It is important to note that because the TIP Report does not see movement as a condition for trafficking, under the US State Department's definition all people in forced labour situations could be considered 'victims of trafficking' (Danailova-Trainor and Laczko 2010: 42).

References

Ahmad, A. N. (2008) 'The labour market consequences of human smuggling: "Illegal" employment in London's migrant economy', *Journal of Ethnic and Migration Studies*, 34 (6): 853–74.

Ahmad, N. (2005) 'Trafficked persons or economic migrants? Bangladeshis in India', in Kempadoo, K., Sanghera, J. and Pattanaik, B. (eds) *Trafficking and Prostitution Reconsidered: New Perspectives on Migration, Sex Work, and Human Rights*, Boulder, CO: Paradigm Publishers, pp. 211–28.

Anderson, B. and O'Connell Davidson, J. (2003) *Is Trafficking in Human Beings Demand Driven? A Multi-country Pilot Study*, December, Geneva: International Organisation for Migration (IOM) Migration Research Series.

Andrees, B. and van der Linden, M. N. J. (2005) 'Designing trafficking research from a labour market perspective: The ILO experience', *International Migration*, 43 (1–2): 55–73.

ASI (2003) *The Migration-trafficking Nexus: Combating Trafficking through the Protection of Migrants' Human Rights*, London: Anti-Slavery International.

Asis, M. M. B. (2008) 'Human trafficking in East and South-East Asia: Searching for structural factors', in Cameron, S. and Newman, E. (eds) *Trafficking in Humans: Social, Cultural and Political Dimensions*, Tokyo: United Nations University Press, pp. 181–205.

Berman, J. (2010) 'Biopolitical management, economic calculation and "trafficked women"', *International Migration*, 48 (4): 84–113.

Brock, D., Gilles, K., Oliver, C. and Sutdhibhaslip, M. (2000) 'Migrant sex workers: A roundtable analysis', *Canadian Woman Studies*, 20 (2): 84–91.

Bruch, E. M. (2004) 'The search for an effective response to human trafficking', *Stanford Journal of International Law*, 40 (1): 1–45.

Caraway, N. (2006) 'Human rights and existing contradictions in Asia-Pacific human trafficking politics and discourse', *Tulane Journal of International & Comparative Law*, 14 (2): 295–316.

Chapkis, W. (2003) 'Trafficking, migration, and the law: Protecting innocents, punishing immigrants', *Gender & Society*, 17 (6): 923–37.

Chuang, J. (2006a) 'Beyond a snapshot: Preventing human trafficking in the global economy', *Indiana Journal of Global Legal Studies*, 13 (1): 137–63.

—— (2006b) 'The United States as global sheriff: Using unilateral sanctions to combat human trafficking', *Michigan Journal of International Law*, 27: 437–94.

Cunningham, H. and Heyman, J. M. (2004) 'Introduction: Mobilities and enclosures at borders', *Identities: Global Studies in Culture and Power*, 11 (3): 298–302.

Danailova-Trainor, G. and Laczko, F. (2010) 'Trafficking in persons and development: Towards greater policy coherence', *International Migration*, 48 (4): 38–83.

Darwin, M., Wattie, A. M., Dzuhayatin, S. R. and Yuarsi, S. E. (2003) 'Trafficking and sexuality in Indonesia-Malaysia cross-border migration', in Darwin, M., Wattie, A. M. and Yuarsi, S. E. (eds) *Living on the Edges: Cross-border Mobility and Sexual Exploitation in the Greater Southeast Asia Sub-region*, Yogyakarta: Center for Population and Policy Studies, Gadjah Mada University, pp. 233–82.

David, F. (2009) 'Research on trafficking in persons in South East Asia: A comment on recent trends, along with remaining gaps and challenges', in IOM (ed.) *Human Trafficking: New Directions for Research*, Geneva: International Organization for Migration, pp. 95–121.

Derks, A. (2000) *Combating Trafficking in South-East Asia: A Review of Policy and Programme Responses*, Geneva: International Organization for Migration.

Ditmore, M. (2005) 'Trafficking in lives: How ideology shapes policy', in Kempadoo, K., Sanghera, J. and Pattanaik, B. (eds) *Trafficking and Prostitution Reconsidered: New Perspectives on Migration, Sex Work, and Human Rights*, Boulder, CO: Paradigm Publishers, pp. 107–26.

Ditmore, M. and Wijers, M. (2003) 'The negotiations on the UN Protocol on Trafficking in Persons', *Nemesis*, 4: 79–88.

Doezema, J. (2005) 'Now you see her, now you don't: Sex workers at the UN Trafficking Protocol negotiation', *Social and Legal Studies*, 14 (1): 61–89.

Emmers, R., Greener-Barcham, B. and Thomas, N. (2006) 'Institutional arrangements to counter human trafficking in the Asia Pacific', *Contemporary Southeast Asia*, 28 (3): 490–511.

Fergus, L. (2005) *Trafficking in Women for Sexual Exploitation*, June, Melbourne: Australian Centre for the Study of Sexual Assault.

Fitzpatrick, J. (2003) 'Trafficking as a human rights violation: The complex intersection of legal frameworks for conceptualizing and combating trafficking', *Michigan Journal of International Law*, 24: 1143–67.

Ford, M. (2006a) 'After Nunukan: The regulation of Indonesian migration to Malaysia', in Kaur, A. and Metcalfe, I. (eds) *Mobility, Labour Migration and Border Controls in Asia*, Basingstoke and New York: Palgrave Macmillan, pp. 228–47.

—— (2006b) 'Migrant labor NGOs and trade unions: A partnership in progress?', *Asian and Pacific Migration Journal*, 15 (3): 299–318.

—— (2007) *Advocacy Responses to Irregular Labour Migration in ASEAN: The Cases of Malaysia and Thailand*, March, Manila: Migrant Forum in Asia and the South East Asian Committee for Advocacy.

Ford, M. and Lyons, L. (2012) 'Labour migration, trafficking and border controls', in Wilson, T. and Donnan, H. (eds) *A Companion to Border Studies*, Oxford: Blackwell.

Frederick, J. (2005) 'The myth of Nepal-to-India sex trafficking: Its creation, its maintenance, and its influence on anti-trafficking interventions', in Kempadoo, K., Sanghera,

J. and Pattanaik, B. (eds) *Trafficking and Prostitution Reconsidered: New Perspectives on Migration, Sex Work, and Human Rights*, Boulder, CO: Paradigm Publishers, pp. 127–48.

GAATW (2007) *Collateral Damage: The Impact of Anti-trafficking Measures on Human Rights around the World*, Bangkok: Global Alliance Against Traffic in Women.

Gallagher, A. T. (2009) 'Human rights and human trafficking: Quagmire or firm ground? A response to James Hathaway', *Virginia Journal of International Law*, 49 (4): 789–847.

Grewcock, M. (2003) 'Irregular migration, identity and the state – the challenge for criminology', *Current Issues in Criminal Justice*, 15 (2): 114–35.

—— (2007) 'Shooting the passenger: Australia's war on illicit migrants', in Lee, M. (ed.) *Human Trafficking*, Cullompton, Devon: Willan Publishing, pp. 178–209.

Grundy-Warr, C., King, R. and Risser, G.(1996) 'Cross-border migration, trafficking and the sex industry: Thailand and its neighbours', *IBRU Boundary and Security Bulletin*, 4 (1): 86–97.

Hausner, S. and Sharma, J. (2011) 'On the way to India: Nepali rituals of border crossing', in Gellner, D. N. (ed.) *Borderlands in South Asia: People, State and Nation at the Margins*, Cambridge: Cambridge University Press.

Hopkins, R. and Nijboer, J. (2004) 'Human trafficking and human rights: Research, policy and practice in the Netherlands', in Zimic, S. Z. (ed.) *Women and Trafficking*, Ljubljana: Peace Institute, Institute for Contemporary Social and Political Studies, pp. 85–98.

Human Rights Watch (2008) *'As If I Am Not Human': Abuses against Asian Domestic Workers in Saudi Arabia*, New York: Human Rights Watch.

Idrus, N. I. (2008) 'Makkunrai passimokolo': Bugis migrant women workers in Malaysia', in Ford, M. and Parker, L. (eds) *Women and Work in Indonesia*, London: Routledge, pp. 155–72.

ILO (2005) *A Global Alliance against Forced Labour*, Geneva: International Labour Organization.

—— (2009) *The Cost of Coercion: Global Report under the Follow-up to the ILO Declaration on Fundamental Principles and Rights at Work*, Geneva: International Labour Organization.

Inglis, S. C. (2001) 'Expanding international and national protections against trafficking for forced labor using a human rights framework', *Buffalo Human Rights Law Review*, 7: 55–104.

IOM (2007) *ASEAN and Trafficking in Persons: Using Data as a Tool to Combat Trafficking in Persons*, Geneva: International Organization for Migration.

Jayagupta, R. (2009) 'The Thai government's repatriation and reintegration programmes: Responding to trafficked female commercial sex workers from the Greater Mekong Subregion', *International Migration*, 47 (2): 227–53.

Jordan, A. D. (2002) 'Human rights or wrongs? The struggle for a rights-based response to trafficking in human beings', *Gender and Development*, 10 (1): 28–37.

Joshi, S. (2005) '"You'll know what we are talking about when you grow older": A third wave critique of anti-trafficking ideology, globalization and conflict in Nepal', in Wilson, S., Sengupta, A. and Evans, K. (eds) *Defending Our Dreams: Global Feminist Voices for a New Generation*, London: Zed Books, pp. 79–94.

Jureidini, R. and Moukarbel, N. (2004) 'Female Sri Lankan domestic workers in Lebanon: A case of "contract slavery"?', *Journal of Ethnic and Migration Studies*, 30 (4): 581–607.

Kapstein, E. B. (2006) 'The new global slave trade', *Foreign Affairs*, 85 (6): 103.

Kapur, R. (2005) *Erotic Justice: Postcolonialism, Subjects and Rights*, London: Glass House Press.

Kaur, A. and Metcalfe, I. (eds) (2006) *Mobility, Labour Migration and Border Controls in Asia*, Basingstoke and New York: Palgrave Macmillan.

Kelly, J. (2005) 'Transnational NGO involvement in the new age of migration: Building a framework for the protection of the human rights of undocumented economic migrants', *Michigan Journal of Public Affairs*, 2 (Summer): 1–30.

Kempadoo, K. (2005) 'Introduction: From moral panic to global justice: Changing perspectives on trafficking', in Kempadoo, K., Sanghera, J. and Pattanaik, B. (eds) *Trafficking and Prostitution Reconsidered: New Perspectives on Migration, Sex Work, and Human Rights*, Boulder, CO: Paradigm Publishers, pp. vii–xxxiv.

Kempadoo, K., Sanghera, J. and Pattanaik, B. (eds) (2005) *Trafficking and Prostitution Reconsidered: New Perspectives on Migration, Sex Work, and Human Rights*, Boulder, CO: Paradigm Publishers.

Kinney, E. C. M. (2006) 'Appropriations for the abolitionists: Undermining effects of the U.S. mandatory anti-prostitution pledge in the fight against human trafficking and HIV/ AIDS', *Berkeley Journal of Gender, Law and Justice*, 21: 158–94.

Laczko, F. (2005) 'Data and research on human trafficking', *International Migration*, 43 (1–2): 5–16.

Lee, M. (ed.) (2007) *Human Trafficking*, Cullompton, Devon: Willan Publishing.

Lerche, J. (2007) 'A global alliance against forced labour? Unfree labour, neo-liberal globalization and the International Labour Organization', *Journal of Agrarian Change*, 7 (4): 425–52.

Lyons, L. and Ford, M. (2009) 'The gendered effects of anti-trafficking discourse for temporary labour migrants in Southeast Asia', *GAATW Alliance News: The Changing Context of Trafficking and Migration in Asia*, pp. 39–43.

—— (2010a) 'Anti-trafficking programs and their impact on temporary labour migrants in Malaysia', paper presented at *International Conference on Forcing Issues: Rethinking and Rescaling Human Trafficking in the Asia-Pacific Region*, Singapore, 4–5 October 2010.

—— (2010b) '"Where are your victims?": Or how sexual health advocacy came to be trafficking in Indonesia's Riau islands', *International Feminist Journal of Politics*, 12 (2): 255–64.

Marshall, P. and Thatun, S. (2005) 'Miles away: The trouble with prevention in the Greater Mekong Sub-region', in Kempadoo, K., Sanghera, J. and Pattanaik, B. (eds) *Trafficking and Prostitution Reconsidered: New Perspectives on Migration, Sex Work, and Human Rights*, Boulder, CO: Paradigm Publishers, pp. 43–64.

McMahon, M. (2005) 'Migratory sex workers: Observations on anti-trafficking measures and public health outcomes on the trans-national superhighway', *Social Alternatives*, 24 (2): 17–19.

McSherry, B. and Cullen, M. (2007) 'The criminal justice response to trafficking in persons: Practical problems with enforcement in the Asia-Pacific region', *Global Change, Peace & Security*, 19 (3): 205–20.

Nederstigt, F. and Almedia, L. C. R. (2007) 'Brazil', in GAATW (ed.) *Collateral Damage: The Impact of Anti-trafficking Measures on Human Rights around the World*, Bangkok: Global Alliance Against Traffic in Women, pp. 87–113.

Nieuwenhuys, C. and Pecoud, A. (2007) 'Human trafficking, information campaigns, and strategies of migration control', *American Behavioral Scientist*, 50 (12): 1674–95.

O'Connell Davidson, J. and Anderson, B. (2006) 'The trouble with "trafficking"', in van den Anker, C. L. and Doomernik, J. (eds) *Trafficking and Women's Rights*, Basingstoke: Palgrave Macmillan, pp. 11–26.

OHCHR (2002) *Recommended Principles and Guidelines on Human Rights and Human Trafficking*, May 2002: UN Office of the High Commissioner for Human Rights.

Ong, A. (2006) *Neoliberalism as Exception: Mutations in Citizenship and Sovereignty*, Durham: Duke University Press.

Ould, D. (2004) 'Trafficking and international law', in van den Anker, C. (ed.) *The Political Economy of New Slavery*, Basingstoke: Palgrave Macmillan, pp. 55–74.

Piper, N. (2003) 'Feminization of labor migration as violence against women: International, regional, and local nongovernmental organization responses in Asia', *Violence Against Women*, 9 (6): 723–45.

—— (2005) 'A problem by a different name? A review of research on trafficking in South-East Asia and Oceania', *International Migration*, 43 (1/2): 203–33.

Pollack, J. (2007) 'Thailand', in GAATW (ed.) *Collateral Damage: The Impact of Anti-trafficking Measures on Human Rights around the World*, Bangkok: Global Alliance Against Traffic in Women, pp. 171–99.

Rogaly, B. (2008) 'Migrant workers in the ILO's global alliance against forced labour report: A critical appraisal', *Third World Quarterly*, 29 (7): 1431–47.

Rosenberg, R. (ed.) (2003) *Trafficking of Women and Children in Indonesia*, Jakarta: International Catholic Migration Commission and the American Center for International Labor Solidarity.

Schloenhardt, A. (2001a) 'Trafficking in migrants in the Asia-Pacific: National, regional and international responses', *Singapore Journal of International and Comparative Law*, 5: 696–747.

—— (2001b) 'Trafficking in migrants: Illegal migration and organized crime in Australia and the Asia Pacific region', *International Journal of the Sociology of Law*, 29: 331–78.

Segrave, M. and Milivojevic, S. (2005) 'Sex trafficking – a new agenda', *Social Alternatives*, 24 (2): 11–16.

Segrave, M., Milivojevic, S. and Pickering, S. (eds) (2009) *Sex Trafficking: International Context and Response*, Cullompton, Devon: Willan Publishing.

Sharma, N. (2005) 'Anti-trafficking rhetoric and the making of a global apartheid', *NWSA Journal*, 17 (3): 88–111.

Skeldon, R. (2000) 'Trafficking: A perspective from Asia', *International Migration*, 1: 7–30.

Sugiarti, K. L., Davis, J. and Dasgupta, A. (eds) (2006) *When They Were Sold*, Jakarta: International Catholic Migration Commission and American Center for International Labor Solidarity.

Surtees, R. (2003) 'Female migration and trafficking in women: The Indonesian context', *Development*, 46 (3): 99–107.

Todres, J. (2006) 'The importance of realizing "other rights" to prevent sex trafficking', *Cardozo Journal of Law and Gender*, 12: 885–907.

Turnbull, P. (1999) 'The fusion of immigration and crime in the European Union: Problems of cooperation and the fight against the trafficking in women', in Williams, P. (ed.) *Illegal Immigration and Commercial Sex: The New Slave Trade*, London: Frank Cass, pp. 189–213.

United Nations (2000) *Convention against Transnational Organized Crime 55/25*, Available at http://www.unodc.org/pdf/crime/a_res_55/res5525e.pdf (accessed 18 January 2008).

UNODC (2003) *Coalitions against Trafficking in Human Beings in the Philippines: Research and Action Final Report*, Vienna: Anti-Human Trafficking Unit: Global

Programme against Trafficking in Human Beings, United Nations Office on Drugs and Crime.

—— (2010) *Human Trafficking FAQs*, Available at http://www.unodc.org/unodc/en/human-trafficking/faqs.html (accessed 19 August 2010).

US Department of State (2000) *Trafficking Victims Protection Act – Minimum Standards for the Elimination of Trafficking in Persons*, Available at http://www.state.gov/g/tip/rls/tiprpt/2007/86205.htm (accessed 18 January 2008).

Weitzer, R. (2007) 'The social construction of sex trafficking: Ideology and institutionalization of a moral crusade', *Politics & Society*, 35 (3): 447–75.

Wong, D. (2005) 'The rumor of trafficking: Border controls, illegal migration, and the sovereignty of the nation-state', in van Schendel, W. and Abraham, I. (eds) *Illicit Flows and Criminal Things: States, Borders, and the Other Side of Globalization*, Bloomington: Indiana University Press, pp. 69–100.

1   Agency by proxy

Women and the human trafficking discourse in the Philippines

Jorge Tigno

Human trafficking is constructed both by states and experts as a problem involving 'a disproportionate number of women', the majority of whom are trafficked for 'sexual exploitation' (Laczko 2005: 9; UNODC 2009: 6) – a view that persists despite the absence of reliable, evidence-based research (Gozdziak and Bump 2008). This focus is understandable in the context of one of the key intentions of the UN Trafficking Protocol, which pays 'particular attention to women and children' (UN 2000: Article 2(a)).[1] When combined with its emphasis on fighting transnational organized crime and illegal migration, the Protocol is able to position human trafficking simultaneously as both a threat to state security and a serious gender issue (Aradau 2004). As a consequence of the incorporation of the gender dimension, the global anti-trafficking discourse as well as the counter-trafficking interventions that emanate from it have become preoccupied with accounts of the vulnerabilities of women and children (Gallagher 2001; Miko 2003; Wong 2005; Anderson and Andrijasevic 2008). For example, the US Department of State's annual Trafficking in Persons (TIP) Report conveys the extent of the human tragedy of trafficking in the form of compelling photographs and anecdotes in which trafficking is depicted as 'a highly gendered phenomenon' that greatly and terribly affects women and children (Dauvergne 2008: 72).

Rarely considered in this gendered positioning of trafficking is how it impacts upon women's agency in the public arena (Caraway 2006). The discourse on trafficking within the Protocol and in numerous other sites of public policy promotes a sense of victimization that effectively 'erases the possibility of women's agency':

> Once one is viewed as a victim, consent is compromised . . . The subject position of victim robs women of voice. This in turn impoverishes debate by silencing one of the most authentic positions from which to hear. It also paternalizes the issue – creating an 'us' group that knows what is best for 'them'.
>
> (Dauvergne 2008: 74)

As women are treated as the direct casualties of trafficking, they are effectively deprived of their agency, which makes it difficult for them to emerge as their own advocates against injustice. Thus the 'victim' identified becomes subservient to the interventions and protection of someone who knows best what is good for the trafficked woman.

Ironically, despite the fact that this victimization narrative permeates the discourse on human trafficking in the Philippines and elsewhere, the UN Trafficking Protocol itself does not contain adequate protection mechanisms for trafficked persons: in early 2000, the UN High Commissioner for Human Rights was prompted to express concern that the provisions in the Protocol concerning the protection of the rights of trafficked persons are effectively compromised by the use of the qualifier term 'in appropriate cases' which is seen to be inconsistent with existing international human rights norms.

An examination of the dynamics by which this process of agency construction (or denial) occurs provides a means to interpret the rhetoric that surrounds the issue of trafficking as it is played out in the Philippines. An interrogation of that rhetoric and its purpose provides a better understanding of the outcomes of public policy interventions that arise to deal with human trafficking and their impact on women's agency. For example, highlighting the health and moral dimensions of human trafficking can lead to the outright criminalization of prostitution, or to the promotion of artificial contraceptives to prevent the spread of sexually transmitted diseases, or to the creation of shelters for women who are trafficking victims. Knowing what informs these public policy interventions may help to explain why they succeed or fail, and why they produce unintended consequences.[2]

This chapter critiques the mainstream view expressed within the anti-trafficking discourse in the Philippines that tends to emphasize the vulnerabilities and subsequent victimization of women and subsequently places counter-trafficking interventions mainly within the construct of 'preparing' women for mobility of their own free choice after 'saving' them from the trafficker and 'rehabilitating' them for a 'normal' life outside the trafficking experience.[3] It argues that rather than empowering women by allowing them to assert their own agency, a sense of agency-by-proxy is established where agency is created *for* the women *by* the state and mainstream women's advocacy groups. This leads to two implications that are not inconsistent with Dauvergne's argument: a presumption of lost agency on the part of the 'victims' and the paternalistic reconstitution of their agency by both the state and (ironically) women's advocacy groups. This chapter finds this conception of agency-by-proxy problematic because it does not fully account for women becoming 'willing victims' of trafficking.

As such, the chapter also has its limits in the sense that it provides only one (albeit critical) interpretation of the anti-trafficking discourse. There can arguably be various other ways of analysing this discourse, including those perspectives that take into account the voices of the women themselves being 'victimized'. Likewise, much has been said and is known in the Philippines about human trafficking from the mainstream feminist perspective. This chapter is not a continuation of that mainstream analysis. However, it does suggest an analysis that can provide the basis for a counter-claim to the mainstream view, which is so problematic.

In broad terms, this chapter examines the notions that drive the way the Philippine state has responded to cross-border human trafficking in general and in particular to the way that trafficked women are positioned within state policy discourses and the responses of feminist groups. The first section describes the labour export programme and how the anti-trafficking discourse can be traced back to it in the context of the feminization of overseas employment from the Philippines. The second section examines the *bagong bayani* (literally 'modern-day hero') rhetoric that the labour export programme gave rise to and how understandings of human trafficking are embedded in it and intermeshed with the narratives of personal martyrdom, sacrifice and survival. The chapter then considers how human trafficking discourses converge with debates about prostitution before examining how illegal recruitment in the overseas employment programme has become a substitute for human trafficking in the Philippines.

The *bagong bayani* tag

The Philippines is thought to be a country of origin for a significant number of trafficked women.[4] It is the third largest exporter of labour after India and Mexico, with anywhere between two and eight million Filipinos living and working outside the country.[5] Nearly a million and a half Filipino workers are deployed overseas on an annual basis to over a hundred countries worldwide. Filipino overseas labour migration has become increasingly feminized since the early 1990s. The proportion of Filipino female workers on new overseas labour contracts increased significantly from 54 per cent of total deployments in 1993 to 74 per cent by 2004 but eventually 'levelled off' at approximately 52 per cent in 2009 (POEA 2007, 2010). The majority of women deployed overseas work in the services sector predominantly as domestic workers, entertainers and health workers. Each year since 2006, the Philippines receives anywhere from 12 billion to as much as 19 billion US dollars in official inward remittances (Bangko Sentral ng Pilipinas 2011).[6] However, such remarkable figures underestimate the actual total remittance inflows as they do not include those transfers that are coursed through unofficial channels such as the personal *padala* (literally 'to send') system and other informal networks. Estimates of the percentage of remittances that are not coursed through the formal banking system can reach as much as 30 per cent of total formal remittance inflows.[7]

Migration from the Philippines is managed from below by a complex web of banking and remittance networks; money changers; training, testing and certification centres; labour recruitment agencies and brokers; courier systems; the real estate developers that sell property to the families of overseas migrants; mass media networks; and political parties and advocacy groups. From above, it is managed by an extensive organization of bureaucrats in the Departments of Labour, Immigration and Foreign Affairs. Initially designed as a stop-gap measure to address the domestic over-supply of labour and to take advantage of demand opportunities particularly in the oil-producing Gulf region, the Philippines labour out-migration programme officially began in earnest in 1974 with the establishment of the Overseas Employment Development Board (OEDB) to promote 'a systematic program for overseas employment of Filipino workers in excess of domestic needs and to protect their rights to fair and equitable employment practices' (Government of the Philippines 1974: Article 17).

In 1982, the programme was further consolidated and institutionalized with the creation of the Philippine Overseas Employment Administration (POEA), the successor of the OEDB. Since that time, the POEA has combined labour migration with worker protection and initiatives to maximize the development impact of remittances. In addition, a range of other agencies and government branches keep track of the outward movement of migrants and the inward movement of their remittances. The most prominent of these include the Commission on Filipinos Overseas (CFO) under the Office of the President, whose mission includes the implementation of special projects and programmes 'to promote the welfare of Filipinos overseas' and 'serve as a forum for preserving and enhancing the social, economic and cultural ties of Filipinos overseas with their motherland' (Government of the Philippines 1980a: Section 3). Others include the Office of the Undersecretary for Migrant and Workers Affairs under the Department of Foreign Affairs, the Economic and Financial Monitoring Group of the Philippines Central Bank (or BSP as it is now known) and the National Statistics Office, which regularly conducts its nationwide surveys of overseas Filipinos.

The economic significance of migration figures prominently in the *bagong bayani* narrative used to valorize Filipino migrants. By the late 1980s, migrant workers leaving primarily for West and East Asia (as distinct from the predominantly professional Filipinos who emigrated to North America in earlier waves) had become celebrated as heroes on account of their remittance contributions. Peculiar to the rhetoric of protection described in the previous section is its pragmatic orientation, namely that the rights and welfare of migrants had to be protected not because they are also human beings (or because it is the state's primary responsibility to do so) but because they give so much for the country economically. The language of the first policy declaration in the Migrant Workers Act conveys such a tone:

> *In the pursuit of* an independent foreign policy *and while considering* national sovereignty, territorial integrity, national interest and the right to self-determination paramount in its relations with other states, *the State shall*, at all times, uphold the dignity of its citizens whether in country or overseas, in general, and Filipino migrant workers, in particular.
>
> (Government of the Philippines 1995 Section 2(a), emphasis added)

This pragmatic language of protecting the dignity of Filipino migrants because they contribute much to 'an independent foreign policy' and the 'national interest' is what essentially frames the state's *bagong bayani* discourse.[8] It was former President Corazon Aquino who first officially enunciated the rhetoric and identified the heroic contributions of overseas migrant workers in 1988 during an address she gave to Filipinos in Hong Kong. A later address made also by Aquino in 1990 shows the primordial importance of economics attached to the 'heroism' of the migrants, greeting the '"new heroes" of [the] country's economy' and going on to say that while they must bear loneliness and sacrifice for their loved ones, they are also helping not only their families but 'above all' they are saving the economy (ABS-CBN News 2009).

Over the last two decades, and coinciding with the feminization of migration from the Philippines, this language of economic heroism has become pervasive in state discourse (Rodriguez 2002: 347) to the extent that it is now the dominant characteristic of the overseas employment programme (Franco 2011). The *bagong bayani* tag becomes a means by which overseas workers are incorporated into the national imaginary and the polity via the provision of certain 'entitlements' conferred upon them (Rodriguez 2002: 342), such as tax exemptions and duty free privileges to returning and departing migrants. In addition, every year since 1989, the POEA has conferred the *Bagong Bayani* Award on Filipino migrants in recognition of their 'extraordinary and exemplary deeds, acts, life, services and contributions'. The awarding ceremony is usually held in the 'Heroes Hall' of Malacañang Palace, the official presidential residence.

Since the mid-1990s, however, the image of the *bagong bayani* has been expanded by a discourse of victimization and survival in the face of the difficult challenges and uncertainties of overseas work. This shift followed the well-publicized death of one woman migrant in March 1995 and the near-execution of another in October of the same year. The first is Flor Contemplacion, a woman from Laguna province in the Philippines convicted of the murder of a four-year-old Singaporean child and another Filipina domestic worker. While criminal cases against male Filipinos overseas were not new, what was unusual about Contemplacion was that she was perceived to be an innocent and hardworking woman in an unforgiving land. The sense of public outcry over Flor Contemplacion's case may very well be the result of a feeling of 'pity' for her and for other Filipino migrant women which in turn generated 'a sense of national community' (Rafael 1997: 274). Whatever its causes, it put pressure on the government to do more to protect vulnerable migrant groups, especially women engaged in domestic work (Rodriguez 2002). The promulgation of the Migrant Workers Act of 1995, a direct result of the furore surrounding the Contemplacion case, was signed in June 1995 just months after her execution.

The other pivotal case was that of Sarah Balabagan, a girl from Mindanao who worked in the United Arab Emirates (UAE) as a domestic worker.[9] In June 1995, shortly after the Migrant Workers Act had been signed into law, Balabagan was charged and convicted of killing her employer and sentenced to be executed. She claimed that she was defending herself from attempted rape. In the public mind-set in the Philippines, like Contemplacion before her, Balabagan embodied the unjust hardships that women migrants have to face overseas. There was a significant public clamour to bring her back home. The Philippine Government lobbied for her sentence to be reduced and she was eventually allowed to return to the Philippines to a hero's welcome in August 1996 after serving part of her prison sentence. In a sense, Sarah Balabagan represented the triumph of the policy to protect vulnerable women migrants in the aftermath of the tragedy of Flor Contemplacion. She had become the embodiment of the victim as survivor (Roces 2009).

Both cases were characterized in the public discourse as personifications of martyrdom, victimization and heroism. Both became suffused into countless other stories of sacrifice by countless Filipino women migrants overseas. The fact that eventually both Contemplacion and Balabagan were 'welcomed' home – the former as an innocent martyr and the latter as a living hero/victim/survivor (Roces 2009) – is a testament to the triumph of a nation over adversity, a key feature of the *bagong bayani* discourse. Filipino migrant workers continue to be seen as people who make the sacrifice of leaving their families in search of better opportunities not only for themselves but also for their loved ones back in the Philippines. In the process, martyrdom and making the transition from victim to survivor have become significant aspects of this label attached especially to women migrants in addition to the economic significance of overseas work. Implied in this heroism/ martyrdom nexus is the idea that the women are particularly vulnerable 'victims' – a view that has since become a key feature of the human trafficking discourse.

Prostitution, the feminist movement and the state

The Philippines discourse on human trafficking can be traced to its association with the rise of the feminist movement. The nationalist feminist movement emerged during the Martial Law period of the 1970s, its leftist orientation betrayed by the way feminist groups within it considered women's issues to be grounded upon a 'nationalist agenda' of anti-imperialism, agrarian reform and nationalist industrialization. But by the late 1980s, the movement had become more and more conscious of and sensitive to women-specific issues such as reproductive health, gender stereotypes and prostitution, without completely abandoning its nationalist roots. The people power revolt of 1986 that installed the country's first ever woman president was a key turning point in the way that the state approached the question of both women and migrants. After 1986, feminist groups actively sought to integrate the women's agenda in the programmes and policies of government for the first time through a series of consultations that were held between nongovernmental women's groups and the National Commission on the Role of Filipino Women (NCRFW), an advisory body under the Office of the President created in the 1970s. The effect of these consultations was that it drew individual feminists and nationalists closer to the government (Sobritchea 2004: 109).[10]

The Catholic Church also became more involved in exerting greater pressure on government to enact measures to protect women in general and overseas women migrants in particular. The Church's advocacy of migrant worker rights in the Philippines actually predates the overseas employment programme. In 1967, the Catholic Bishops Conference of the Philippines (CBCP) created the Commission on Immigration and Tourism and the Commission on the Apostolates of the Sea and Air to minister to the spiritual needs of people on the move. In 1972, the CBCP merged the two by creating the Episcopal Commission on Migration and Tourism (ECMT). The emergence of the nationalist-feminist groups and the traditional power of the Church have become the major influences not only in the way the state engages with the migration discourse and the problem of trafficking but also in the way it looks upon the social issue of prostitution. As a consequence, a feminist/moralist discourse began to take root in the policy discourses of the state particularly on matters concerning prostitution and women in migration. This can be seen in the enactment of the Anti-Mail Order Bride Act of 1990, the first article of which mandates that the state 'take measures to protect Filipino women from being exploited in utter disregard of human dignity in pursuit of *economic* uplift-ment' (Government of the Philippines 1990: Section 1, emphasis added).

In popular discourse in the Philippines, prostitution – like mail-order marriage – is framed as something that is forced upon women, an understanding that is also deeply rooted in the feminist discourse on the victimization of women by a patriarchal society. Prostitution in colonial Philippines was chastised yet tolerated and kept 'in the shadows' (Ofreneo and Ofreneo 1998: 100). Under the American occupation in the early part of the twentieth century, Americans were prohibited from visiting brothels, although such an order was honoured in the breach. While prostitution was illegal, laws in the country at the time did not penalize the brothel owners, pimps, and the men who patronized the brothels (Ofreneo and Ofreneo 1998).

In seeking to deal with these kinds of prostitution, historically, official pol-icy has adopted a gendered view. For example, the Revised Penal Code of 1980 applies the term 'prostitute' exclusively to women:

> For the purposes of this article, women who, for money or profit, habitu-ally indulge in sexual intercourse or lascivious conduct, are deemed to be prostitutes.
>
> (Government of the Philippines 1980b: Article 202 (5), Book Two)

This penal article is included in a chapter entitled 'Offenses against Decency and Good Customs' (Government of the Philippines 1980b: Chapter Two, Book Two). The statute strongly implies two things: that prostitution is not only illegal but also immoral, and that women cannot willingly choose to become prostitutes. Ironi-cally, the historical and contemporary understanding of prostitution in the Philip-pines is that it is seen as a problem that harms women yet the policy response is to punish them instead of their male patrons.

> Philippine laws are punitive towards women in prostitution . . . The existing laws aim to suppress prostitution . . . The intent of existing anti-prostitution laws is prohibitionist – prohibiting women from engaging in prostitution. It is also based on moral condemnation of prostitution, stating that it is 'morally degrading; a social malady that must be curbed for the public good; corrupts moral fiber of society; a menace to the good customs of people'.
>
> (Sancho 1999: 39)

In contemporary times, conservative religious-based groups in the Philippines continue to condemn prostitution as an evil and prostitutes as immoral. When the HIV-AIDS pandemic began in the Philippines, 'the religious prayed' and called it 'a heaven-sent plague to punish the sinners' (Santos 1997: 1). By contrast, progressive feminist groups see prostitution as a form of institutional violence against women in which prostituted women are victims who continue to be vulnerable as long as traditional (masculine and paternalistic) values dominate society. For them, prostitution is violence against women, and prostitutes are seen as 'social victims of a culture that glorified women's suffering for the family' (Roces 2009: 274).

Most progressive women's groups argue that prostitution is 'a structural issue related to patriarchy and poverty' and that no woman would consent to engage in sex work were she not forced by poverty and desperation (Santos 1997). This position reflects the mainstream view in Philippine society, which denies women agency once they are engaged in sex work. Most feminist groups in the country find it inconceivable that a woman could willingly choose to become involved in sex work: it must be 'because poverty forced women to become involved in a transaction in which they are clearly the victims' (Sancho 1999; Roces 2009: 274). Moreover, according to this view, it is capitalist patriarchy that compels these women to engage not only in sex work, but also domestic work.[11] The active and dominant presence of women in these lines of work is seen as an 'obvious manifestation' of 'the feudal-patriarchal system, which has been effectively and efficiently maintained by the mechanisms and values of a capitalist-dominated world' (Santos 2004: 39).

The dominant progressive feminist organizations thus look upon prostitution as a moral or social evil that has been forced upon women by an uncaring society. From this standpoint, prostitution is not considered legitimate work, nor is it something that can be regulated. Prostitutes need to be rehabilitated, re-educated and reformed so that they can lead a 'normal' life. In the view of these feminist groups, the women are also seen as brave survivors. But before they can be survivors they must be seen as victims, whose agency is defined for them by such groups. This social narrative of victimhood becomes the key argument made by women's groups in the Philippines in pushing for the passage of anti-trafficking legislation (Roces 2009). It is not inconceivable for mainstream women's groups to make the leap from prostitution to human trafficking using the same analytical frame.

From prostitution to trafficking

Trafficking was first described in contemporary Philippine legal discourse in 1992 through RA 7610, An Act Providing for Stronger Deterrence and Special Protection against Child Abuse, Exploitation, and Discrimination, and for Other Purposes, a law in which 'child trafficking' was specifically defined as 'trading and dealing with children' as well as 'the act of buying and selling of a child for money, or for any other consideration, or barter' (Government of the Philippines 1992: Section 7). The child trafficking law essentially referred to children treated as chattel property, although it positions the act of trafficking clearly in the context of being forced into prostitution or to inflict sexual abuse. The definition of trafficking was formally extended to adults a year after the Philippines signed and ratified both the UN Trafficking and Smuggling Protocols, when RA 9208, An Act to Institute Policies to Eliminate Trafficking in Persons Especially Women and Children, Establishing the Necessary Institutional Mechanisms for the Protection and Support of Trafficked Persons, Providing Penalties for its Violations, and for Other Purposes was passed.

The Anti-Trafficking Act is a consolidation of two versions that emanated from the Senate (SB 2444) and the House of Representatives (HB 4432) that dealt with human trafficking within the framework of prostitution and the sexual exploitation of women and children. A major coalition of women's groups, the Coalition against Trafficking in Women, Philippines (CATWP) which is affiliated with the Asia-Pacific Coalition against Trafficking in Women (CATW-AP), vigorously pushed for the passage of the law. CATW-AP, which was established in 1993 in Manila, and relies on the Philippines for its organizational strength, adopts the position that trafficking and prostitution are one and, like nationalist feminist groups, that 'socio-economic, political, and gender inequalities' have contributed to the continued sexual exploitation of women (FOKUS 2007: 8). Its focus is on saving 'abused, trafficked, and prostituted women' and its services include 'training and education; research and publication; advocacy campaigns; referral of trafficking cases; and group building' (Sobritchea 2004: 117).[12]

Roces (2009: 270–1) observes that in lobbying for the anti-trafficking law, the dominant feminist groups in the Philippines used the victim narrative to push for its passage because (a) prostitution is considered as violence against women and (b) that the 'women's experiences of prostitution were constructed in a history of continuing oppression and violation' within a patriarchal social construct.[13] This implied that if the so-called prostitutes were 'victims' then 'they could not possibly exude sexuality; instead they were victims of male desire'. This signalled a significant departure from the traditional view that criminalizes prostitutes as immoral elements of society, shifting attention to society and to men that perpetrate prostitution (Roces 2009: 275). However, such a view did not represent a complete departure from the traditional view since it is still the women who are vulnerable to becoming 'victims' of prostitution and being trafficked. The anti-trafficking law has effectively become the 'master metaphor' for the illicit, the criminal and the immoral (Wong 2005: 71). In the words of Sancho:

> In the Philippines, suppressing trafficking in women is equated with suppressing prostitution. The existing definitions of what trafficking is are quite hazy because it is made synonymous with prostitution. Thus, anti-trafficking measures include enforcement of anti-prostitution laws.
>
> (Sancho 1999: 40)

As Roces suggests, much of the discussion surrounding the passage of the Anti-Trafficking Act centred on the problem of prostitution as violence against women and the need to protect them. The Act essentially follows the provisions of the UN Trafficking Protocol but, in addition, enumerates certain acts of human trafficking such as mail-order marriages and child trafficking as well as engaging in prostitution, pornography, sexual exploitation, forced labour, slavery, involuntary servitude or debt bondage (Section 3).[14] These acts are already identified in earlier statutes such as the Philippine Mail Order Bride Act (RA 6955) of 1990, the Anti-Child Abuse and Exploitation Act (RA 7610) of 1992; and the Revised Penal Code.

The positioning of prostitution and pornography involving women and children as focal points in human trafficking statutes in the Philippines is no surprise considering that the victimization of women (and girls) for purposes of sexual exploitation and prostitution occupies a dominant space in Philippines trafficking discourse. The focus on sexual exploitation also explains the prominence of social welfare assistance agencies that provide shelter, halfway houses and other forms of direct and indirect support (for example, psychological and evangelical counselling, information dissemination and legal advice) to prostituted women and minors who invariably have become (or are potential) trafficking victims.[15] This again implies that women are weaker and more vulnerable to exploitation (in the context of a prevailing patriarchy) such that they require all the resources of the state and society to take care of them.

Feminist groups, notably CATW-AP and the General Assembly Binding Women for Reforms, Integrity, Equality, Leadership, and Action (GABRIELA), a coalition of organizations and institutions established in 1984, now with over 100 members – which is not a member of CATW-AP – quickly responded to the passing of the Act. Along with the NCRFW, these organizations spearheaded information dissemination and awareness campaigns to prevent women and girls from the Philippines from being victimized by traffickers. These groups are also engaged in advocacy efforts to promote women's rights and to enact stronger legislation to stop and prevent the sexual exploitation of women.

Groups like Bantay Bata (Child Watch) are also involved in collaborative efforts with government agencies to rescue children from abusive and exploitative conditions. However, the Visayan Forum Foundation (VFF) is one of the few organizations in the Philippines to focus on domestic work and slavery (especially involving children), and not specifically on sexual exploitation and prostitution, in the way that it understands and deals with human trafficking.[16] Both mainstream women's groups and the Anti-Trafficking Act assume that a woman becomes a victim against her choice and without agency, and must now be rehabilitated in order to fit into 'mainstream' society. Such a view is not inconsistent with traditional notions attached to prostitutes by feminist and Church groups in the Philippine context. However, the use of the narrative of victimhood becomes more problematic as prostitution and trafficking are elided with illegal migration and recruitment.

The meshing of trafficking and illegal recruitment

Over the last 30 years, the problem of illegal recruitment had become a serious concern for many Filipinos. Migrants see the recruitment stage as the biggest hurdle to their overseas deployment, which also incurs the biggest costs. Private recruitment entities dominate the labour migration industry (representing at least 95 per cent of total annual deployments). In this market-dominated landscape, unscrupulous agents abound, eager to take advantage of the over-supply of domestic labour relative to the availability of overseas jobs.

From the mid-1980s through the 1990s, an average of 700 illegal recruitment cases were received each year by the POEA (with over 1,000 cases in 1984, 1985 and 1989) involving an average of 1,500 worker-victims (with a high of over 3,000 victims in 1985). Although the number of cases had fallen to 250 and 488 (involving some 1,100 victims and 54 establishments) in 2005 and 2006 respectively, this does not mean that illegal recruitment activities have actually declined. Between 2003 and 2004, the POEA cancelled the licenses of 142 recruitment entities for various recruitment violations and malpractices (Abella 2006: 51). As of the end of 2009, there were still 1,349 licensed agencies in good standing (POEA 2009: 14) – a number that does not include the countless other fly-by-night recruiters. Interventions to address and prevent such illegal recruitment activities are based on the assumption that migrants do not have sufficient information, awareness or knowledge to detect and avoid fraudsters. This assumption ignores the possibility that workers may have chosen to be recruited or deployed through illegal means. Moreover, legally recruited migrants are just as likely to become victims of traffickers as illegally recruited ones. Irregular migration is also a function of the unavailability or inaccessibility to migrants of official, legal or regular channels of recruitment and deployment. The inability or unavailability of proper and effective access by migrants to official or legal channels of recruitment and deployment can convince potential migrants to resort to illicit and illegal means of departure and entry. To rationalize illegal recruitment entirely as a function of information asymmetry is to oversimplify and misrepresent the problem.

To further complicate matters, illegal recruitment is often conflated with human trafficking. In fact, it is not uncommon for Philippine authorities to use the terms interchangeably. When the Philippines Government declared 1997 to be Anti-Trafficking of Migrants Year, the executive order signed by President Fidel Ramos at the time called on government agencies to 'adopt measures, including allocation of its resources, to the drive against *illegal trafficking*' (Ruiz-Austria 2006: 100, emphasis in original).[17] The redundant use of the term 'illegal' to describe trafficking demonstrates the extent to which it has become conflated with illegal recruitment and human smuggling, something typical of the discourse in the Philippines before the advent of the UN Trafficking Protocol (Ruiz-Austria 2006: 100). It is significant to note that the 1997 Anti-Trafficking of Migrants Year aimed to address the problems associated more with illegal labour recruitment than with human trafficking *per se*.

Trafficking and illegal recruitment continue to be seen to be two sides of the same coin. In September 2010, the chair of the Senate Foreign Relations Committee urged the Department of Foreign Affairs to:

> create channels to improve our rankings by the United States in anti-human trafficking performance, asserting that our high conviction rates on illegal recruitment must offset our low convictions under the Anti-Trafficking in Persons Act for purposes of making the Philippines eligible for foreign assistance.
>
> (Senate of the Philippines 2010)

The reason for this peculiar understanding of the relationship between human trafficking and illegal recruitment is the general conception that illegally recruited workers are more likely to experience exploitation and abuse abroad. This argument can lead to a position where only those illegally recruited can actually be trafficked, ignoring the possibility that even those who go through legal channels of recruitment are also susceptible to being tricked, exploited and abused. And since illegal recruitment is thought to lead to a person being trafficked and exploited, it is also thought that the only way that trafficking can be avoided is by preventing illegal recruitment.

Once it is assumed that trafficking and illegal recruitment are interchangeable, a problem arises with regard to women's agency. In particular, there appears to be an incompatibility between the way that trafficking is constructed (using the victim narrative in which the migrant loses her sense of agency) and its relationship to illegal recruitment (where the migrant becomes a 'willing' victim). For some, this incompatibility is resolved by timing. During the recruitment process it is possible to say that the migrant had a choice and a sense of agency but later on because of trafficking that sense of agency had now been lost as the migrant becomes a victim of the trafficker. But such an argument can be problematic when former victims of trafficking become traffickers themselves or when migrants are victimized repeatedly.[18] This suggests that their representation as 'innocent victims' does not sit well with the idea that the women would repeatedly 'return to a situation where they knew they could once again be dehumanized, exploited and abused' (Roces 2009: 274–5).

As a result, despite active information campaigns on how to avoid unscrupulous recruiters, reports in the mass media confirm that people continue to be 'victimized' by unscrupulous agents. On the one hand, it may be said that private recruitment agencies are always able to find new and better ways to distort the information that goes to the worker-applicants and avoid detection and capture. But on the other hand, the strong desire to go abroad becomes a compelling reason for would-be migrants to knowingly become victims of recruitment proposals that are often and obviously fraudulent. Many migrants are reluctant to file charges against recruiters – in not a few cases, these so-called 'victims' are not so much interested in having the illegal recruiters arrested and jailed as they are interested in getting their money back (Esplanada 2002). As soon as their money is returned the workers desist from pursuing their cases against the recruiters, indicating an underlying sense of agency as law enforcement agencies are turned into collection agents by those victims (Esplanada 2002; Hilotin 2003).

Conclusion

Wrapped around the anti-trafficking discourse in the Philippines are a complex and complicated set of notions and narratives of migrant martyrdom, the immorality of prostitution and the language of patriarchy as well as how trafficking overlaps with illegal recruitment. The interplay of these notions within the anti-trafficking discourse in the Philippines has had a profound impact on reinterpretations of the agency of women, particularly and especially overseas migrants, in relation to how they are looked upon by the state and feminist groups. From the point of view of the state, female migrant workers deserve and need to be protected. And because they are seen to be weak, they are believed to be unable to express their own agency, so that agency must be established for them by the state. The enactment of the Migrant Workers Act of 1995 as a result of the high-profile cases of Contemplacion and Balabagan and the special emphasis on 'women and children' in the Anti-Trafficking Act of 2003 provide the legal bases for this assertion.

Trafficking and prostitution have become interchangeable in the Philippines context. Dominant nationalist feminist groups strongly associate trafficking with prostitution, patriarchy, violence and the exploitation of women. The idea of genuinely choosing to engage in sex work is considered unlikely – if not impossible – in the context of an exploitative patriarchy where women are treated as inferiors and all trafficked women are represented as victims. Anti-trafficking/anti-prostitution programmes have become the location for a feminist discourse in which feminist groups assign *their* agency to the trafficked/prostituted women by 'rescuing' them and 'rehabilitating' them towards establishing a 'normal life' on their behalf. As Caraway (2006: 307) points out, 'women's rights are at risk of being violated by so-called rescue missions, despite the good intentions of would-be rescuers.' The emphasis on rescue, rehabilitation and reintegration into mainstream society reveals a peculiar understanding of victimhood on the part of the state and women's groups in the Philippines that displaces genuine agency with one that assumes that the woman's agency has been lost due to exploitation, prostitution and patriarchy and now needs to be regained or reconstituted on her behalf.

The peculiarity of the anti-trafficking discourse in the Philippines also lies in the slippage between trafficking and illegal recruitment (Anderson and Andryijasevic 2008: 138). This is largely based on the assumption that trafficking in the Philippines stems mainly from illegal recruitment and which is also seen to be a function of information asymmetry and limited choice. However, to account for illegal recruitment merely as a function of insufficiency of information is to oversimplify the problem and how it is actually linked to human trafficking and migrant agency. Providing the right kind of information to the migrant does not automatically prevent illegal recruitment. The desire to live and work overseas is so strong and compelling that migrants are willing to forego authorized recruitment channels. Complicating this fact is the conflicted way that illegal recruitment is understood by government authorities in the Philippines. On the one hand, the 'victim' needs to be 'rescued' from the recruiter/trafficker. But on the other hand, the victim is the 'client' who is 'caught' just before boarding the plane.

All in all, the anti-trafficking discourse in the Philippines attests to the further victimization of women where their own sense of agency is displaced and defined for them largely by the state and feminist groups. The women in the anti-trafficking narrative are both glorified and reduced to victimhood, their heroism necessarily preceded by their victimization. This displacement of migrant agency reinforces 'notions of female dependency and purity' that has the effect of marginalizing rather than empowering the women concerned (Doezema 2002: 23).

Ironically, the emphasis on rescue and rehabilitation has the unexpected effect of compromising women's rights. In order to address this, anti-trafficking protocols must necessarily be informed by the importance of upholding the totality of the human rights of trafficked persons to eventually make them advocates of their own welfare and empower them.

Notes

1 Collapsing the two distinct categories (i.e. women and children) leads to serious issues of agency as even adult women are assumed to be like children with limited reasoning faculties and therefore deserving of the protection of the state and society (Doezema 2002).

2 It is not uncommon to find former 'victims' who have become recruiters (UNODC 2009: 6) or women who have been exploited and abused returning to their exploitative situations (Roces 2009: 274).

3 This is the revised version of a paper presented at the Tenth International Women in Asia Conference, 'Crisis, Agency, and Change', 29 September–1 October 2010, The Australian National University (ANU), Canberra. Research for this paper was made possible by an Australian Leadership Award Fellowship (ALAF) grant from the Australian Agency for International Development (AusAID), taken at the Department of Political and Social Change at the ANU from July to November 2010. This chapter is based on insights gathered during earlier fieldwork, supplemented by analysis of relevant policies and pronouncements; a critical survey of the existing literature on human trafficking from the Philippines; and consultations with experts in the academic sector and Philippine embassy officials. The arguments and positions stated in this chapter do not reflect the views of any particular institution, and the author is responsible for all claims.

4 The Philippines is described as a country of origin, transit and destination for trafficking victims. However, the rhetoric surrounding the discourse on trafficking assigns the Philippines the role of a source of trafficked victims going abroad, notwithstanding the fact that trafficking also takes place internally from rural to urban areas. For purposes of this chapter the Philippines is treated as a source country.

5 The higher estimate comes from the government's approximations on stocks of Filipinos overseas. It includes documented as well as undocumented or irregular migrants but does not account for double counting or natural attrition due to deaths. The lower estimate is made by the National Statistics Office (NSO) based on its 2009 Survey of Overseas Filipinos, which tracks the number of Filipinos who have worked overseas within a given period (NSO 2010).

6 For the whole of 2010, official remittance inflows totalled nearly US$19 billion. The figure clearly exceeds the amount of official development assistance the Philippines gets.

7 The Bangko Sentral ng Pilipinas began reporting on informal remittance flows in 2001. However, since 2005 the proportion of remittances that pass through the informal system has gone down considerably to about 5 per cent (Philippine Daily Inquirer 2009).

8 Franco (2011) provides an excellent account of how the *bagong bayani* discourse has been used by the state to justify labour export in the midst of criticisms against the government programme and calls for the protection and promotion of the rights and welfare of overseas Filipino migrant workers.

9 Sarah Balabagan was under-aged and thus should not have been working overseas.

10 Before 1986, the movement had eschewed collaboration, which it saw as co-optation. The consultations eventually triggered what Sobritchea (2004) describes as

the 'collaboration' debate within the feminist movement that traces its roots to the nationalist movement of the late 1970s.

11 Ironically, while calls from the country have risen to protect and promote the rights and welfare of Filipino migrant domestic workers in other countries, not much has been said about protecting the rights of local household workers. Most middle-class feminist groups in the Philippines are silent on the idea of protecting and granting more rights to domestic workers in the country, whom many of them employ.

12 As far as the Philippines is concerned, CATW-AP dominates the landscape in the way that trafficking is equated with prostitution and prostituted women are actually victims of violence. Aside from CATW-AP, there are other feminist groups operating in the Philippines, most notably the Global Alliance Against Trafficking in Women (GAATW) which is a coalition of some 30 organizations and national coalitions in 11 countries in the Asian region. It has only one member in the Philippines, the Buhay Foundation for Women and the Girl Child, founded in 2000. While it recognizes prevailing and persistent 'socio-political and economic realities', the Buhay Foundation advocates a more rights-based approach to human trafficking by ensuring safe and fair migration procedures and workplaces and adopts the position that women should be given 'life choices' and the 'right to self determination' (Buhay Foundation 2008).

13 Roces (2009: 270) also observes that this victim construct was used to lobby for the legislation but argues that women's groups in the Philippines 'preferred to use the narrative of advocacy, agency and empowerment when fashioning former prostitutes and survivors of trafficking into feminist activists'.

14 The Anti-Trafficking Law defines pornography to be 'any representation' that shows 'indecent' acts by 'a person engaged in real or simulated explicit sexual activities or any representation of the sexual parts of a person for primarily sexual purposes' (Government of the Philippines 2003, Section 3 (h)).

15 In a preliminary survey conducted among NGOs in the Philippines in 2002, respondents were asked what they thought trafficked victims needed the most. Their top responses dealt with programmes to protect victims such as legal and financial assistance, resettlement assistance, and health care/counselling including the establishment of psychosocial and welfare services (Tigno 2002).

16 Since its establishment in 1991, the main focus of VFF has been on helping women and girls who have become trafficked and abused within the Philippines as household domestic workers although it also provides assistance to victims of trafficking found at the Manila International Airport. VFF provides shelter and halfway houses to facilitate the rehabilitation and reintegration of victims of trafficking through psychosocial counselling, legal aid and 'life skills training' (VFF 2008).

17 It is not only the Philippines that has made this mistake. At the time the Trafficking Protocol was being drafted in early 1999, several other states used the term 'illegal trafficking' in their proposals. For further details refer to the *Travaux Préparatoires* of the negotiations of the United Nations Convention against Transnational Organized Crime and the related protocols.

18 For instance, Roces (2009: 274–5) finds cases of women who have 'returned to Japan six or seven times . . . at different clubs' after supposedly experiencing abuse and exploitation problematic and not in consonance with the victim representation inherent in the trafficking discourse.

References

Abella, M. (2006) 'Policies and best practices for management of temporary migration', paper presented at the International Symposium on International Migration and Development, Population Division, Department of Economic and Social Affairs, United Nations Secretariat Turin (28–30 June 2006).

ABS-CBN News (2009) 'Fan bares Cory's message to OFWs', ABS-CBN News.com. Online. Available at http://www.abs-cbnnews.com/ofw/08/03/09/fan-bares-corys-message-ofws (accessed 23 December 2010).

Anderson, B. and Andrijasevic, R. (2008) 'Sex, slaves and citizens: The politics of anti-trafficking', *Soundings*, 40: 135–45.

Aradau, C. (2004) 'The perverse politics of four-letter words: Risk and pity in the securitisation of human trafficking', *Journal of International Studies*, 33 (2): 251–77.

Bangko Sentral ng Pilipinas (2011) 'Overseas Filipinos' remittances'. Online. Available at http://www.bsp.gov.ph/statistics/keystat/ofw.htm (accessed 10 March 2011).

Buhay Foundation (2008) 'Vision, mission and objectives – Buhay Foundation for Women and the Girl Child'. Online. Available at http://buhayfoundationlifechoices.blogspot.com/2008/07/vision-mission-and-objectives-buhay.html (accessed 20 December 2010).

Caraway, N. (2006) 'Human rights and existing contradictions in Asia-Pacific human trafficking politics and discourse', *Tulane Journal of International and Comparative Law*, 14 (1): 295–316.

Dauvergne, C. (2008) *Making People Illegal: What Globalization Means for Migration and Law*, Cambridge: Cambridge University Press.

Doezema, J. (2002) 'Who gets to choose? Coercion, consent, and the UN Trafficking Protocol', *Gender and Development*, 10 (1): 20–7.

Esplanada, J. (2002) 'Uncooperative victims hamper fight vs. illegal recruiters', *Philippine Daily Inquirer*, 9 January 2002.

Forum for Women and Development (FOKUS) (2007) *Evaluation of Coalition Against Trafficking in Women – Asia Pacific – The Philippines*. Online. Available at http://www.norad.no/en/Tools+and+publications/Publications/Publication+Page?key=117496 (accessed 31 October 2010).

Franco, J. (2011) 'The politics of language in labor export: A discourse historical analysis of *bagong bayani* and overseas employment policies', unpublished PhD dissertation, Department of Political Science, University of the Philippines.

GABRIELA (n.d.) 'GABRIELA's history'. Online. Available at http://www.members.tripod.com/~gabriela_p/ (accessed 23 December 2010).

Gallagher, A. (2001) 'Human rights and the new UN protocols on trafficking and migrant smuggling: A preliminary analysis', *Human Rights Quarterly*, 23 (4): 975–1004.

Government of the Philippines (1974) Labour Code of the Philippines, Manila: Department of Labour and Employment.

—— (1980a) An Act Creating the Commission on Filipinos Overseas and for Other Purposes, Manila: Republic of the Philippines.

—— (1980b) The Revised Penal Code of the Philippines, Manila: Republic of the Philippines.

—— (1990) An Act to Declare Unlawful the Practice of Matching Filipino Women for Marriage to Foreign Nationals on a Mail-order Basis and Other Similar Practices including the Advertisement, Publication, Printing or Distribution of Brochures, Fliers and Other Propaganda Materials in Furtherance Thereof and Providing Penalty Therefor, Manila: Republic of the Philippines.

—— (1992) An Act Providing for Stronger Deterrence and Special Protection against Child Abuse, Exploitation, and Discrimination, and for Other Purposes, Manila: Republic of the Philippines.

—— (1995) An Act to Institute the Policies of Overseas Employment and Establish a Higher Standard of Protection and Promotion of the Welfare of Migrant Workers, their

Families and Overseas Filipinos in Distress, and for Other Purposes, Manila: Republic of the Philippines.

—— (2003) An Act to Institute Policies to Eliminate Trafficking in Persons Especially Women and Children, Establishing the Necessary Institutional Mechanisms for the Protection and Support of Trafficked Persons, Providing Penalties for its Violations, and for Other Purposes, Manila: Office of the President.

Goździak, E. and Bump, M. (2008) *Data and Research on Human Trafficking: Bibliography of Research-Based Literature*, Washington, DC: Georgetown University.

Hilotin, J. (2003) 'Filipino job seekers walk into illegal recruitment trap', *Asia Africa Intelligence Wire*, 11 November 2003. Online. Available at http://www.accessmylibrary.com/coms2/summary_0286-19337537_ITM (accessed 24 December 2010).

Laczko, F. (2005) 'Introduction: Data and research on human trafficking', *International Migration*, 43 (1 and 2): 5–16.

Miko, F. (2003) 'Trafficking in women and children: The US and international response', in Troubnikoff, A. (ed.) *Trafficking in Women and Children: Current Issues and Developments*, New York: Nova Science Publishers, pp. 1–30.

National Statistics Office (NSO) (2010) 'OFWs counted at 1.9 million'. Online. Available at http://www.census.gov.ph/data/pressrelease/2010/of09tx.html (accessed 30 November 2010).

Ofreneo, R. and Ofreneo, L. (1998) 'Prostitution in the Philippines', in Lean Lim Lin (ed.) *The Sex Sector: The Economic and Social Bases of Prostitution in Southeast Asia*, Geneva: International Labour Office, pp. 100–29.

Philippine Daily Inquirer (2009) 'Remittances via non-bank channels shrinking', 2 February 2009.

Philippine Overseas Employment Administration (POEA) (2007) '2007 employment statistics'. Online. Available at http://www.poea.gov.ph/stats/stats2007.pdf (accessed 10 January 2009).

—— (2009) *Annual Report 2009*, Mandaluyong City: POEA.

—— (2010) 'OFW deployment per skill and country'. Online. Available at http://www.poea.gov.ph/stats/Skills/Skill_Country_Sex/Deployment%20per%20Skill,%20Country%20and%20Sex%202009.pdf (accessed 19 May 2010).

Rafael, V. (1997) '"Your grief is our gossip": Overseas Filipinos and other spectral presences', *Public Culture*, 9 (2): 267–91.

Roces, M. (2009) 'Prostitution, women's movements, and the victim narrative in the Philippines', *Women's Studies International Forum*, 32 (4): 270–80.

Rodriguez, R. (2002) 'Migrant Heroes: Nationalism, citizenship and the politics of Filipino migrant labour', *Citizenship Studies*, 6 (3): 341–56.

Ruiz-Austria, C. (2006) 'Conflicts and interests: Trafficking in Filipino women and the Philippine government policies on migration and trafficking', in Beeks, K. and Amir, D. (eds) *Trafficking and the Global Sex Industry*, Lanham, MD and Oxford: Lexington Books, pp. 97–118.

Sancho, N. (1999) 'The legal system on prostitution and trafficking and impact on the women affected: The Philippine case', paper presented during the NGO Consultation with UN/IGOs on Trafficking in Persons, Prostitution and the Global Sex Industry, Geneva, 21–2 June 1999. Online. Available at http://www.imadr.org/en/pdf/99GenevaConsultation.pdf (accessed 6 March 2011).

Santos, A. (1997) 'Patriarchy, poverty, prostitution and HIV/AIDS: The Philippine experience', paper read at the 4th International Congress on AIDS in Asia and the Pacific, Manila, 25–9 October 1997.

—— (2004) 'Do women really hold up half the sky? Notes on the women's movement in the Philippines', in Sobritchea, C. (ed.) *Gender, Culture, and Society: Selected Readings in Women's Studies in the Philippines*, Seoul: Ewha Womens University Press and Asian Center for Women's Studies, pp. 23–43.

Sayres, N. (2004) *An Analysis of the Situation of Filipino Domestic Workers*, Makati City, Philippines: International Labour Organization. Online. Available at http://www.ilo.org/wcmsp5/groups/public/---asia/---ro-bangkok/---ilo-manila/documents/publication/wcms_124895.pdf (accessed 28 May 2011).

Senate of the Philippines (2010) 'Loren: Conviction rate in illegal recruitment shows RP serious in fight vs. human trafficking', Senate Press Release. Online. Available at http://www.senate.gov.ph/press_release/2010/0903_legarda1.asp (28 September 2010).

Sobritchea, C. (2004) 'Women's movement in the Philippines and the politics of critical collaboration with the state', in Lee Hock Guan (ed.) *Civil Society in Southeast Asia*, Singapore: Institute of Southeast Asian Studies, pp. 101–22.

Tigno, J. (2002) 'A survey on trafficking and smuggling in human beings from the Philippines and the involvement of organized crime groups: Examining the experiences and perspectives of victims and non-governmental organizations (NGOs)', paper presented at the Expert Meeting on the Coalitions Against Trafficking in Human Beings in the Philippines – Phase I, Philippine Center on Transnational Crime, Manila, 18–19 March 2002.

UN Office on Drugs and Crime (UNODC) (2009) *Global Report on Trafficking in Persons*, Vienna: Policy Analysis and Research Branch, UNODC.

Visayan Forum Foundation, Incorporated (VFF) (2008) 'About the Visayan Forum'. Online. Available at http://www.visayanforum.org/portal/index.php?option=cms&mode=view&id=4 (accessed 30 November 2010).

Wong, D. (2005) 'The rumor of trafficking: Border controls, illegal migration, and the sovereignty of the nation-state', in van Schendel, W. and Abraham, I. (eds) *Illicit Flows and Criminal Things: States, Borders, and the Other Side of Globalization*, Bloomington and Indianapolis: Indiana University Press, pp. 69–100.

2 International politics, anti-trafficking measures and sex work in Cambodia

Larissa Sandy

Timed to coincide with Cambodia's National Anti-Human Trafficking Day, 35,000 people packed into Phnom Penh's Olympic Stadium on 12 December 2008 for a free concert featuring top selling local and international artists. Multi-platinum alternative rock bands like Placebo and Click Five rocked the crowds supported by Australian pop singer Kate Miller-Heidke and the much-adored local pop artist Preap Sovath. The Olympic Stadium concert was the last in a series held across the country as part of the global MTV EXIT (End Exploitation and Trafficking) campaign. This campaign began with MTV Europe in 2004, and expanded to include MTV Asia Pacific in 2008, in partnership with the United States Agency for International Development (USAID). In front of the stadium on that same evening, Cambodia's sex workers launched their 'NO EXIT: Stop Trafficking and Decriminalise Sex Work' campaign. Sex workers and their supporters protested against MTV EXIT and the high-profile series of events and multi-media productions, which included a series of documentaries that featured the stories of women who had been trafficked for sexual exploitation. Local sex workers protested against their lack of inclusion in the MTV EXIT campaign, expressing the opinion that MTV was not able to broadcast their views as they had received funding from USAID for the concerts and special programmes. In addition, they raised concerns about the MTV campaign, which overwhelmingly failed to pay any attention to the gross violations of their rights under Cambodia's new anti-trafficking laws.

Cambodia has long been identified as a human trafficking 'hotspot' (see Molland in this volume) and, after sustained pressure from the US and other governments, in February 2008 the Royal Government of Cambodia promulgated its Law on the Suppression of Human Trafficking and Sexual Exploitation. It is patently obvious that Cambodia's anti-trafficking legislation was expressly adopted in response to the US Government's policy of eradication under sustained pressure from the Trafficking in Persons (TIP) Report and threat of economic and other sanctions. The passing of this law, which criminalizes sex work and equates it with human trafficking, saw sex workers arrested and brothels closed down across the country. Indeed, as a result of the new law, brothel raids and rescues have become the major form of intervention against trafficking in the country.

In this chapter I examine the phenomenon of human trafficking in Cambodia and chart local and international responses to the issue, which culminated in the promulgation of the 2008 Human Trafficking Law.[1] In contrast to other parts of Southeast Asia, where it is increasingly accepted that trafficking can occur in various migration processes and sites, Cambodia's Human Trafficking Law is limited to – and by – an almost exclusive focus on sex work. This conflation between sex work and human trafficking has had serious consequences. Having forced sex workers to move through illicit channels, the law leaves them vulnerable, stigmatized and illegitimate (Kapur 2005: 35). In addition, it provides no impetus to address and transform the abusive practices that structure and shape Cambodia's sex industry. I argue that these changes, along with international policies and funding, have strengthened the dominant discourse of trafficking and, in doing so, have further compounded the stigmatization, marginalization and oppression of sex workers.

The 'cross-border flows' of anti-trafficking measures

Cambodia's Human Trafficking Law casts all sex work as by nature forced and views the practice as a form of sexual exploitation – a position that is at odds with the views of many local sex workers who see working in the industry as an income-generating activity or form of labour. This understanding is not unique to Cambodia but rather is a key feature of the global sex workers' rights movement, which emerged in the 1970s out of the American civil rights movement (Leigh 1997; Alexander 1998; Kempadoo 1998). The sex workers' rights movement saw the development of a reactive but self-identified discourse in which it was argued that sex work is a legitimate occupation for consenting adults. After its inception, this fledgling discourse gained traction internationally, as sex workers around the world started arguing for the legitimacy of their work and inclusion in society. Through this activity, they began to challenge the one-dimensional views on sex work expressed by radical feminists, public health officials and governments (Pheterson 1989). Speaking for themselves without mediation by radical feminists or public health officials, many sex workers criticized the hegemonic logic that excluded them from discussions and theorizations about sex work. Further, through the neologism 'sex work', and the discourse that had formed around this term, sex worker activists were able to form alliances with groups of similarly oppressed workers, as well as with other feminists, scholars and NGO workers sympathetic to their cause. In countries like Australia and elsewhere, the discourse became instrumental in shaping government responses to sex work as public health officials began to take some of its key messages on board.

Underpinning the 'sex as work' paradigm, the dichotomy of free and forced labour soon became one of the dominant models for understanding sex work. This framework, which attempted to distinguish between voluntary and forced sex work, was initially developed by sex worker activists who then engaged in a debate with radical feminists and others who viewed all sex work as forced. In this debate, sex workers pushed for a differentiation between voluntary and forced monetized sexual exchanges, as they advanced their position as politicized sex workers who were not coerced into working in the industry. Like sex workers elsewhere, Cambodian sex workers define the provision of sexual services as a trade or profession, with many expressing the view that sex work is a job in which the performance of sexual labour is a means through which to earn a living (Sandy 2006). For these women, many of whom are local migrants, working in the sex industry is a way of expanding livelihood strategies. The free/forced dichotomy has also been influential in shaping other local understandings of sex work. According to Derks *et al.* (2006), most research on sex work in Cambodia seeks to distinguish between those who have 'voluntarily' entered sex work and those who were 'forced' into the industry. A large body of this research has been carried out by local and international NGOs, which suggests that the free/forced framework has also shaped understandings in this sector.

For other researchers and NGOs, however, women's participation in sex work is necessarily forced.[2] Such understandings do not view sex work as a form of work or a trade/profession but as a form of sexual exploitation and thus a form of violence against women, and within this understanding, sex workers are not considered as women with agency – however limited or constrained this may be – but rather rendered as hapless victims who need to be saved (Sandy 2007; Tigno in this volume). This discourse of sexual exploitation is not concerned with, nor does it speak of, labour and migrant rights or creating safer working environments for women. Instead, it emphasizes the need to rescue and rehabilitate women and girls from sex work, with the ultimate aim of abolishing the sex industry. These two incompatible understandings of the practice have struggled for dominance in local and international sex work debates. While there are many factors at play in shaping this discursive terrain, a key factor shaping this battleground has been shifts in international policy and funding.

Another core feature of the debate within Cambodia has been its focus on the number of trafficked women and girls. Most research and estimates on trafficking in the country have been ideologically driven, with the result that available statistics are not reliable or verifiable. No reliable, original data sets exist and most estimates have been produced by NGOs working in the field, based largely on anecdotal evidence and questions about 'how big' they thought the problem was. In late 2001, estimates held that between 80,000 and 100,000 trafficked women and between 5,000 and 15,000 children were involved in sex work in Cambodia. Steinfatt (2003) traces this figure to the *Cambodia Human Development Report* (UNDP 2000), where it appeared as an estimate of the number of sex workers in the country. The subsequent conflation of sex workers and victims of trafficking led to a massive over-estimation of the number of women and girls trafficked in the country. It also directed attention and anti-trafficking efforts to focus exclusively on sex work. A small number of empirical studies, including two studies based on a nation-wide census of sex workers (Royal Government of Cambodia 1997; Steinfatt 2003), provide substantially lower estimates on the number of sex workers and forced labourers in the sex industry.[3] While the report issued by the Cambodian government did not attempt to estimate the number of women trafficked for sex work, Steinfatt's study did. His study attempted to quantify the means of entry into sex work by distinguishing between the number of indentured (debt-bonded) and non-indentured labourers.[4] Through this method, he concluded that just over 20 per cent of women and children working in Cambodia's sex industry were indentured or trafficked, the overwhelming majority of whom were Vietnamese. This led to his estimation of approximately 2,000 women and children trafficked into the Cambodian sex industry (Steinfatt 2003).[5]

It appears, then, that the hyper-inflated claim of 80,000–100,000 trafficked women in Cambodia is based on a flawed reasoning that equates all sex work in the country with trafficking. Such reasoning accords with local discourse and practice, which has seen the issue of trafficking constructed as inextricably linked to sex work. The following passage appears on the opening page of a report on trafficking written in the early 1990s, a time when the issue was starting to draw a significant amount of attention inside and outside of the country and which marks the origins of contemporary trafficking discourse:

> 17 year old Supanee was sent by her impoverished family in Kompong Speu province to Phnom Penh to find her grandmother who would help her find a good job. Supannee [sic] did not know where to find her grandmother's home and asked a moto taxi driver for assistance. The driver took her to a brothel manager for $2.00. Supanee was then sold to another brothel manager in the area for $40.00 and forced into having sex with clients patronising the brothel. The clients paid $1.50 to the brothel manager for each encounter and Supanee received half. Supanee's story is not uncommon, she is one of the hundreds to become a victim of the lucrative slave and bonded labour sex trade.
>
> (CWDA 1994: 1)

In this statement, we can see that the subject was constructed around a particular mythology of trafficking, with the practice being discussed by means of 'moralist language and emotive stories [which do little to] contribute to a deeper understanding of the patterns, context or extent' of trafficking (Derks *et al.* 2006: 9). As highlighted by Sanghera (2005), this trafficking story is commonly told across Southeast Asia, and exhibits some of the key assumptions informing the mainstream trafficking discourse. These assumptions, which are often packaged as 'facts', include the notion that the trafficking of women and girls is rapidly increasing and that a large number of the 'victims' are trafficked primarily for the purpose of sex work. Poverty is often claimed to be the root cause of trafficking, and thus women's entry into sex work is regarded as necessarily forced. Women who claim that they have chosen to do sex work are described as having a kind of false consciousness: in other words, all women working in the sex industry are victims who need to be rescued, regardless of their own conceptualization of their status. Consequently, police raids and rescues are believed to be the logical mechanism through which to reduce the number of trafficking victims and rehabilitation is seen to be an unproblematic strategy (Sanghera 2005: 5).

The key actors in the creation of this particular mythology of trafficking in Cambodia were local and international NGOs. As their concern with trafficking was almost exclusively limited to women and children forced into the sex industry, female sex workers quickly became the critical site for intervention. However, in the mid-1990s, this fledgling discourse was overshadowed by emerging concerns about HIV-AIDS due to a supposed shift in the epidemic from 'core groups' to 'generalized' as HIV prevalence peaked at 2 per cent in 1998.[6] In Cambodia, as elsewhere in the region, it was assumed that sex work was a factor fuelling HIV transmission, and in this re-labelling of the epidemic, women working in the sex industry came to be viewed as a priori infected and thus largely responsible for the alarming rise in HIV. As a result, the 'risk group' framework came to dominate approaches to sex work, with interventions designed to regulate and control the industry taking precedence (Marten 2005) – a move that was also consistent with international policies and funding.

Shifts in international policy brought about a revived concern for human trafficking in the early 2000s. Two key policy changes contributing to this process were the US Government's anti-prostitution pledge (see the Introduction to this volume) and the TIP Reports. These instruments strengthened the local trafficking discourse and opened more of a foothold for it in approaches to sex work. This shift had significant consequences for Cambodian sex workers. For example, the Women's Network for Unity (WNU) is a sex worker collective advocating a policy of decriminalization. The WNU was founded in 2000, and by late 2001 had become a focal point for sex worker programmes in the country. After the US Government introduced its requirement that recipients of US development aid sign an anti-prostitution pledge in 2003, six of the seven local and international NGOs that had been collaborating with the WNU re-worked or dropped their programmes on sex worker empowerment and stopped working with this sex worker collective for fear that continued collaboration would jeopardize their funding.

Two years later, Cambodia was down-graded from Tier 2 to Tier 3 in the TIP rankings, a move that was accompanied by sanctions on non-humanitarian and non-trade-related aid, which came into effect in October 2005. In the 2004 TIP Report Cambodia had been ranked as a Tier 2 country, with the US Government recognizing that, while not fully complying with the minimum standards, it was 'making significant efforts to do so despite considerable resource constraints' (US Department of State 2004). But then on 7 December 2004 Phnom Penh police and a French anti-trafficking NGO, Acting for Women in Distressing Circumstances (Agir pour les Femmes en Situation Précaire, AFESIP), raided the Chai Hour II Hotel, which traded as a karaoke bar and massage parlour. During the raid, 83 women and girls were 'rescued' and subsequently detained by the police before being transferred to an AFESIP shelter. Several individuals were also arrested on various trafficking offences, most of whom were later released without charge. The following day approximately 30 people forced open the entrance gate at the AFESIP shelter and the women fled from the compound. AFESIP, the US State Department, French Government and the European Union condemned the Cambodian Government's lack of response to what they described as a 'raid' on the NGO shelter and the US threatened to downgrade Cambodia on the TIP list if the government continued to take no action. The Cambodian Government countered these allegations with claims that the hotel owner and some of the women asserted that they had been illegally detained by AFESIP. On 13 December a complaint was filed in the Cambodian courts on behalf of the 83 women employed at the hotel, demanding AFESIP pay each woman US$20,000 for incorrectly identifying them as sex workers and holding them against their will. The women also protested outside the US Embassy, speaking out against what they saw as US interference in their case (*Cambodia Daily Weekend* 2005).

Cambodia's relegation to Tier 3 was short-lived. In the following year the US Government placed the country on the Tier 2 Watch List on the basis of a determination that Cambodia was again 'making significant efforts' to combat trafficking (US Department of State 2006). The year in question was marked by high-profile raids and rescues led by the International Justice Mission, a USAID-funded evangelical Christian organization, which effectively shut down Svay Pak, a notorious Vietnamese brothel district on the outskirts of Phnom Penh. In the past, Svay Pak had been subject to numerous clean-up campaigns by the municipal authorities, and its brothel shanties and child sex workers were starting to attract significant attention in the international media. In one high-profile story the NBC's Dateline team, in an undercover investigation assisted by the International Justice Mission, described the district as a 'dark place where sexual predators can gain access to terrified children for a handful of cash' (Dateline 2005). However, the 2006 report also made explicit reference to the lack of a comprehensive anti-trafficking law in Cambodia, suggesting that the government should pass and enact such legislation (US Department of State 2006). Cambodia remained on the Tier 2 Watch List in the 2007 report primarily because the government 'failed to show evidence of increasing efforts to combat trafficking in persons' (US Department of State 2007). Specific mention was again made to the lack of anti-trafficking legislation, reinforcing the message that the passage of an anti-trafficking law was one of the steps the country must take in order to regain Tier 2 status (US Department of State 2007).

Clearly under pressure from the US, Cambodia passed the anti-trafficking law that was many years in the making in time for the 2008 round of TIP reporting. The enactment of this legislation saw the country lifted from the Tier 2 Watch List to Tier 2, thereby avoiding the re-imposition of sanctions. In line with the US Government's policy on sex work – but also local authorities' long-standing opposition to the industry, which they view as undesirable and detrimental to 'good' Khmer customs and traditions – a key feature of the new anti-trafficking legislation was its criminalization. The Ministry of Interior had attempted to pass remarkably similar legislation in August 2002 (Royal Government of Cambodia 2002), but had been forced to shelve the draft legislation in face of the fierce opposition and protest they encountered from sex workers and NGOs. However, this was before the era of the TVPA and US funding restrictions on sex work-related projects, which effectively silenced NGO opposition to the 2008 law.[7]

Prior to the passing of the law, the four instruments that regulated formal sex work – the Constitution, Penal Code, 1996 Human Trafficking Law and 100% Condom Use Policy – had led to the de facto legalization of brothels and brothel-based sex work. Of these, the only legal text that came close to outlawing sex work was the Constitution, which prohibited 'the commerce of human beings, their exploitation by prostitution and obscenity which affects the reputation of women' (Article 46 as cited in Jennar 1995: 15). This article rendered illegal the 'commerce of human beings' (trafficking) and 'their exploitation by prostitution' (trafficking for forced labour in the sex industry and prostitution-related activities such as brothel keeping and living on the earnings) but not the commercial sex act itself. Article 10 in Chapter Two of the new law removed this ambiguity. The relevant passage decrees that:

> A person who unlawfully removes another for the purpose of profit making, sexual aggression, production of pornography, marriage against will [*sic*] of the victim, adoption or *any form of exploitation* shall be punished with imprisonment for 7 years to 15 years.
>
> (Royal Government of Cambodia 2008: 5, emphasis added)

Sex work is criminalized under the 2008 law because it defines the provision of sexual services, referred to in the legislation as a 'commercial sex act', as a form of exploitation associated with trafficking:

> The [term] 'any form of exploitation' . . . [in] this law shall include the exploitation of the prostitution of others, pornography, commercial sex act, forced labour or services, slavery or practices similar to slavery, debt bondage, involuntary servitude, child labor or the removal of organs.
>
> (Royal Government of Cambodia 2008: 5)

The law constructs trafficking as a threat to the nation's peace and security, and as a result, border control and restrictions on migration also become intrinsic to its logic. The law's emphasis, which serves to curtail women's mobility,[8] reflects the international location of trafficking within the framework of border control and organized crime. Research suggests that the role of organized crime groups in trafficking may be exaggerated. As Lee (2007: 7) has argued, there are 'diverse agents and beneficiaries of human trafficking . . . for example, the more nebulous crime networks operating in particular locales; short-lived mom and pop type operations; opportunistic freelance criminals; and intermediaries and employers otherwise engaged in legitimate businesses'. Despite a growing body of evidence which suggests that organized crime groups may not play as large a role in human trafficking as assumed, international instruments and governmental laws and policies continue to construct trafficking within the framework of organized crime. As Lee (2007) comments, an important aspect of the institutionalization of such approaches has been the 2000 UN Convention against Transnational Organized Crime, to which the UN Trafficking Protocol is attached. The trafficking-as-organized-crime approach is premised on the threat that organized crime groups pose and takes border control as the basis of the state's sovereignty (Lee 2007: 6). The approach is often tied to geopolitical disputes about the integrity of the nation-state and neighbouring countries, and central to this is the idea of 'irregular' migration and, for the Cambodian Government, the lack of social control over subjects who are 'not in place' (FitzGerald 2008).

In the Cambodian context, this emphasis on the dangers of mobility legitimates the tighter controls and increased surveillance introduced in the Human Trafficking Law. Article 8 makes illegal any offer to introduce or provide transportation to a person for work in the sex industry, even if the person in question consents to or asks for an introduction, transport or employment in the sector. Article 10 has the potential to render all migration or movement for sex work illegal and Article 12 to render illegal the employment of women for sex work. Even more disconcerting, the legislation contains preventative measures targeted at 'at-risk' women and girls, who are defined as 'being in danger of prostitution' rather than persons at risk of being trafficked (Royal Government of Cambodia 2008: 10). Under these measures, women and girls could potentially be institutionalized without adequate evidence that they are 'in danger of prostitution', as the law does not contain any provisions specifying what might count as evidence in such cases. When read in concert with the law's elastic definition of sex work, it is clear that in addition to criminalizing this practice, the legislation is also aimed at controlling women's bodies in order to protect them from making what is judged to be bad or dangerous decisions in a context where sex, commerce and travel are typically viewed as male domains. As a result, it both potentially applies to any person considering employment in the sex industry, even in a voluntary capacity, and ignores those at risk of being trafficked for other forms of forced labour or servitude.

Not surprisingly, Cambodia's Human Trafficking Law locates trafficking within the framework of organized crime, imposing heavier penalties for crimes committed by an organized group than by individuals. As with debates about estimates of the numbers of victims of trafficking, the narrative of trafficking as transnational organized crime has largely been constructed from unsubstantiated statements which suggest that criminally sophisticated organized crime groups are the driving force behind trafficking in the country. It is common to see statements to the effect that little is known about trafficking networks alongside claims about their seriousness. For example, an early UNICEF report stated: 'There is no independent investigation into child trafficking networks in the country. From all indicators, they are very well organized and more and more people are beginning to profit from them' (UNICEF 1995: 6). This narrative belies the reality described in research that has documented the phenomenon as involving family and kin networks rather than organized crime groups (Derks 1998; Derks *et al.* 2006; Sandy 2006; Molland 2008). The deployment and reinforcement of this imagery, which conjures up pictures of predatory and dangerous criminal gangs that prey upon vulnerable, weak and powerless women and children, is influenced by the need of government and non-government organizations to justify the 'war on trafficking' (Murray 1998). Border control and the fight against organized crime is fundamental to this 'war', which has seen a proliferation of anti-trafficking agencies in Cambodia, with more than 200 government ministries, agencies and local and international organizations now working on trafficking. The campaign has also led to the creation of the National

Taskforce on Human Trafficking in March 2007 and to the promulgation of the Cambodian Human Trafficking Law.

The aftermath

Standing on the frontlines are Cambodia's sex workers, for whom the costs of the war being waged on trafficking have been particularly high. At the same time, as elsewhere, Cambodian sex workers' oppression as workers has become a force for mobilization in the struggle for better working conditions (Law 1997; Kempadoo 1998; Sandy in press). Sex workers have responded to the Human Trafficking Law by demanding the repeal of the law and an end to police raids and the forced rehabilitation of sex workers, and the recognition of commercial sex as work and of sex workers' status as workers.

The promulgation of the Human Trafficking Law not only threatened, but also led to the widespread violation of, the rights and liberties of sex workers, many of whom faced arbitrary arrest and detention without due process and restrictions on mobility. Brothel raids and rescues resulted in the removal of adult sex workers against their will, with compulsory rehabilitation in government or NGO-run centres.[9] In the first six months of implementation 121 brothels were shut down in Phnom Penh, 52 in Banteay Meanchey and 42 in Battambang (see Figure 2.1). By May 2008 fewer than 40 brothels remained open in the nation's capital. NGOs working in the field claimed that during this process hundreds of sex workers were arrested and kept in detention until a family member or brothel owner bailed them out for between US$40 and US$80 in Phnom Penh alone. Those who were less fortunate were forced into rehabilitation centres (*Cambodia Daily* 2008). The

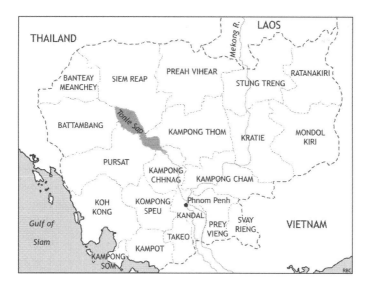

Figure 2.1 Cambodia

rehabilitation centres used included the Prey Speu and Koh Kor Social Affairs Centres run by the Phnom Penh Social Affairs Department under the Ministry of Social Affairs, Veterans and Youth Rehabilitation. This was not the first time that the Koh Kor Social Affairs Centre had been put to such uses. In the early 1980s the government of the People's Republic of Kampuchea established secret 're-education camps' for sex workers, after which women were forced to live in the countryside (Gottesman 2003; Sandy 2006). During periodic crackdowns sex workers were routinely arrested and detained in these 'reform centres', including one run by the Phnom Penh Municipality on the island of Koh Kor for re-education and rehabilitation (CWDA *et al.* 1995; UNICEF 1995).[10] According to Gottesman, many of the sex workers sent to Koh Kor were brutally beaten and raped, with some dying in detention (Gottesman 2003: 166–7, 265).

Sex workers 'rescued' during the 2008 raids also suffered serious abuse. Many were arrested without sufficient evidence, as the authorities regarded being caught with a condom as evidence of the charge of prostitution (Keo 2009). Some of those detained by the police were held without charge and sent to rehabilitation centres for indefinite periods of time. A number of sex workers reported being physically and sexually assaulted in the police stations, including in gang rapes perpetrated by the police. Other workers were forced to pay bribes to be released or had their earnings confiscated from them. At rehabilitation centres sex workers faced further inhumane treatment, including brutal beatings and rapes, with some dying in the centres and many being denied crucial life saving anti-retroviral medicines (Keo 2009: 7–12).

Another important consequence of the passing of the Human Trafficking Law has been the lack of attention paid to eradicating abusive practices in the sex industry that violate sex workers' rights. As documented in the World Charter for Prostitutes' Rights and elsewhere, a key issue facing sex workers is the recognition of sex work as a profession and, by extension, recognition of the right to practise that profession. Sex worker activists have also demanded the decriminalization of sex work in order to give legal protection to those working in the industry and access to mechanisms to promote improved working conditions. At the core of labour rights issues for sex workers is the protection of work standards, the right to privacy and freedom from forced labour or servitude, as well as the abolition of laws imposing sex work 'zones' – the key claim being that sex workers have the right to choose their place of work and residence and to provide services under conditions determined by themselves and not others (Ditmore 2006). The 2008 law has promoted none of these things, instead, forcing sex workers to travel and work in ways that have dramatically reduced their safety and well-being. The legislation also undermined the country's 100% Condom Use Policy, leading to the virtual collapse of HIV prevention efforts, which had served as a mechanism through which brothel-based sex work could be regulated in the country before the introduction of the law.[11]

The implementation of the Human Trafficking Law, and abuses perpetrated against sex workers by the police as a result, has led to bitter opposition from sex worker activists to the law, which they claim has introduced new forms of repression in their lives (Women's Network for Unity and the Asia Pacific Network of Sex Workers 2008). In their protests against the Human Trafficking Law, Cambodian sex workers were joined by sex workers and their supporters globally. Local sex workers coordinated a National Day of Action (4 June) and gathered at a temple to pray for the law to be repealed. Protests were also held at the UN high-level meeting on HIV-AIDS. In addition, testimonies from Cambodian sex workers were featured in a documentary produced by the Women's Network for Unity and the Asia Pacific Network of Sex Workers for the 2008 AIDS Conference in Mexico.

In an attempt to clarify the intent and diminish some of the harms associated with implementation of the Human Trafficking Law, sex workers and activists called for guidelines to be developed. In October 2008 the government responded to this pressure and issued guidelines on enforcement. Yet, these guidelines have only muddied the waters, as they claim that:

> *prostitutes are to be regarded as victims* of procurement for prostitution. Prostitution *is not a crime*; thus the individual *prostitutes are not punished* as offenders under the new legislation.
>
> (Excerpt from Guidelines on Enforcing the Law on Human Trafficking and Sexual Exploitation cited in Keo 2009: 17, emphasis in original)

This statement contradicts the 2008 Human Trafficking Law, which is explicit in its criminalization of sex work and regard of sex workers as criminals. The law punishes sex workers as offenders with provisions on solicitation pertaining only to workers while the guidelines make it clear that sex workers are also viewed as victims. However, in practice the guidelines have had little effect. In March 2010 Prime Minister Hun Sen renewed his call for increased efforts to eradicate brothels, nightclubs and karaoke parlours as part of the nation's counter-trafficking efforts. In response, the police extended their focus beyond brothels and began raiding cafes and massage parlours on the suspicion that they were being used for prostitution (*Phnom Penh Post* 2010). Only female sex workers were detained during this operation – the owners of the premises remained at large. This series of events suggests that sex work is still seen as a crime in the eyes of the authorities, and the sex workers themselves as criminals.

Conclusion

The equation of sex work and trafficking in Cambodia has led to a simplistic understanding of a complex situation, the results of which are interventions that are doing more harm than good. There is no doubt that trafficking is a serious and heinous crime. It is indeed necessary to fight against trafficking in persons; however, as the experience of sex workers in Cambodia demonstrates, this should not be at the expense of their safety and rights. As it stands, Cambodia's legislation and responses to trafficking demonstrate the confluence of confused and conflicted attitudes towards sex work: a conservative sexual morality in which sex workers are viewed as deviants and criminals combined with a protectionist approach toward women and children that casts them as victims. This has led to a situation where sex workers (read: women and girls) are deemed to need constant male or state protection from harm, and as a result they must not be allowed to exercise their right to movement or right to earn a living in the manner they choose.

Reflecting on the Human Trafficking Law, Keo Tha of the WNU has commented that: '[sex workers] are sandwiched right now – we are oppressed by the police, the law and rising living costs' (*Straits Times* 2008). In the frontlines of the war on trafficking, local sex workers have indeed been sandwiched – firstly, as women who made what they saw as the best choice from within a very narrow range of options available to them in the transition to a market economy (Sandy 2007, 2009) and, secondly, as sex workers caught up in the politics of international aid. Sex work is part of a vast informal economic sector in Cambodia. Many sex workers are migrants who have left their home villages to earn a living as Cambodia makes the transition to a market economy. Some workers are forced into the industry through economic necessity, whereas others make choices (albeit constrained), deciding that sex work is the best option for them (Derks 2004; Sandy 2007).

For the time being there is no way out for local sex workers from a situation that has developed as a consequence of the government's anti-trafficking efforts and the US TVPA approved legislation. These current anti-trafficking interventions, which are based on the ideology of rescuing and rehabilitating 'victims', do little to address and transform abusive and exploitative practices in the sex industry that violate sex workers' rights. In fact, the deployment of this framework has seen the introduction of conservative and draconian legislation in Cambodia and paternalistic interventions that are doing little to improve the situation for migrant sex workers. Sex workers have argued, instead, for a labour rights approach to be taken in regulating the sector and preventing trafficking. As they recognize, the labour migration framework, which emphasizes the social, economic and cultural factors underpinning migration, would more adequately respond to their issues and concerns. It is also a framework in which we can consider sex workers' diverse experiences and move away from the almost exclusive focus on more obvious forms of coercion that capture so much voyeuristic attention.

Notes

1 The literature and data search undertaken for this chapter involved desk-based research on Cambodia's new Human Trafficking Law, including commentary from anti-trafficking groups and sex worker organizations and observations from fieldwork in Cambodia undertaken from November 2001 to April 2004.

2 See, for example, Brown (2000) and Hughes (2000), and the publications of anti-trafficking organizations such as Acting for Women in Distressing Circumstances (Agir Pour les Femmes en Situation Précaire, AFESIP) and the Coalition Against Trafficking in Women (CATW).

3 In 1997 the RGC estimated that almost 15,000 women worked in Cambodia's brothels, while in 2003 Steinfatt concluded that almost 19,000 women worked in the sex trade in 2002–3. While comparison of these two studies is complicated by the fact that the 1997 report counted only brothel-based sex workers and Steinfatt counted women working in the formal and non-formal sectors of the industry, both recorded significantly lower numbers of female sex workers compared with NGO estimates and those reported in 2000 by the United Nations. Additional estimates on the number of sex workers include a 2003 National AIDS Division of the Ministry of Health count of approximately 17,000 sex workers (Steinfatt n.d.) and a Steinfatt *et al.* (2002) estimate of 20,829 sex workers in 2002.

4 In the Cambodian sex industry debt bondage or indenture is a practice in which brothel owners pay women a sum of money ranging from US$100 to US$3,000 and, after receiving the advance, women enter into a period of debt bondage and pay off the debt by receiving clients (Sandy 2009). Debt bondage is widely understood as a form of unfree labour as sex workers mortgage their future labour power against a loan from brothel owners, after which they are not free to leave their jobs until the debt is repaid. In the sex trafficking discourse and international instruments such as the UN Trafficking Protocol, the practice is considered to fall under the scope of trafficking.

5 Steinfatt *et al.* (2002) reported an indentured percentage of 31 per cent in Phnom Penh, with 2,488 women and children trafficked for forced labour in the sex industry. Other studies that have attempted to estimate the extent of indenture include a paper by the Cambodian Women's Development Association (CWDA 1994), which estimated an indenture percentage of 47 per cent, with reference to this statistic being produced from a CWDA survey on prostitution in Phnom Penh, the results of which were unavailable to this author. According to Brown (2000), up to half of all sex workers in Cambodia were bonded in 2000. However, she provides no information on how this statistic was derived.

6 HIV was first detected in Cambodia in 1991, and for many years it was argued that the country faced potentially the worst HIV-AIDS epidemic in Asia.

7 Local press clippings indicate that there was little public protest from the NGO sector with the passage of the legislation in 2008.

8 While Article 24 specifies that men and women might provide sexual services, in the public mind sex workers are considered as women. In addition, there are no gender-neutral terms of reference for sex workers. The common term used to refer to women working in the industry is *srei khouc* (prostitute). It is a gender-specific term that is not applied to men and literally means a spoilt, rotten or bad woman. The term for sex worker, *srei roksii phlauvphet*, is literally a woman (*srei*) making a living (*roksii*) from her vagina (*phlauvphet*), which is also gender-specific. Male sex workers, referred to as *proh lukkhleun* (a man selling his body), are largely absent in the local trafficking discourse, the issue confined to the HIV-AIDS discourse and male-to-male sexual practice, and the idea that men are trafficked has not gained a strong foothold in the national consciousness.

9 Crackdowns and sex worker 'rehabilitation' has long been a key feature of the Cambodian Government's conflicted attitude towards sex work and response to the industry. Indeed, local precedent for this method of controlling and regulating sex work was established during the first decade of independence from French rule when Kram 60-CE, a law prohibiting brothels in the Kingdom, was promulgated in 1961. In addition, throughout the 1950s and 1960s the port city of Sihanoukville was the only city in which sex work was legally permitted, while outlawed in the rest of the country (Williams 1969; Sihanouk 2003; Sandy 2006). However, by 1963 prohibition had proved impossible to enforce and the government introduced a licensing system, with unlicensed workers sent for rehabilitation (Williams 1969; Sandy 2009). Since the late 1990s the Phnom Penh Municipal Authority has launched numerous crackdowns on the sector as they attempted to 'clean up' rapidly transforming urban spaces.

10 According to the Cambodian League for the Promotion and Defense of Human Rights (LICADHO), the government-run Koh Kor Social Affairs Center was built on the site of a former Khmer Rouge-era prison and execution camp. On 17 and 19 June 2008, LICADHO staff visited the Koh Kor site and images taken of detainees and the conditions in which they were held can be viewed at: www.licadho-cambodia.org/album/view_photo.php?cat=40. Those detained at Koh Kor at the time of LICADHO's visit included sex workers, beggars, people who use drugs, and homeless and mentally ill people.

11 The 100% Condom Use Policy, a public health measure executed as part of the government's National HIV-AIDS Strategy, was designed to control and monitor condom use in brothels. As this policy did not have the status of a law, it was superseded by the 2008 Human Trafficking Law. The wide-reaching ramifications of the Human Trafficking Law drew strong criticism from those working in the HIV-AIDS sector, with the laws severely hampering their prevention efforts.

References

Alexander, P. (1998) 'The international sex workers' rights movement', in Delacoste, F. and Alexander, P. (eds) *Sex Work: Writings by Women in the Sex Industry* (2nd edn), Berkeley, CA: Cleis Press, pp. 14–18.

Brown, L. (2000) *Sex Slaves: The Trafficking of Women in Asia*, London: Virago.

Busza, J. (2004) 'Sex work and migration: The dangers of oversimplification – A case study of Vietnamese women in Cambodia', *Health and Human Rights*, 7 (2): 231–49.

Cambodia Daily, The (2008) 'Brothel raids, arrests worry health workers', 1 May.

Cambodia Daily Weekend (2005) '2004: The year in review', 1–2 January.

Cambodian Women's Development Association (CWDA) (1994) 'Cambodia country report', paper prepared for the International Workshop on the Traffic and Migration in Women, Phnom Penh, Cambodia.

Cambodian Women's Development Association, Human Rights Task Force on Cambodia, Human Rights Vigilance of Cambodia, Indradevi and Krousar Thmey (1995) 'Report on prostitution and traffic of women and children', Outcomes of a workshop-conference, Phnom Penh, Cambodia, 4–5 May.

Dateline (2005) Children for Sale. NBC News. Online. Available at http://www.msnbc.msn.com/id/4038249/ (accessed 4 January 2010).

Derks, A. (1998) *Trafficking of Vietnamese Women and Children to Cambodia*, Phnom Penh: Centre for Advanced Studies and the International Organization for Migration.

—— (2004) 'Khmer women on the move: Migration and urban experiences in Cambodia', unpublished PhD thesis, Radboud University, Nijmegen.

Derks, A., Henke, R. and Ly, V. (2006) *Review of a Decade of Research on Trafficking in Persons, Cambodia*, Phnom Penh: Centre for Advanced Study.

Ditmore, M. (2006) *Encyclopedia of Prostitution and Sex Work*, Santa Barbara, CA: Greenwood Publishing.

FitzGerald, S. (2008) 'Putting trafficking on the map: The geography of feminist complicity', in Munro, V. and Della Giusta, M. (eds) *Demanding Sex: Critical Reflections on the Regulation of Prostitution*, Aldershot: Ashgate, pp. 23–46.

Gottesman, E. (2003) *Cambodia after the Khmer Rouge: Inside the Politics of Nation Building*, New Haven, CT: Yale University Press.

Hughes, D. (2000) '"Welcome to the rape camp": Sexual exploitation and the internet in Cambodia', *Journal of Sexual Aggression*, 6 (1/2): 1–23.

Jennar, R. (1995) *The Cambodian Constitutions (1953–1993)*, Bangkok: White Lotus.

Kapur, R. (2005) 'Cross-border movements and the law: Renegotiating the boundaries of difference', in Kempadoo, K., Sanghera, J. and Pattanaik, B. (eds) *Trafficking and Prostitution Reconsidered: New Perspectives on Migration, Sex Work and Human Rights*, Boulder, CO: Paradigm, pp. 25–41.

Kempadoo, K. (1998) 'Introduction: Globalizing sex workers' rights', in Kempadoo, K. and Doezema, J. (eds) *Global Sex Workers: Rights, Resistance, and Redefinition*, New York: Routledge, pp. 1–28.

Keo, C. (2009) *Hard Life for Legal Work: The 2008 Anti-trafficking Law and Sex Work*, Phnom Penh: CACHA.

Law, L. (1997) 'A matter of "choice": Discourses on prostitution in the Philippines', in Manderson, L. and Jolly, M. (eds) *Sites of Desire, Economies of Pleasure: Sexualities in Asia and the Pacific*, Chicago, IL: University of Chicago Press, pp. 233–61.

Lee, M. (2007) 'Introduction: Understanding human trafficking', in Lee, M. (ed.) *Human Trafficking*, Cullompton, Devon: Willan Publishing, pp. 1–25.

Leigh, C. (1997) 'Inventing sex work', in Nagel, J. (ed.) *Whores and Other Feminists*, New York: Routledge, pp. 226–31.

Marten, L. (2005) 'Commercial sex workers: Victims, vectors or fighters of the HIV epidemic in Cambodia?', *Asia Pacific Viewpoint*, 46 (1): 21–34.

Molland, S. (2008) 'The perfect business? Traffickers, victims and anti-traffickers along the Mekong', unpublished PhD thesis, Macquarie University.

Murray, A. (1998) 'Debt-bondage and trafficking: Don't believe the hype', in Kempadoo, K. and Doezema, J. (eds) *Global Sex Workers: Rights, Resistance, and Redefinition*, New York: Routledge, pp. 51–64.

Pheterson, G. (1989) *A Vindication of the Rights of Whores*, Seattle, WA: Seal Press.

Phnom Penh Post (2010) 'Cafes raided in brothel crackdown', 12 March.

Royal Government of Cambodia (1997) *Report on the Problem of Sexual Exploitation and Trafficking in Cambodia*, Phnom Penh: National Assembly, Commission on Human Rights and Reception of Complaints.

—— (2002) Draft Law on the Suppression of Human Trafficking and Sexual Exploitation [in Khmer]. Phnom Penh: Royal Government of Cambodia.

—— (2008) Law on Suppression of Human Trafficking and Sexual Exploitation. Unofficial translation. Online. Available at http://www.no-trafficking.org/content/Laws_Agreement/cambodia%20new%20law%20on%20trafficking%20&%20sexual%20exploitation%20-%20english.pdf (accessed 4 January 2010).

Sandy, L. (2006) '"My blood, sweat and tears": Female sex workers in Cambodia – victims, vectors or agents?', unpublished PhD thesis, Australian National University.

—— (2007) 'Just choices: Representations of choice and coercion in sex work in Cambodia', *Australian Journal of Anthropology*, 8 (2): 194–206.

—— (2009) '"Behind closed doors": Debt-bonded sex workers in Sihanoukville, Cambodia', *Asia Pacific Journal of Anthropology*, 10 (3): 216–30.

—— (in press) 'International agendas and sex worker rights in Cambodia', in Ford, M. (ed.) *Social Activism in Southeast Asia*, Abingdon and New York: Routledge.

Sanghera, J. (2005) 'Unpacking the trafficking discourse', in Kempadoo, K., Sanghera, J. and Pattanaik, B. (eds) *Trafficking and Prostitution Reconsidered: New Perspectives on Migration, Sex Work and Human Rights*, Boulder, CO: Paradigm, pp. 3–24.

Sihanouk, N. (2003) 'Le problème de la prostitution au Cambodge', *Etudes Cambodgiennes*, 4 June. Available at http:www.norodomsihanouk.info/messages/ec%200406.htm (accessed 2 March 2006).

Steinfatt, T. (2003) 'Measuring the number of trafficked women and children in Cambodia:

A direct observation field study, part III', Phnom Penh: Royal University of Phnom Penh.

—— (n.d.) *Methodological Issues in Trafficking Research.* Online. Available at http://www.unescobkk.org/fileadmin/user_upload/hiv_aids/Documents/Workshop_doc/Seminar_promoting/Methodological_Issues_in_Trafficking_Research_-_Thomas_Steinfatt.pdf (accessed 19 October 2009).

Steinfatt, T., Baker, S. and Beesey, A. (2002) 'Measuring the number of trafficked women in Cambodia: 2002, part 1', paper presented at The Human Rights Challenge of Globalization in Asia-Pacific-US: The Trafficking in Persons, Especially Women and Children. Globalization Research Center, University of Hawai'i-Manoa, 13–15 November.

Straits Times (2008) 'New sex law brings problems', 26 December.

UNDP (2000) *Cambodia Human Development Report 2000*, Cambodia: Ministry of Planning.

UNICEF (1995) 'The trafficking and prostitution of children in Cambodia: A situation report', *Regional Workshop on Trafficking in Children for Sexual Purposes*, 12–15 December, Phnom Penh.

US Department of State (2004) *Trafficking in Persons Report*, Washington, DC: US Department of State.

—— (2006) *Trafficking in Persons Report*, Washington, DC: US Department of State.

—— (2007) *Trafficking in Persons Report*, Washington, DC: US Department of State.

Williams, M. (1969) *The Land in Between: The Cambodian Dilemma*, Sydney: Collins.

Women's Network for Unity and the Asia Pacific Network of Sex Workers (WNU-APNSW) (2008) *Caught Between the Tiger and the Crocodile*. Online. Available at http://blip.tv/file/1159149 (accessed 28 November 2009).

3 The inexorable quest for trafficking hotspots along the Thai–Lao border

Sverre Molland

I am sitting with Thou, an official working for an anti-trafficking programme in Vientiane, Lao People's Democratic Republic. We have just discussed several case studies from my fieldwork on trafficking into the commercial sex industry along the Thai–Lao border. The case studies point to a common phenomenon on both sides of the border: occasionally sex workers use deception and debt bondage to recruit acquaintances into the industry, and in a minority of cases the recruiter and/ or the recruit are under the legal age of 18. While Thou reacts with a mixture of excitement and surprise to my case studies, she is also familiar with the narratives I reproduce. She has heard similar stories from Vietnam. Unlike many other inform-ants, however, Thou immediately sees the implication for law enforcement:

> How can we deal with this? The perpetrator might be a young woman from the same village, even underage? And, as both the victim and perpetrator come from the same community, even the same village, what does this mean for anti-trafficking programming?

Yet, even as we contemplate these issues, in the very same interview Thou re-asserts the taken-for-granted assumption that traffickers belong to well-organized mafia-like organizations. Commenting on current trafficking trends in Laos, Thou proclaims: 'Because of the growing number of anti-trafficking projects in the south we now believe that the traffickers have relocated and now target the north.'

Thou's comment reflects a double narrative which is commonplace amongst anti-trafficking programmes in Laos. On the one hand, individuals who work for anti-trafficking programmes recognize that human trafficking can be an infor-mal affair involving members of the community in which traffickers recruit. On the other hand, traffickers are simultaneously depicted as an external other: they are faceless, malevolent creatures possessing fluid attributes with the mystical ability to adapt to new situations arising from changes in the market or interven-tions from trafficking programmes. This double narrative is intimately bound up with institutionally produced (and sanctioned) spatial imaginaries amongst devel-opment aid programmes which seek to combat trafficking in persons.

Human trafficking is a relatively new object of programmatic interven-tion within the development sector. As trafficking refers to the non-consensual movement of migrants for the purpose of exploiting their labour, its deterritorial nature challenges the *habitus* of development programmes which are always demarcated in spatial terms (i.e. one always has a project *site*). In Laos, many anti-trafficking projects are run by community-based development programmes that are accustomed to implementing activities in rural villages. As a result, anti-trafficking programmes find themselves in an odd situation: the phenomena they are attempting to combat occur miles away from where they are based, and therefore the object of their intervention exists outside the confines of a traditional development programme. This requires two things: they must identify exactly *what* constitutes their target and *where* this target can be located. In other words, they need to identify 'hotspots'.

This chapter explores how anti-trafficking projects along the Thai–Lao border produce spatial notions of agglomeration in the context of larger cross-border migration flows.[1] In it, I begin by illuminating the different ways in which the local anti-trafficking sector produces specific notions of what is, and what is not, considered 'hot'. I then explore the spatial part of this equation, that is, the 'spots', drawing attention to source communities and international borders, as well as to segments within labour markets. Finally, I examine the effects of the emphasis on hotpots within the anti-trafficking sector and consider its implication on cross-border migration. I argue that the way anti-trafficking programmes place emphasis on hotspots does not so much reflect the social reality in which they seek to intervene as represent a discursive necessity. In this sense, anti-trafficking programming is detached from its object. This is not to suggest that human trafficking, with all its definitional hurdles, has no materiality. However, as this case shows, its materiality is in effect subordinated to this discursive reality.

Economism and hotspots

Numerous scholars note that definitions and estimations of human trafficking can be manipulated politically to serve both anti-prostitution and anti-immigration agendas (Gallagher 2001; Anderson and O'Connell Davidson 2003; Kempadoo 2005; Doezema 2007). These points are well taken. However, to explain anti-trafficking efforts in light of policies on prostitution and immigration is to omit one of the key actors involved in shaping the meanings associated with 'trafficking' and in operationalizing anti-trafficking responses – namely development aid programmes. Since the late 1990s, the Mekong region has witnessed a considerable increase in anti-trafficking projects that are implemented through development aid programmes. Although these programmes often work closely with state actors, their mode of operation, ideological underpinnings and policy objects are not always congruous. Whereas states tend to emphasize the importance of border control to curb trafficking, many anti-trafficking programmes argue that it is precisely border controls that allow traffickers to flourish. Nevertheless, nation-states and development institutions share a doxic means–ends rationality which straddles controversies regarding both sex work and migration policy.

Aid programmes are similar to states in the sense that they are ideologically highly modernist as they attempt to engender planned, orchestrated change (Stirrat 2000; de Sardan 2005; Lewis and Mosse 2006). An important part of such orchestrated change is to identify clear objects of programmatic intervention. Binary distinctions underpin the work of government and development programmes that seek to combat human trafficking, whether this work entails the investigation, arrest and prosecution of traffickers; the provision of support for victims; or delivery of awareness-raising campaigns in communities deemed at risk of human trafficking. Although human trafficking can vary in degree (egregious cases of exploitation, number of trafficked victims, etc.), an anti-trafficking project must determine what fits and what counts. To identify someone as 'somewhat' of a trafficked victim will not do, as NGOs, UN agencies and government bodies ultimately need to make decisions about whether migrants and recruiters fit the definitions they are working with and consequently warrant programmatic action (such as assistance, arrest, vocational training and so on). Such binary distinctions result in an individuated conceptualization of how trafficking operates that has important implications for how trafficking is understood in spatial terms.

Trafficking reports ubiquitously portray trafficking in terms of a market (Ruggiero 1997; Schloenhardt 1999; Scheper-Hughes 2000; Anderson and O'Connell Davidson 2004; Shangera 2005; Agustín 2007; Gallagher 2006; ILO 2006). Economic language is commonly used in these reports as well as by anti-trafficking project officers in their everyday work. For example, they refer to the ways in which traffickers maintain supply (victims) in order to meet demand (exploiters) within a marketplace. These economic metaphors reinforce the tendency to portray victims and traffickers as atomized actors within a market. Elsewhere (Molland 2010), I have explored how this economic imagery is conceived in the social body (who is vulnerable?). In this chapter I place specific focus on spatial notions of vulnerability (where does trafficking take place?). What is at stake is not merely a question of traffickers, exploiters and their victims, but a question of where they are. It is in this context that it becomes possible to talk about hotspots.

I will now turn to how Lao anti-trafficking programmes evoke several understandings of both *spots* and what is deemed *hot* in order to show that underpinning these notions is a strong assumption that trafficking in persons operates first and foremost according to a unified market logic.

What's hot?

The first two anti-trafficking projects in the Lao PDR were launched in 2000. They were both part of regional UN programmes and their project rationales were underpinned by rapid assessment-style studies which pointed to large-scale migration from Laos to Thailand as well as larger migration flows in the Mekong region. The reports documented cases of debt bondage, deceitful recruitment as well as exploitative labour conditions (Caouette 1998; Wille 2001), which the authors acknowledge are based mostly on anecdotal data. There has been a remarkable increase in the number of anti-trafficking projects in the Lao PDR since the release of these reports, which in turn have resulted in several new anti-trafficking studies.

Both the academic literature and these development reports confirm what the initial rapid assessment studies suggest: although many Laotians migrate voluntarily and describe positive experiences working in Thailand, some labour migrants experience debt bondage, deceptive recruitment and exploitative labour conditions (Phetsiriseng 2001; ILO 2003; IOM 2004; Doussantousse and Keovonghit 2006; Haughton 2006; UNIAP *et al*. 2004; UNICEF and Ministry of Labour and Social Welfare 2004). These accounts were supported by evidence that showed large-scale movements across the border. A comprehensive survey by the International Labour Organization (ILO) states that 6.9 per cent of the total population in three southern provinces had migrated, of whom 80.5 per cent had crossed the border to Thailand (ILO 2003).[2] Another report showed that as much as 20 per cent of the entire village population in some villages engage in seasonal cross-border migration (UNIAP and Ministry of Labour and Social Welfare 2001). At the time there were no documented cases of internal trafficking, nor was there much attention to internal migration. As a result, it was widely assumed that exploitation – regarded as the common outcome of human trafficking – was taking place across the border. Lao anti-trafficking projects were thus confined to dealing with one thing: departure. Hence, initial anti-trafficking projects in Laos were primarily focused on source communities.

As human trafficking is defined retrospectively, since trafficking is manifest only when a migrant faces exploitation (Shangera 2005), it becomes extremely difficult from the standpoint of a village community to make distinctions between labour migration and human trafficking. One of the criteria used by several anti-trafficking projects in determining where anti-trafficking activities are to be implemented was the prevalence of migration in village communities. In other words, in identifying spots deemed to be 'hot', the emphasis was placed squarely on out-migration (as opposed to labour exploitation itself). Although some anti-trafficking programmes were keenly aware of the difficulty in equating labour migration with human trafficking (e.g. UNIAP *et al*. 2004), others were less willing or able to recognize this distinction (cf. Phetsiriseng 2001). Hence, in the first few years of Lao anti-trafficking programming there was a tenacious interest in defining what is hot in order to domesticate spots.

The criteria for determining what constitutes spots were applied uncritically and liberally to anything from villages with high levels of migration to communities with endemic poverty – a tendency that was reinforced by the Lao Government's own priorities. Combating trafficking fits within the Government's overall poverty reduction strategy (Lao People's Democratic Republic n.d.). It is common for officials to equate the fight against human trafficking with rural development under the rubric of prevention. That is, they believe that by bringing development to villages they can deter labour migration to Thailand. Collaborating with international organizations to combat trafficking thus coincided with two government objectives: curbing migration to Thailand and boosting rural development projects.

Several aid organizations happily supported this line of thinking because they were already familiar with rural development. It also allowed them to 'combat' trafficking without becoming embroiled in the sensitivities and the possible dangers associated with dubious forms of labour migration recruitment.[3] A fact sheet from the ILO project entitled *Micro-finance Interventions to Combat the Worst Forms of Child Labour including Trafficking* (ILO-IPEC 2002) illustrates this trend. Except for mentioning the word 'trafficking' briefly in the introduction, the rest of the document is full of advice on 'marketing research', 'monitoring' and 'enterprise development'. The actual issues of human trafficking, labour exploitation and migration are ignored. If it were not for the project title one would be at a loss to know that this was in fact a 'trafficking intervention'.

The ILO is far from alone in implementing such programmes. Several aid organizations launched counter-trafficking projects which in real terms addressed problems of rural development often in combination with awareness-raising, for example, through the use of posters warning against the dangers of trafficking. In this way, what is deemed 'hot' is a mixture of the presence of migration and the lack of development in rural communities. Hotspots allow aid programmes to shape their target in terms of generic socio-economic indicators similarly (if not identically) to traditional rural poverty reduction programmes. As Laos is one of Asia's poorest countries it is not difficult to find targets for anti-trafficking interventions within such a framework. In the early days of Lao anti-trafficking interventions 'trafficking prevention' could be anything from weaving, funds for fish ponds, pig raising, building a footbridge to allow farmers easier access to farmland, vocational training, micro-finance, exports of mushrooms, funding of village schools, hairdressing courses and vaccination of chickens.[4] In short, such anti-trafficking projects were (and some still are) rural development projects in disguise.

This type of project implementation soon came under considerable criticism within the anti-trafficking community. One of the first explicit criticisms surfaced in a field report by the UNIAP project (Ginzburg 2002), which questioned the blurring of anti-migration and harm reduction strategies amongst anti-trafficking projects:

> [Rural community development] activities even take organisations away from trying to understand the complexities of the trafficking situation, and push them to rely on (simplistic?) assumptions regarding the links between migration and trafficking . . . I . . . note that poverty reduction was a stated global objective years before the anti-trafficking agenda came to the forefront and that 'poverty alleviation programmes' have not always met the expectations of those who had initiated them. Designing economic interventions that reach those 'most at risk of being trafficked' may prove as difficult as designing interventions that reach 'the poorest of the poor'.
>
> (Ginzburg 2002: 10)

This critique was later followed by others (Haughton 2006; Molland 2005). There is now a growing realization within the anti-trafficking community in Laos that by

engaging in community development – what some anti-trafficking actors causti-
cally label the 'stay where you are approach' (Marshall and Thatun 2005) – attention is drawn away from the problem of migrant labour exploitation.

Several trafficking and migration-related studies conducted in Laos in recent
years suggest that although human trafficking is taking place, it does so within the
context of a much larger migration pattern which is often – at least in the eyes of
villagers – beneficial both economically and socially (Caouette 1998; Phetsiriseng
2001; UNIAP and Ministry of Labour and Social Welfare 2001; Wille 2001;
ILO 2003; UNIAP *et al.* 2004; UNICEF and Ministry of Labour and Social Welfare
2004; Doussantousse and Keovonghit 2006). It is also difficult for projects to
justify anti-trafficking activities in village communities without being able to demonstrate that their target communities are indeed prone to trafficking. Although it
is indeed the case that trafficking is occurring (or has occurred) in villages where
anti-trafficking programmes operate, the scale and frequency varies and its documentation is opaque. Nor is there much evidence to support the assumption that
poverty or lack of jobs at home necessarily has much to do with why migrants
leave in the first place (Feingold 1997; Ginzburg 2002, 2004; Muttarak 2004;
Haughton 2006; Rigg 2006; Huijsmans 2007), or why some end up in exploitive
situations.

Many anti-traffickers in Laos have gradually realized that it is perhaps somewhat far-fetched to think that by vaccinating chickens and pigs in a Lao village
they prevent rape and physical abuse of Laotians in Bangkok sweatshops and
brothels. To be fair, there is no doubt that political sensitivities are part of the
reason aid programmes have often focused on community development. Many
aid workers are keenly aware of this constraint and do what they can to lobby the
government to change its perception of anti-trafficking work. Governments are far
more accommodating when research can serve socio-economic development in
rural village communities than when aid organizations uncover labour abuse and
exploitation. This is not to dismiss the role aid programmes play in encouraging
micro finance and vocational training as a means to combat human trafficking.
However, there is no doubt that the spatial *habitus* of aid programmes, the idea of
having a defined geographic area – a project site – where one does something one
already knows how to do, contributes to this end.

In response to these challenges there has been a gradual shift from understanding anti-trafficking work as focusing on prevention towards understanding it
as promoting harm reduction or 'safe migration'. In other words, the focus has
shifted towards those factors which may make a migrant vulnerable to exploitation, as opposed to considering annihilation of movement as a success. Consequently awareness-raising material has changed from preventing movement
(the message being 'don't go!') to making departure safer ('go safely!'); and
increased interest has been paid towards the ways in which projects can empower
migrants. And, in parallel to all this, the Thai and Lao Governments have made
slow but gradual steps in implementing a Memorandum of Understanding which
seeks to legalize labour migration. This shift meshes with broader trends in the
international anti-trafficking sector, where there has been increasing attention to

'the demand side of trafficking'. It is in this context that the ubiquitous use of economic terminology and a market metaphor is invoked.

Where are the spots?

The notion of a market in trafficked persons is well-depicted by Shangera, the former trafficking advisor to the United Nations' Human Rights Commissioner:

> The sites of work that draw this supply of migrant livelihood-seekers are contingent upon demand from particular sectors of the economy for certain types of labor that would enable maximization of profit . . . The drive for maximizing profit under a competitive economic regime fields a demand for workers who are the most vulnerable and therefore the most exploitable and controllable.
>
> (Shangera 2005: 7)

Trafficking is here understood as a fallout of the twin forces of supply and demand and echoes old-school migration theory derived from classical economics where migration is seen as a response to market disequilibrium (Massey 1998). The depiction of migration as a response to market disequilibrium is also evident in the Lao anti-trafficking sector:

> Trafficking occurs across provincial and national boundaries, and over long distances, creating a flow of people moving from poorer areas to more prosperous ones. Due to the increase in cross-border movement and migration, previously remote areas are now exposed to rapid social changes. This has disrupted traditional lifestyles, and made communities especially vulnerable to the problem of trafficking.
>
> (Asia Regional Cooperation to Prevent People Trafficking 2003: 9)

The aforementioned strategy to provide vocational training and micro-credit schemes in villages with out-migration also reflects a profound internalization of classic market theory. It is not only that such projects (perhaps naively) assume that by removing incentives for leaving the village a 'trafficking situation' is hence prevented. By providing opportunities at home, these projects reason, one is contributing to labour market equilibrium – if equal opportunity exists at home, then why leave?

This tendency to articulate human trafficking in terms of a market is intertwined with spatial notions of vulnerability produced by international borders. Most Lao anti-trafficking projects are located in border areas. Five are part of regional anti-trafficking programmes (implying the importance of borders), and many have 'cross border' in the title of their project.[5] The border also contributes to the way migration is imagined amongst anti-trafficking programmes. This is most potently expressed in the use of maps in trafficking reports as well as project websites. Such maps include dots to indicate both source and destination points, but also numerous arrows to indicate cross-border flows and trafficking routes.

A UNICEF report from 2004 is exemplary of this trend (UNICEF and Ministry of Labour and Social Welfare 2004). The report was the first nationwide research into child trafficking in Laos. It covered all provinces in Laos with a sample of 149 villages. The research claims to have uncovered 253 trafficking cases and in its foreword makes it clear that child trafficking is one of UNICEF's priorities:

> The report's case studies provide a vivid portrayal of the extreme vulnerability to exploitation of children who are growing up in a country with low socio-economic indicators, situated at the crossroads of a fast-developing region.
>
> (UNICEF and Ministry of Labour and Social Welfare 2004: 7)

The report includes maps which show big arrows at several cross-border checkpoints indicating hotspots and trafficking routes (see Figure 3.1).

In contrast to the village-based projects discussed earlier, which fail to identify spots (i.e. where trafficking is taking place) or define what is hot (i.e. the conceptual conflation of migration, poverty and trafficking), these maps clearly locate hotspots in spatial terms (i.e. cross-border checkpoints). But are these spots really hot?

Trafficking reports, such as this one, do not explain exactly what warrants the insertion of an arrow indicating a trafficking hotspot on a map. There is no explicit methodology behind such visualized data. Indeed, the frequent use of such arrow-littered maps is puzzling as it is relatively easy to question their validity. For example, the UNICEF report places a large arrow indicating a trafficking route at the Nong Khai border checkpoint. This is the main land crossing between Laos and Thailand where thousands of people cross the border on a weekly basis. However, the report only describes three cases involving Nong Khai as either a destination or transit point for trafficking. Furthermore, the 253 trafficking cases uncovered by the research team are based on a sample of 149 villages which means that on average there are only 1.69 trafficked victims per village. A careful reading of the report reveals that most of the case studies were not current. Many cases were four years old and in some cases up to eleven years old at the time the research was carried out.

Given the fact that villages were purposely selected based on which villages local government officials thought were trafficking-prone, it becomes difficult to accept that this study shows any trafficking trends or hotspots at all.[6] Yet, the report fails to reflect on such obvious limitations in its methodology and sees no difficulty in proclaiming that it 'identifies trafficking routes and methods, and those actively involved and whose complicity fuels the crime of child trafficking' (UNICEF and Ministry of Labour and Social Welfare 2004: 6).

This UNICEF report is by no means unique in this regard. Several other anti-trafficking reports from the Mekong region engage in the seemingly compulsive production of such maps, some of which include comprehensive use of Geographic Information Systems data (e.g. ILO 2003; UNESCO Bangkok n.d.).

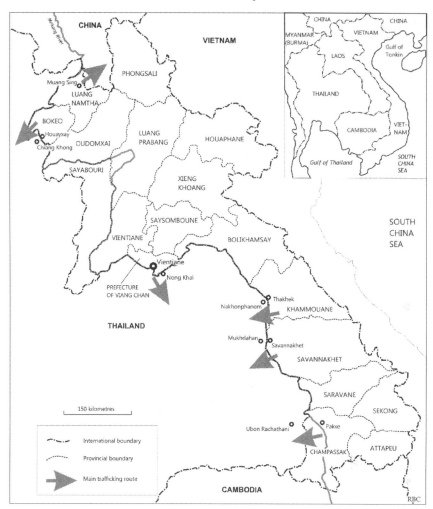

Figure 3.1 UNICEF map of trafficking 'hot-spots' in Laos

Such maps appear in reports and project websites and include topographical information such as elevation and different types of roads ('roadfoot', 'roadcart', 'road', etc.). It is never explained exactly why such data is relevant to anti-trafficking efforts yet they remain central to visualized representations of trafficking trends and can be considered a form of modernist aesthetic (Stirrat 2000) that is commonplace within the broader aid community.

Perhaps the boldest usage of trafficking maps in Laos is produced by the UNIAP project. In the project's second phase attempts were made not only to collate data on trafficking for the purpose of visual presentation of trafficking trends, but also to mirror this with a visual representation of anti-trafficking programmes. The UNIAP project was based on the premise that this would enable a strategic framework of analysis in which it was possible to assess to what extent anti-trafficking programmes targeted the correct geographic areas, thereby identifying gaps and duplication within the anti-trafficking effort. I was part of this process when I worked as a project advisor for the Lao office of UNIAP. Although to my knowledge the results of this 'strategic analysis exercise' has yet to see the light of day, its remnants remained for some time on UNIAP's website.[7] The collation of trafficking data is also shown on a trafficking data sheet where various human trafficking routes are depicted with coloured arrows (UNIAP 2008).

As with the UNICEF report, the methodology employed in the UNIAP report is easily refuted. The collation of various trafficking statistics represents what Anderson has termed the 'dustbag approach' to trafficking statistics where one 'hoovers up apples, pears and packets of crisps and cannot tell them apart when they are mushed up' (Anderson 2008: 3). And the attempt to generate maps to pinpoint anti-trafficking activities in relation to actual trafficking trends resembles some sort of childhood fantasy of total control over miniature worlds (see Scott 1998) reflected by play with model railroads and cardboard games.

The way these reports are written does not simply reflect trafficking 'on the ground'. This is not to say that there is nothing which resembles what is conventionally meant by trafficking along the border – indeed, these reports and other trafficking research provide specific examples of human trafficking. Nor is it to deny that deceptive recruitment is taking place or that agents facilitate cross-border movements of Laotians.[8] However, the extent to which the combination of movement, non-consensual recruitment and the intention of placing a migrant in an exploitative labour situation constitutes a systematic and therefore patterned undertaking by traffickers remains unclear and highly anecdotal at best.

In other words, I question the idea that trafficking constitutes identifiable clusters, legible trends, observable hotspots and enduring routes. It is the tendency to articulate trafficking in terms of agglomeration which needs to be interrogated. How the usage of maps fits the depictions of trafficking cited earlier: the notion of a frictionless marketplace where trafficked victims 'flow' (indicated by arrows) from source communities ('supply') to destination points ('demand'). These examples reveal the contours of a particular logic: trafficking programmes insist on ideal types and generic forms of models that presuppose agglomeration, and in doing so 'slip from the model of reality to the reality of the model' (Bourdieu 1977: 29). This phenomenon is particularly pertinent when it comes to the 'demand side' which has placed the spots clearly in the camp of traffickers and exploiters – that is at 'destination points'.

Destination points: where is the demand?

Discussing, writing and designing interventions that target the demand side of trafficking has become fashionable within development programmes. Demand is frequently a topic in anti-trafficking workshops, and is regarded by many to constitute the cutting edge of anti-trafficking responses (Molland in press). At first glance, the point is well taken. Given the fact that poverty is widespread in Laos it appears unrealistic to 'turn off the tap' by addressing socio-economic problems within communities with high levels of out-migration. An emphasis on exploitative employers and traffickers allows for a far more targeted focus on what many believe is the real problem of human trafficking: that is, labour exploitation and dubious recruitment practices.

The challenge of demand-side reduction for an anti-trafficking project is captured by Anderson and O'Connell Davidson (2004: 26) in one of the best-known demand-side studies amongst anti-traffickers:

> ... there is no reason to assume that individuals who wish to exploit others are only or specifically interested in trafficked persons. It is hard to imagine an abusive plantation manager or sweatshops owner turning down the opportunity to subject a worker to forced labour or slavery-like practices because s/he is a 'smuggled person' rather than a 'victim of trafficking', and harder still to imagine a client refusing to buy the sexual services of a prostitute on the same grounds. It makes more sense to assume that the niceties of international and national law on trafficking, and the details of a person's journey into vulnerability and unfreedom, are irrelevant to those who exploit or consume their labour/services.

Neither migration nor labour exploitation in itself accounts for the demand side of trafficking. From a trafficking project's point of view, the question then becomes: 'Why does a factory owner employ trafficked labour as opposed to voluntary labour?' Or: 'Why does a brothel owner employ trafficked women as opposed to voluntary sex workers?' In other words, the reasons for trafficking are directly associated and linked to the *modus operandi* of business enterprise.

The notion of where demand is greater comes in different (and often competing) flavours: some commentators argue that trafficking is more common in the 'low end' of a given labour sector characterized by marginal profit margins (Anderson and O'Connell Davidson 2004). Because of their low profits, it is reasoned, employers are more likely to recruit trafficked labour as it becomes difficult to recruit voluntary labour for sub-standard wages. Others suggest the exact opposite: trafficking is found where traffickers can reap huge profits, often pointing to niche commodities such as the sale of virgins (Hughes 2000). As is the case with the process of pinpointing spots in both source communities and border zones, the way the anti-trafficking sector envisages spots in destination points is conjectural and is rarely based on solid empirical research.

Within the Lao anti-trafficking sector, demand reduction is relatively new and no reports have attempted to explicitly theorize exactly what 'demand' entails. Nor has any Lao-based anti-trafficking project attempted to investigate empirically why employers in a given sector engage trafficked labour. Instead, they focus on traffickers. In other words, in order to identify spots through the prism of demand, they focus on traffickers, brokers and recruiters:

> Another explanation [for the limited reduction of trafficking] has been the comparison of trafficking to a squishy balloon, where pressure applied in one

place simultaneously leads to a local reduction in the problem and its 'ballooning up' in another place, with traffickers dynamically adjusting to changing environments. Thus, through displacement of the problem, every actor or organization working on trafficking will have genuine 'success stories' to tell, yet the problem's overall magnitude will remain intact. Displacement can be geographical (with traffickers targeting other villages, provinces or countries), social (with traffickers targeting different social groups), or a displacement in time (for example with traffickers waiting until an intervention is over).

(UNIAP *et al.* 2004: 6)

Traffickers are depicted as frictionless with the ability to presciently move to areas that are most profitable, or offer minimal chance of detection. Trafficking is depicted as a mechanical zero-sum game with clear cause and effect relationships. Indeed, the metaphor is derived from the laws of physics. Traffickers are assumed to be highly calculating and the fact that traffickers are always referred to in plural implies both a conspiratorial and organizational aspect to their operations. For example, UNICEF suggests that elements of organized crime are central to Thai–Lao trafficking:

Lao traffickers have regular contacts on the Thai side. Information pieced together from interviews with trafficking victims seems to indicate these contacts are highly organized and appear to be formed into a complex of mafia-type groups, the largest of which are in Bangkok, but with a considerable number of locations outside the capital as well. This is evidenced by the wide variety of destinations outside of Bangkok to which Lao victims are trafficked, in all regions of the country ranging from the far south to the far north, as well as to provinces such as Chonburi in the eastern region.

(UNICEF and Ministry of Labour and Social Welfare 2004: 23)

The simple fact that Lao trafficked victims end up in different locations in Thailand is taken as evidence for the existence of mafia groups. Indeed, the report even admits to engage in purely speculative musings, adding that: 'The degree to which these groups may be interrelated is unknown' (UNICEF and Ministry of Labour and Social Welfare 2004: 23).

Such depictions contrast with my own ethnographic research into recruitment along the Thai–Lao border. During the fifteen months I spent studying the commercial sex industry along the Thai–Lao border I uncovered no clear evidence of mafia-style operations. By far the most common type of recruiters were sex workers themselves who recruit friends and acquaintances on their return to their home villages. Occasionally this involved deception and debt bondage arrangements. In contrast to the imagery of traffickers acting in a highly calculative fashion, the conduct of Lao traffickers (if we can call them such) is better understood as a form of bad faith where deceptive recruitment is camouflaged as a form of assistance (Molland in press). As one Lao recruiter says, 'I am helping. I feel sorry for them because they are so poor.' Lao 'traffickers' do not engage in human trafficking as a full-time activity; rather it is the result of opportunism and circumstance.

To be fair, several Lao anti-trafficking programmes are quite aware that trafficking can often be an informal affair amongst community members. What this means is that they vacillate between different understandings of trafficking. This is evident in the statements of key informants who work within anti-trafficking programmes. When asked what comprises a trafficking trend, Peter, who works for a large anti-trafficking programme in Laos, looked baffled for a moment and then said: 'Look, we must be careful talking about trends in the Lao context.' Only minutes before Peter had been discussing how his project was considering exploring the impact of large infrastructural projects on trafficking trends. Similarly, John, who works within the legal sector in Laos to strengthen the criminal justice process in relation to human trafficking, expressed frustration over the difficulty of getting government officials in training workshops to realize that when a mother sells her daughter to a beer shop then 'this is trafficking!'. Yet, earlier in the very same interview, John suggested that if there are only two or three girls involved 'then it is perhaps not [trafficking], but if it is 200 to 300 girls then yes, that would be trafficking'. Similarly, while Thou initially recognized that sex workers are involved in recruiting friends and acquaintances, she also employed the notion of trafficking being orchestrated by organized crime gangs who are capable of relocating their geographical operations in order to minimize risk and maximize profit.

The necessity of agglomeration

In a celebrated (and critiqued) analysis of development aid in Lesotho, Ferguson (1990) argued that development aid programmes are shaped by a discursive internal logic rather than by the social world that they seek to alter. Drawing on Foucault, he suggests that aid programmes can only articulate their object in terms of what the project is capable of delivering. The result of this, according to Ferguson, is that development aid tends to take on a technocratic character, emphasizing technical solutions (the provision of tractors, training in new harvest techniques and so on) rather than addressing questions of power and politics (i.e. entrenched elites and patron–client relationships). This does not render aid delivery benign. Although development programmes describe themselves in apolitical terms, they carry with them, Ferguson says, concrete although often unintended political effects.

Similarly, I argue that anti-traffickers such as Thou cling to the notion of prescient traffickers who can swiftly relocate to maximize their profits because it is a discursive necessity. Trafficking programmes manage scarce resources and need to place their efforts where they envisage they will have the most impact. It is difficult for an anti-trafficking project to justify spending those scarce resources in an area if it is clear that there have only been a few reported cases of human trafficking. De-centred, infrequent and ad hoc trafficking will not do for an anti-trafficking project because it does not allow for a 'hook' on which a project can design an intervention – in other words, trafficking must be made legible

(Scott 1998) and receptive to policy intervention. It therefore becomes impera-tive for an anti-trafficking project to make allusions to agglomerations ('this border crossing is a hotspot for trafficking', 'this village is vulnerable to traffick-ing', 'trafficking is more prone in the low-end brothels'). And the metaphor of a market is particularly well suited as a vessel to communicate notions of trends and hotspots because it gives a sense of coherence and meaning to anti-trafficking projects and provides cause–effect relationships which allow aid workers to design interventions.

Anti-trafficking programmes in Laos are detached from the social world of migrants because the discursive necessity for agglomeration and its accompany-ing focus on hotspots and market metaphors has led to a tendency to depict the intentional subject in a utilitarian fashion (i.e. the rational maximizing agent). The effect of this is that agency is understood as being external and prior to social action (Emirbayer and Mische 1998) thereby drawing attention *away* from social relation-ships. Advocating for strengthened law enforcement, even if this includes the death penalty, is made conceivable when it is claimed that traffickers use 'demand-supply basics' (Aye 2002: 3) and 'dynamically [adjust] to changing environments' (UNIAP *et al.* 2004: 6).[9] It is less certain whether Lao anti-trafficking programmes would be so eager to launch law enforcement-style projects if more consideration were given to the fact that, at least when it comes to the sex industry along the border, recruiters are often themselves young sex workers who recruit sporadically and opportunisti-cally (as opposed to methodically and with calculation). So far the introduction of the death penalty has not resulted in executions (it only applies in egregious cases) and given the extremely limited dissemination and knowledge of Lao laws amongst its citizens and officials it is doubtful whether it has been a meaningful deterrent. Although arrests of traffickers have been made, the number is still relativity small compared to the enormous numbers of migrants, and it is difficult to argue that they have resulted in significant changes for migrant populations and Lao labour migrants at large.

Conclusion

As I have indicated throughout this chapter, what is extraordinary is the way anti-trafficking programmes in Laos in many respects remain detached from their object of intervention. Although this may be surprising it is worth noting that '[k]nowledge and action mobilize extremely dissimilar registers of legitimation' (de Sardan 2005: 199) and there are often wide discrepancies between discourse and practice within the development sector (Lewis and Mosse 2006).

It is not just that anti-trafficking programmes are defined with reference to their own discursive logic. As Mosse (2004: 646) has pointed out, the success (and the continuation) of projects does not primarily depend on turning policy into reality, but 'upon the stabilization of a particular interpretation' of success. As human trafficking is inherently a de-territorial development challenge, the mismatch between ideal types models and the local unfolding of migration can be glossed over because the notion of a frictionless market allows anomalies to be explained by the model: hence, absence of clear evidence of trafficking-prone villages can be turned into evidence for frictionless and calculating traffickers thus:

> There is a growing acknowledgement of the displacement, or push-down pop-up (PDPU) effect surrounding trafficking. This name is used to describe a phenomenon whereby the problem is reduced or pushed down in one place, only to emerge somewhere else. Trafficking is a dynamic phenomena and traffickers can quickly adjust to changing environments, in particular, but not only, by shifting geographic focus of their activities. Evidence of PDPU raises questions about the efficacy of a range of current programs and its acknowledgement is fundamental to developing more effective interventions.
>
> (Marshall and Thatun 2005: 44)

However, it is not just that 'this raises questions about the efficacy of a range of current programs'. Although the shortcomings of anti-trafficking projects are acknowledged, the assumption that traffickers flit across borders to bring supply to meet demand in a mysterious and prescient manner is sustained, thereby legitimizing the development of more effective interventions. As this exploration of the use of hotspots has shown, it is doubtful whether policy initiated to combat trafficking has significantly influenced migration flows along the Thai–Lao border. Rather, the imagery of hotspots has become central to the programmatic reproduction of anti-trafficking programmes themselves.

Notes

1 The material presented in this chapter is based on 15 months' fieldwork on migration and sex commerce along the Thai–Lao border. It is also drawn from my previous role as a project advisor for the Lao office of the UN Inter-agency project to Combat Human Trafficking in the Greater Mekong sub-Region (UNIAP). Although I address the question of the actual social practice of recruitment, migration and sex commerce along the Thai–Lao border elsewhere (Molland 2008), the empirical horizon for this chapter is primarily the anti-trafficking programmes that operate in the Lao PDR. I would like to thank Rosemary Wiss and Roy B. C. Huijsmans for valuable comments and criticisms of earlier drafts of this paper.

2 The report's methodology is unclear in terms of how it collates data on migration. Some survey questions refer to the past, whereas others refer to the present. For example, one part of the questionnaire asks: 'In your family, is there any member works [*sic*] in other places?'; another part asks: 'Have you traveled and lived elsewhere for more than 3 months outside the village in past 3 years?'.

3 With their emphasis on providing reliable and time-bound development to rural communities, many development projects avoid activities that may be politically sensitive. This could include addressing recruitment practices within village communities. Aid programmes are worried that migrant brokers, or 'traffickers' are well-connected. Hence, attempting to disrupt brokering activities directly may place field staff at risk. In addition, it is politically unacceptable to raise direct questions of dubious recruitment and the possible complicity of local government officials.

4 All examples are from anti-trafficking projects operating in Laos. I witnessed one representative from a UN project solemnly suggest in a meeting that one possible avenue to combat trafficking could be to employ more people on anti-trafficking projects.

5 For example, Save the Children Australia's trafficking programme bears the title: 'Cross Border Project against Trafficking and Exploitation of Migrant and Vulnerability of Young People'.
6 There are other serious shortcomings in this report. Although it claims to use the definition of human trafficking contained in the UN Trafficking Protocol, the author appears to misunderstand important aspects of the definition. At times the report seems to suggest that *any* movement of children constitutes a case of trafficking.
7 This visual representation of anti-trafficking programmes was removed after a revamp of the project website in 2007.
8 I personally encountered cases while doing ethnographic research within the sex industry along the Thai–Lao border (Molland in press).
9 Over the last few years increasing attention has been given to law enforcement within the Lao anti-trafficking sector with the advent of the Asia Regional Trafficking in Persons Project (ARTIP) in 2003 followed by UNODC in 2005. ARTIP is funded by the Australian Government and works primarily within police and the legal sector in order to strengthen the criminal justice response to trafficking. In Laos, a large part of their work includes training the Lao police on the investigation, arrest and prosecution of traffickers. UNODC also works with the legal sector. Their main counterpart in Laos is the Ministry of Justice.

References

Agustín, L. M. (2007) *Sex at the Margins: Migration, Labour Markets and the Rescue Industry*, London and New York: Zed Books.

Anderson, B. (2008) 'Sex, slaves and stereotypes', *Global Networks*, 8 (3): 367–71.

Anderson, B. and O'Connell Davidson, J. (2003) *Is Trafficking in Human Beings Demand Driven? A Multi-Country Pilot Study*, Geneva: IOM International Organization for Migration.

—— (2004) *Trafficking – A Demand Led Problem? Part I: Review of Evidence and Debates*, Stockholm: Save the Children Sweden.

Asia Regional Cooperation to Prevent People Trafficking (2003) *Gender, Human Trafficking, and the Criminal Justice System in the Lao PDR*, Vientiane: ARCPPT.

Aye, N. N. (2002) 'Can we outsmart traffickers?', *Step by Step: UN Inter-Agency Project Newsletter*, 3 and 7.

Bourdieu, P. (1977) *Outline of a Theory of Practice*, Cambridge: Cambridge University Press.

Caouette, T. M. (1998) *Needs Assessment of Cross-border Trafficking in Women and Children: The Mekong Sub Region*, Bangkok: UN Working Group on Trafficking in the Mekong Sub-Region.

Carrier, J. G. and Miller, D. (1998) *Virtualism: A New Political Economy*, Oxford: Berg.

De Sardan, J. O. (2005) *Anthropology and Development: Understanding Contemporary Social Change*, London: Zed Books.

Doezema, J. (2007) 'Who gets to choose? Coercion, consent, and the UN Trafficking Protocol', *Gender and Development*, 10 (1): 20–7.

Doussantousse, S. and Keovonghit, B. (2006) *Migration of Children and Youth from Savannakhet Province, Laos to Thailand: A Research Study*, Vientiane: World Vision Lao PDR.

Emirbayer, M. and Mische, A. (1998) 'What is agency?', *American Journal of Sociology*, 103 (4): 962–1023.

Feingold, D. (1997) *The Hell of Good Intentions: Some Preliminary Thoughts on Opium in the Political Ecology of the Trade in Girls and Women*, Philadelphia: Ophidian Research Institute.

Ferguson, J. (1990) *The Anti-politics Machine: 'Development,' Depoliticization, and Bureaucratic Power in Lesotho*, Cambridge: Cambridge University Press.

Gallagher, A. (2001) 'Human rights and the new UN protocols on trafficking and migrant smuggling: A preliminary analysis', *Human Rights Quarterly*, 23 (4): 975–1004.

—— (2006) 'Recent legal developments in the field of human trafficking: A critical review of the 2005 European convention and related instruments', *European Journal of Migration and Law*, 8: 163–89.

Ginzburg, O. (2002) *Building Projects on Assumptions*, Bangkok: UN Inter-Agency Project on Trafficking in Women and Children in the Mekong sub-Region (UNIAP).

—— (2004) *Reintegration of Victims of Trafficking: Defining Success and Developing Indicators: Cambodia, Laos, Myanmar, Vietnam*, Bangkok: IOM.

Haughton, J. (2006) *Situational Analysis of Human Trafficking in the Lao PDR with Emphasis on Savannakhet*, Vientiane: World Vision Lao PDR.

Hughes, D. (2000) 'The "Natasha" trade: The transnational shadow market of trafficking in women', *Journal of International Affairs*, 53 (2): 625–51.

Huijsmans, R. (2007) 'Approaches to Lao minors working in Thailand', *Juth Pakai: Perspectives on Lao Development*, 8: 18–33.

ILO (2003) *Labour Migration Survey in Khammuane, Savannakhet and Champasak*, Vientiane: Ministry of Labour and Social Welfare, Lao PDR and ILO.

—— (2006) *Demand Side of Human Trafficking in Asia: Empirical Findings*, Geneva: ILO.

ILO-IPEC (2002) *Technical Intervention Area Summary Notes: TIA-3; Micro-Finance Interventions to Combat the Worst Forms of Child Labour, including Trafficking*, Bangkok: ILO-IPEC.

IOM (2004) *From Lao PDR to Thailand and Home Again: The Repatriation of Trafficking Victims and Other Exploited Women and Girl Workers: A Study of 124 Cases*, Bangkok: IOM.

Kempadoo, K. (2005) 'Introduction: From moral panic to global justice: Changing perspectives on trafficking', in Kempadoo, K., Sanghera, J. and Pattanaik, B. (eds) *Trafficking and Prostitution Reconsidered: New Perspectives on Migration, Sex Work, and Human Rights*, London: Paradigm Publishers, pp. vii–xxxiv.

Lao People's Democratic Republic (n.d.) *National Growth and Poverty Eradication Strategy (NGPES)*, Vientiane: Government of Laos.

Lewis, D. and Mosse, D. (2006) 'Theoretical approaches to brokerage and translation in development', in Lewis, D. and Mosse, D. (eds) *Development Brokers and Translators: The Ethnography of Aid and Agencies*, Kumarian Press, pp. 1–26.

Marshall, P. and Thatun, S. (2005) 'Miles away: The trouble with prevention in the Greater Mekong Sub-region', in Kempadoo, K., Sanghera, J. and Pattanaik, B. (eds) *Trafficking and Prostitution Reconsidered: New Perspectives on Migration, Sex Work, and Human Rights*, London: Paradigm Publishers, pp. 43–63.

Massey, D. S. (1998) 'Contemporary theories on international migration', in Massey, D., Arango, J., Hugo, G. and Kouaouci, A. (eds) *Worlds in Motion: Understanding Migration at the End of the Millennium*, Oxford: Clarendon Press, pp. 244–77.

Molland, S. (2005) 'Human trafficking and poverty reduction: Two sides of the same coin?', *Juth Pakai: Perspectives on Lao Development*, 4: 27–37.

—— (2010) 'The value of bodies: Deception, helping and profiteering in human trafficking along the Thai-Lao border', *Asian Studies Review*, 34 (2): 211–29.

——(in press) *The Perfect Business? Anti-trafficking and the Sex Trade along the Mekong*, Honolulu: University of Hawai'i Press.

Mosse, D. (2004) 'Is good policy unimplementable? Reflections on the ethnography of aid policy and practice', *Development and Change*, 35 (4): 639–71.

Muttarak, R. (2004) 'Domestic service in Thailand: Reflection of conflicts in gender, class and ethnicity', *Journal of Southeast Asian Studies*, 35 (3): 503–29.

Phetsiriseng, I (2001) *Preliminary Assessment on Trafficking of Children and Women for Labour Exploitation in Lao PDR*, Vientiane: ILO.

Rigg, J. (2006) 'Moving lives: Migration and livelihoods in the Lao PDR', *Population, Space and Place*, 13 (3): 163–78.

Ruggiero, V. (1997) 'Trafficking in human beings: Slaves in contemporary Europe', *International Journal of the Sociology of Law*, 25 (3): 231–44.

Scheper-Hughes, N. (2000) 'The global traffic in human organs', *Current Anthropology*, 41 (2): 191–224.

Schloenhardt, A. (1999) 'The business of migration: Organised crime and illegal migration in Australia and the Asia-Pacific Region', *Adelaide Law Review*, 21: 81–114.

Scott, J. C. (1998) *Seeing like a State: How Certain Schemes to Improve the Human Condition Have Failed*, New Haven, CT: Yale University Press.

Shangera, J. (2005) 'Unpacking the trafficking discourse', in Kempadoo, K., Sanghera, J. and Pattanaik, B. (eds) *Trafficking and Prostitution Reconsidered: New Perspectives on Migration, Sex Work, and Human Rights*, London: Paradigm Publishers, pp. 3–24.

Stirrat, R. L. (2000) 'Cultures of consultancy', *Critique of Anthropology*, 20 (1): 31–46.

UNESCO Bangkok (n.d.) 'Trafficking and HIV/AIDS Project', Retrieved from http://www.unescobkk.org/en/culture/our-projects/protection-of-endangered-and-minority-cultures/trafficking-and-hivaids-project/projects/gis-linked-social-sentinel-surveillence-project/unesco-gis-map-collection-new/lao-pdr/

UNIAP (2008) 'SIREN Human Trafficking Data Sheet', Beijing: UNIAP.

UNIAP and Ministry of Labour and Social Welfare (2001) *Trafficking in Women and Children in the Lao PDR: Initial Observations*, Vientiane: Ministry of Labour and Social Welfare, Lao PDR and UNIAP.

UNIAP, UNICEF Laos and Ministry of Labour and Social Welfare (2004) *Trace: Trafficking from Community to Exploitation*, Vientiane: UNIAP, UNICEF, Ministry of Labour and Social Welfare.

UNICEF and Ministry of Labour and Social Welfare (2004) *Broken Promises Shattered Dreams: A Profile of Child Trafficking in the Lao PDR*, Vientiane: Ministry of Labour and Social Welfare, Lao PDR and UNICEF.

Wille, C. (2001) *Thailand-Lao People's Democratic Republic and Thailand-Myanmar Border Areas: Trafficking in Children into the Worst Forms of Child Labour: A Rapid Assessment*, Geneva: ILO-IPEC.

4 Counter-trafficking and migrant labour activism in Indonesia's periphery

Michele Ford and Lenore Lyons

Worldwide, the anti-trafficking agenda has generated an enormous growth in the number of NGOs, government organizations and international agencies working to prevent human trafficking, assist in the prosecution of traffickers, and aid in the rescue and return of 'victims'. Indonesia is no exception. There, as elsewhere in Southeast Asia, international agencies and donor countries have played a significant role in shaping both NGO and government approaches to human trafficking. International NGOs and inter-governmental organizations have partnered with local NGOs and local governments to develop policy and legislative responses, as well as prevention and rehabilitation programmes. These efforts are a response to the UN Trafficking Protocol and the subsequent pressure from the United States to comply with its annual Trafficking in Persons (TIP) reports, which identify Indonesia as a major source country.[1]

Particularly influential in the development of Indonesia's anti-trafficking strategy was a series of joint projects funded by USAID and implemented by the American Center for International Labor Solidarity (Solidarity Center) and the International Catholic Migration Commission (ICMC). Over a nine-year period, these very different organizations worked together to implement three separate USAID-funded projects which sought to develop a national response to human trafficking in Indonesia in response to its poor performance in the TIP Reports. Along with the initiatives of intergovernmental organizations like the International Organization for Migration (IOM), these projects transformed the way in which local NGO activists have understood and responded to temporary labour migration.

This chapter documents the pivotal role played by Solidarity Center/ICMC projects in changing the way human trafficking was imagined and handled not only in the metropolitan core but also in key locations in Indonesia's far-flung peripheries. Through a detailed account of these projects and their implementation in the Riau Islands, the chapter demonstrates the extent to which the anti-trafficking frame has shaped the evolution of individuals' and organizations' ways of conceptualizing and responding to the issues of labour exploitation and mobility in Indonesia.[2]

Counter-trafficking initiatives in the Riau Islands

The islands of Bintan, Batam and Karimun are part of Kepri Province (Provinsi Kepulauan Riau), which lies in the Straits of Malacca to the north-east of Sumatra (see Figure 4.1). These islands are a transit zone for documented and undocumented labour flows to Malaysia and Singapore, as well as the nearest point for repatriation of workers whose contracts have ended or undocumented migrants who have been deported (Lyons and Ford 2007). They have also attracted large numbers of internal migrants in search of work since the formation of the Indonesia-Malaysia-Singapore Growth Triangle in 1990. In that time, a large commercial sex industry catering to both Indonesian and foreign men has sprung up alongside the islands' manufacturing and tourist zones.[3]

As the commercial sex industry grew, it began to attract international donor funding for HIV-AIDS prevention and by 2001 there were at least three NGOs in the islands working to improve sex workers' reproductive health. Yet although HIV-AIDS and reproductive health had attracted international interest for some time, the islands' role as a major transit zone for international labour migrants was of little interest until the signing of the UN Trafficking Protocol.[4] The Coalition Against Trafficking in Women (CATW), which played an influential lobbying role in the drafting of the Protocol, first identified the Riau Islands as a key site of trafficking for sexual exploitation in Indonesia in a report released in 2002.[5]

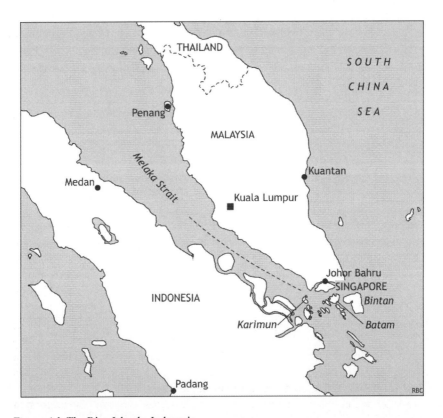

Figure 4.1 The Riau Islands, Indonesia

Around the time that CATW wrote this report, the IOM began a repatriation programme in which all the major islands in Kepri were identified as sites for 'victim identification'.[6] Through this programme, funding was provided on a case-by-case basis for trafficked victims to be repatriated and to receive a reintegration disbursement to start a small business in their place of origin (Lindquist 2008).

Despite this international interest, there were no dedicated local anti-trafficking NGOs in operation in the islands and the concept of 'human trafficking' was little understood by NGOs working in HIV-AIDS prevention or on labour migration issues. Indeed, most NGOs working on reproductive health and/or HIV-AIDS prevention in the islands felt the impact of USAID proscriptions against providing assistance to sex workers well before they understood the links between the US anti-prostitution and anti-trafficking agendas (Lyons and Ford 2010). The situation began to change as international organizations began to see the potential benefits of working with local NGOs to pursue counter-trafficking activities, and the Foundation for Friends of Health and Humanity (Yayasan Mitra Kesehatan dan Kemanusiaan, YMKK) was approached to become involved in counter-trafficking activities after Indonesia signed the UN Trafficking Protocol in December 2000 (Lindquist and Piper 2007: 142–3).[7] The strategy of using existing NGOs to pursue anti-trafficking activities became even more apparent with the first Solidarity Center/ICMC-led project, which began in October 2001.

'Creating an Enabling Environment to Overcome Trafficking of Women and Children in Indonesia' – known as the Counter Trafficking Project (CTP) for short – was funded by USAID as part of its global anti-trafficking programme (Rosenberg 2006: 6). The stated aims of this two-year project were to help the government to improve policies and legislation; to support the counter-trafficking programmes of NGOs, trade unions and universities; to improve information flows and networking amongst stakeholders; and to strengthen worker networks to counter trafficking of marginalized workers (Rosenberg 2003b: 261–3).[8] The CTP sought to achieve these aims through a 'multi-faceted approach', providing technical and financial assistance and training to government agencies, NGOs and trade unions. Its goal was to strengthen these groups and support their 'efforts to establish a proactive framework of counter-trafficking initiatives' (Rosenberg 2003b: 261). Much of the project's resources were devoted to capacity building and the development of the National Plan of Action for the Elimination of Trafficking of Women and Children and a purpose-specific national law to deal with trafficking.[9] The project team also ran training sessions for members of recipient organizations and officials from different levels of government. A vital element of this work was a study tour by project officers and central government officials to twelve targeted provinces. This tour formed the basis for an influential 300-page report, entitled *Trafficking of Women and Children in Indonesia* (Rosenberg 2003b), which not only provided the blueprint for Indonesia's response to human trafficking, but also influenced the approach taken by the US Office to Monitor and Combat Trafficking in Persons – and through it, the response of other international organizations, including the IOM.

The CTP report, which describes labour trafficking as 'the predominant form of trafficking' in Indonesia, identifies the Riau Islands as a destination for domestic trafficking and a transit zone for trafficking abroad. Like the CATW report before it, it describes Batam and Tanjung Balai Karimun as key destinations for women and girls trafficked from other parts of Indonesia into the commercial sex industry. It also notes Batam's role as a hub for international trafficking for commercial sex (Agustinanto 2003: 178–9). When asked about Batam's prominence in the project, Ruth Rosenberg, the CTP Project Manager in the Jakarta office of ICMC, responded that 'Batam chose itself' (Interview, July 2003), which suggests that the island's position as a trafficking 'hotspot' (see Molland in this volume) was already well established prior to the project. By contrast, the report made no mention of the neighbouring island of Bintan, which was also a major transit point for labour migration and a destination for sex workers in the early 2000s.

The absence of any mention of Bintan in the report can be explained by the fact that there were no NGOs working on trafficking, HIV-AIDS prevention or international labour migration on the island in 2001. The CTP report was based on secondary sources, many produced by local NGOs (Interview with Ruth Rosenberg, July 2003). Consequently, the presence or absence of NGOs had a significant impact on the data collected and the conclusions reached. Bintan was omitted not because no human trafficking took place there but because there were no NGOs to report it. Existing NGOs were also the main recipients of CTP funding for anti-trafficking initiatives. In the Riau Islands, three NGOs and a new NGO coalition – all based on Batam – received funding through the CTP's grant scheme (Rosenberg 2003b: 276–7). YMKK undertook to provide shelter, counselling and medical assistance for victims of sex trafficking. The Commission for Migrants (Komisi Migran dan Perantau, Karya Migran) received support to provide shelter, counselling and repatriation for returned migrant workers. A third NGO, the Service Centre for Female Overseas Migrants in Batam (Pusat Pelayanan Tenaga Kerja Wanita di Batam, PP Nakerwan), was funded to run an awareness-raising campaign to 'improve conditions for migrant workers in the holding centers and to stop trafficking-like practices'. The NGO forum that received funding for awareness-raising with local government officials was set up by the head of the Setara Kita Foundation (Yayasan Setara Kita), a former YMKK staff member. Called Forum 182, it was tasked with convincing local government to commit resources to counter-trafficking and to raise public awareness (Rosenberg 2003b: 276–7).

The Riau Islands were also among the group of 13 target provinces selected for inclusion in the second of the Solidarity Center/ICMC projects, which ran for 26 months from September 2004. This project, entitled 'Strengthening the Initiatives of Government and Others Against Human Trafficking' (SIGHT), received US$2 million in financial support from USAID. The bulk of the project focused on the development of vulnerability reduction strategies and service provision for victims in the regions. At the national level, project staff provided technical assistance on the Anti-Trafficking Bill, first to the Ministry of Women's Empowerment and then to members of parliament.[10] They also provided advice on Law No. 39/2004 on the Protection of Migrant Workers and their Families and trained provincial labour inspectors on its use in the detection of trafficking cases. Standard Operating Procedures for return, recovery and reintegration developed in conjunction with the Ministry of Women's Empowerment as part of the project were then piloted in Kalimantan, Sumatra, Sulawesi and Bali. Project staff also worked with officials from the Ministry of Women's Empowerment and the Coordinating Ministry for Social Welfare to assist local and provincial governments to form the taskforces mandated in the National Plan of Action.

As a consequence of IOM activity and the CTP and SIGHT projects, by 2006 the Riau Islands had reached what one activist described as 'the peak of the anti-trafficking fever' (Interview, 2009). Several dedicated anti-trafficking NGOs were operating both in Batam and in the new provincial capital, Tanjung Pinang, located on the island of Bintan. As one NGO activist observed:

> Suddenly there were so many NGOs dealing with trafficking. It was like a magnet. Everyone's attention shifted. Everyone wanted to work on it. The ones that used to deal with other issues all shifted focus and a whole bunch of new ones emerged.
>
> (Interview, November 2006)

During the life of the SIGHT project the primary focus in the Riau Islands was on providing and strengthening shelter services, as well as sensitizing local governments to the issue of trafficking and supporting their counter-trafficking measures. On the island of Batam, where all the CTP projects had taken place, YMKK was funded to provide technical assistance for the provision of shelter services and other forms of assistance to the Batam Women's Empowerment Bureau. As part of this project staff distributed leaflets raising awareness of the shelter to police stations, port facilities, and in the red-light and entertainment districts. They also developed a manual and a set of Standard Operating Procedures for the shelter and trained shelter staff on its use, as well as assisting the bureau in its negotiations with other government agencies.

Two additional projects were funded in Karimun and Bintan, which had not been a focus for the CTP. In Tanjung Balai Karimun, a twelve-month project to raise public and local government awareness about human trafficking and to provide assistance to trafficked women was run by the Women's Health and Education Foundation (Yayasan Kaseh Puan), which, like YMKK, had previously worked in HIV-AIDS prevention. During this time Kaseh Puan also received funding from the IOM for repatriation and reintegration (Interview with Rina Lestari, December 2006).[11] In Tanjung Pinang, a private shelter run by a newly established NGO called the Kemala Bintan Foundation (Yayasan Kemala Bintan) was funded for a period of one year. Kemala Bintan was also tasked with raising awareness of trafficking and assisting the local Women's Empowerment Bureau to establish a counter-trafficking programme (Solidarity Center/ICMC 2006: 63–8).

The Riau Islands received even closer attention in the third and final project undertaken by the Solidarity Center and ICMC, which attracted a further US$1.2 million from USAID between March 2007 and September 2009. Entitled 'Anti-Trafficking in Persons in Indonesia' (ATP), this project aimed to provide technical assistance at the national level and to 'accelerate the development of integrated counter-trafficking efforts' in eight strategic locations, which were then to serve as models for replication in other districts (Solidarity Center/ICMC 2009: 3). Batam, Tanjung Pinang and Tanjung Balai Karimun were three of the eight locations identified.

As part of the ATP, project staff supported the development of implementing regulations for Law No. 21/2007 on the Eradication of the Crime of Trafficking in Persons and a series of Standard Minimal Services for victims of trafficking, as well as continuing work on the revision of the Standard Operating Procedures formulated as part of SIGHT. Project staff also provided technical support for the development of a new National Plan of Action for the period 2009–2014. In addition to advocating stronger prosecutory measures for traffickers, one of the review committee's key recommendations was that the labour migration system be reformed and that widespread education be conducted on debt bondage (Solidarity Center/ICMC 2009: 17–19). On receipt of the evaluation, ICMC and the Solidarity Center took active carriage of the early drafting of the new National Plan of Action, which addressed the majority of recommendations contained in the report. In addition, attempts were made by project staff to sensitize the staff of the National Board for the Placement and Protection of Overseas Workers (Badan Nasional Penempatan dan Perlindungan Tenaga Kerja Indonesia, BNP2TKI) to the issue of debt bondage, which the project partners defined as a form of trafficking (Solidarity Center/ICMC 2009: 58).

In addition, local NGOs were commissioned to serve as technical advisors to local government with the aims of increasing local knowledge and understanding of national anti-trafficking laws and regulations; establishing local counter-trafficking taskforces; and developing local plans of action on trafficking (Solidarity Center/ICMC 2009: 22–3). In the Riau Islands, an NGO was funded in each municipality to provide technical support to the local government in the formation of taskforces and the drafting of local action plans. In Batam, 17 months' funding was allocated to Setara Kita, the lead NGO in the anti-trafficking forum set up under the CTP. Kaseh Puan was funded for the same period to facilitate the project in Tanjung Balai Karimun. As Kemala Bintan, the project's previous partner in Tanjung Pinang, had collapsed with the end of SIGHT funding, project staff turned instead to the Sirih Besar Foundation (Yayasan Sirih Besar), which had a record of working with local government to improve conditions for irregular migrant workers deported to Tanjung Pinang, and also with the IOM on the rescue and repatriation of victims of trafficking (Solidarity Center/ICMC 2009). As part of an additional component of the project, shelter staff in the three municipalities received intensive training from Rifka Annisa, the NGO behind a long-established women's crisis centre in Yogyakarta. In Batam and Tanjung Pinang, this initiative involved staff running government shelters, but in Tanjung Balai Karimun it focused on Kaseh Puan.

Setting the anti-trafficking agenda

A key feature of the Solidarity Center/ICMC's interlinked projects has been their framing of trafficking. As ICMC coordinator Ruth Rosenberg notes in the CTP's final report, by the early 2000s important changes had already occurred in the international approach to human trafficking, with shifts in emphasis from recruitment to exploitation; from coercion to 'with or without consent'; from prostitution to informal and unregulated labour; from violence against women to violation of human rights; and from trafficking in women to illegal migration (Rosenberg 2003a: 12–13). It is significant that, at a time when many international NGOs remained heavily focused on trafficking for sexual exploitation, the project's first report places equal, if not greater, emphasis on trafficking for forced labour. This emphasis is particularly significant because – unlike the Solidarity Center, which came to the project convinced that labour trafficking rather than trafficking for sexual exploitation was the major concern in the Indonesian context (Interview with Rudy Porter, June 2008) – ICMC did not initially have a great deal of focus on migrant labour (Interview with Ruth Rosenberg, July 2003).

In the CTP report's introduction, Rosenberg leaves readers in no doubt of the importance of labour migration as a form of trafficking in the Indonesian context:

> Although trafficking for sexual exploitation certainly exists in Indonesia, far more women are trafficked for other forms of labor. Of the nearly a half million Indonesians who migrate officially for work each year, 70% are women (Hugo, 2001: 109); many more are thought to migrate through irregular channels. A large majority of the women migrate for work as domestic helpers; others for work in restaurants, factories or plantations. From research as well as NGO accounts of migrant workers, we know that many of these women find themselves facing conditions of exploitation, debt bondage, confiscation of identification, and restrictions on their movement that constitute trafficking.
>
> (Rosenberg 2003a: 12–13)

Labour migration is accorded an equally prominent position in the remainder of the report, in which the first two of five chapters on forms of trafficking deal with female overseas migrants. The central importance accorded to labour migration by ICMC and the Solidarity Center is particularly apparent in the 'Trafficking Framework' presented on page 15 of the CTP report (see Figure 4.2). This framework incorporates the key dimensions of the definition of trafficking contained in the UN Protocol – process, means and purpose – in a schema designed to help determine whether trafficking has taken place. According to the report's authors, if one condition from each column is met, then the phenomenon meets the definition of trafficking.

This framework represented a major shift in Indonesian understandings of human trafficking by creating space for discussion of overseas domestic work as trafficking. Although the CTP produced other results, this discursive shift was by far the most significant outcome of this project, as it set the parameters for government policy and increasingly for civil society activism. Prior to the CTP, Indonesian Government discourses around trafficking remained firmly centred on the sexual exploitation of women (Wahyuningrum 2007). The subsequent shift

Process	+	Means	+	Purpose
Recruitment OR Transportation OR Transferring OR Harboring OR Receiving	AND	Threat OR Coercion OR Abduction OR Fraud OR Deceit OR Deception OR The Abuse of Power	AND	Prostitution OR Pornography OR Violence / Sexual Exploitation OR Forced Labor OR Slavery/Similar Practices
1	+	1	+	1

Figure 4.2 ICMC/Solidarity Center Trafficking Framework

Source: Rosenberg (2003a: 15).

in Indonesia's official position clearly reflected the CTP's emphasis on labour migration. This is nowhere more evident than in the five-year 2002 National Plan of Action, which states that:

> Trafficking in women and children within the meaning of this National Plan of Action encompasses all forms of actions undertaken by perpetrators of trafficking that have one or more of the elements of recruiting, transporting between regions and countries, transferring, sending, receiving and temporary placement or placement at their destination of women and children. It includes using threats, verbal and physical abuse, abduction, fraud, deception, misuse of vulnerability (e.g. if someone has no alternative, is isolated, addicted to drugs, trapped in debt), giving or receiving payments or profits in cases involving women and children who are used for prostitution and sexual exploitation (including pedophilia), legal or illegal migrant workers, child adoptions, fishing platform work, mail order brides, domestic helpers, begging, pornography, drug dealing, selling of body organs as well as other forms of exploitation.
>
> (KPP 2002 cited in Misra 2003: 220)

According to Wahyuningrum (2007: 12), a former employee of the Solidarity Center who had worked on the CTP, the focus on women and children in the first National Plan of Action was the product of international precedents and pressures (specifically the UN Trafficking Protocol and the US Trafficking Victims Protection Act); the widely held view that women and children are more vulnerable to exploitation than men; and a strong push from women's groups to 'keep the focus on women'. Yet while the CTP focused only on women and children, its final report clearly stated that this 'should not be read as a comment on the prevalence or seriousness of trafficking of men in Indonesia' (Rosenberg 2003a: 15). By the time the draft anti-trafficking law had entered the parliament, there was not only evidence of a strong recognition of human trafficking for purposes other than sexual exploitation, but also acknowledgement that victims of trafficking could conceivably be male.

The national policy framework developed during this period further confirms that labour trafficking had come to be regarded as a central focus of Indonesia's response to human trafficking. Documents produced by the Coordinating Ministry for People's Welfare – the body tasked with coordinating the counter-trafficking programmes of different ministries – were heavily influenced by the first Solidarity Center/ICMC report. For example, it is cited heavily in *The Elimination of Trafficking in Persons in Indonesia, 2004–2005*. The definition of human trafficking provided in this document also explicitly reflects the CTP's emphasis on international labour migration:

> Trafficking in persons can victimize anyone: adults and children, men or women who normally live in vulnerable conditions, for example: men, women and children from poor families who came from rural or urban slums; those who are not educated and have limited knowledge; those who are caught up in serious economic, political, and social problems; family members dealing with financial crisis, such as their husbands/parents lose their income, their husbands/parents are gravely ill, or dead; dropout children; victims of physical, psychological, sexual violence; job seekers (including migrant workers); women and street children; abductees; divorced women as a result of having married at an early age; those who are pressured by their parents or neighborhood to work; even sex workers think that working overseas promises higher income.
>
> (Republic of Indonesia 2005: 4)

As in the CTP report, specific reference is also made in this document to the potential for trafficking within the formal labour export system:

> Labor recruitment companies, with their network of agents/brokers in many areas, are traffickers when they facilitate the falsification of ID cards and passports and illegally confine potential migrant workers at the safe house, and put them in a different job than the one promised or introduce them by force to sex industry.
>
> (Republic of Indonesia 2005: 6)

The emphasis placed on labour trafficking during the CTP is reiterated and strengthened in *When They Were Sold: Trafficking of Women and Girls in 15 Provinces of Indonesia* (Sugiarti *et al.* 2006), the companion volume to

Trafficking of Women and Children in Indonesia produced as part of the second Solidarity Center/ICMC project, SIGHT. In the background section of this massive 432-page report, the initial discussion on human trafficking in Indonesia immediately orients readers to the question of labour migration, stating that trafficking discourse in Indonesia was 'primarily fuelled by the plight of Indonesian women abused abroad – in domestic work and prostitution' (Sugiarti *et al.* 2006: 14). In the Solidarity Center/ICMC Trafficking Framework (Figure 4.2) an important addition is that of debt bondage to the column on ways and means.[12] The overview of trafficking that follows includes a section that identifies ten major purposes of human trafficking in Indonesia, the first of which is domestic work abroad. The other forms of trafficking mentioned (in the order in which they appear in the report) are prostitution/entertainment work abroad; marriage to foreigners; workers in construction sites, plantations and others; domestic work in Indonesia; domestic prostitution; baby selling; organized begging rings; contract marriages; and 'other forms of trafficking'.[13]

The inclusion of 'workers in construction sites, plantations and others' in *When They Were Sold* represents a significant departure from the 2003 report, as these categories deal primarily with male workers. The focus on labour migration, including male labour migrants, continues in the report's final chapter on emerging issues related to trafficking, the first of which is debt bondage and the second the placement of migrant workers in Malaysia, followed by sections on law enforcement and the counter-trafficking efforts of government, NGOs and civil society (Sugiarti *et al.* 2006: 319–94). The emphasis in the report on addressing debt bondage as a way of preventing labour trafficking is somewhat at odds with the focus of much of the SIGHT project on victim assistance. However, it clearly represented a further attempt to shift the focus in Indonesian understandings towards the recognition of the potential for the trafficking of labour migrants within, as well as outside, the official labour migration system.

Influence on local NGOS

Indonesian NGOs both assisted in the formulation of the Solidarity Center/ICMC approach and were influenced by it. In the CTP report, practices associated with labour trafficking were elaborated in a schema generated by a coalition of Indonesian NGOs led by Solidaritas Perempuan, a women's NGO with a long history of migrant labour activism and ties to the Global Alliance Against Trafficking in Women (GAATW), the international NGO alliance set up in opposition to CATW, which had lobbied for the inclusion of forms of human trafficking not related to sexual exploitation in the UN Trafficking Protocol (see Ditmore 2005; Doezema 2005). The Solidaritas Perempuan schema provides a more specific overview of the elements of trafficking in each stage of the labour migration process in ways that firmly focus attention on the state's formal labour export programme (see Table 4.1). The schema identifies the roles performed by state authorities and registered labour brokers and agents in facilitating 'trafficking' at all stages of the formal labour export programme – an emphasis that stands in stark contrast to

Table 4.1 Trafficking and exploitative practices within the Indonesian labour export system

Stage	Identified Elements of Human Trafficking	Perpetrator
Recruitment	False information about jobs Falsification of official documents (ID card, passport, family permission) Illegal fees / debt bondage	Broker Recruiting agency Village chief Immigration officer
Pre-departure	Restrictions on freedom of movement Sexual harassment and assault Debt bondage	Recruiting agency Centre management Local authorities
In destination country	Work conditions or type of employment violates contract and/or verbal agreement with the worker, including placement in brothels Assignment to new employer in the recipient country carried out without worker's consent, and in some cases, through coercion and physical abuse, including for prostitution Physical, psychological and sexual abuse Illegal confinement Withholding of identification and immigration documents Debt bondage Reduced or withheld wages	Employer Placement agency Embassy officer Immigration officer Police
Upon return	Deception, extortion, and sexual harassment upon arrival at airports or other transportation transit areas	Government officer Police Airport authorities Broker Mafia/thugs

Source: Solidaritas Perempuan (2002), reproduced in Misra (2003: 54).

the traditional focus of governments and labour trafficking activists on irregular labour migration.

The link between labour migration and trafficking is also made explicit in a training manual produced by the Solidarity Center/ICMC for NGO workers and other laypersons involved in assisting victims of trafficking. According to the text accompanying a reproduction of the Solidarity Center/ICMC Trafficking Framework, 'If one condition from each of the three categories is met, the result is trafficking. The consent of the victim is irrelevant if one of the identified means of trafficking is employed' (ACILS and ICMC 2004: 6). This reference to 'consent' reflects the use of that term in the UN Trafficking Protocol, which stipulates that consent is irrelevant once the use of deception, force or other prohibited means is established. In emphasizing the irrelevance of consent, the training manual reinforces the assertion that documented migrant workers who have actively pursued overseas employment are victims of trafficking if they have been deceived about the nature of their work. The manual also provides a series of iconic examples of abuse which migrant workers face, namely the issue of falsified documents by recruiters; the prevalence of debt bondage; employer retention of passports and other documents; and poor working conditions, explaining how each potentially puts migrant workers at risk of becoming victims of trafficking (ACILS and ICMC 2004: 7).

The understanding of trafficking promoted by the Solidarity Center/ICMC Framework has had an uneven effect on NGO activities at the national and local levels in Indonesia. In Jakarta, labour migration gradually came to be framed as a form of trafficking, as experienced NGO activists began both to engage intellectually with the concept of trafficking and to adjust to the new realities of funding in their field. In some cases, this involved a process of contestation and accommodation, as a number of prominent activists were concerned by the potential impact of the anti-trafficking framework on migrant labour activism. At best, they feared that it robbed migrant workers of agency. At worst they believed its deployment effectively shifted migrant labour abuses into the private realm of organized crime, thus absolving the state of responsibility (Interviews, 2003). In peripheral locations like the Riau Islands, Solidarity Center/ICMC projects, in tandem with funding from organizations like the IOM, created a new generation of anti-trafficking activists. As discussed above, the NGOs in Batam and Tanjung Balai Karimun that became involved in the Solidarity Center/ICMC projects were all either already operating in related fields such as HIV-AIDS prevention or service provision for overseas labour migrants, or were set up by activists from those NGOs. With the advent of the CTP, these organizations were rapidly transformed into anti-trafficking NGOs. In Tanjung Pinang, activists not only first learned of trafficking from ICMC, but engaged in NGO work for the first time through a counter-trafficking project. For this group of NGO workers, their understanding of activism was shaped almost entirely through their engagement with the SIGHT and ATP projects.

The Solidarity Center/ICMC projects very rapidly led to a fundamental re-orientation of the way that these local activists acted – and thought – about sex work and labour migration. Since 2001 there have been remarkable changes in the ways in which sex work is framed by established NGOs in the Riau Islands. As late as 2004, Kaseh Puan's work focused exclusively on assisting brothel-based sex workers to improve their sexual health. The NGO's director, Rina, first learnt about trafficking from the ICMC team when it came to the Riau Islands as part of the CTP survey. But it was only when Kaseh Puan assisted a Jakarta-based NGO to show a CTP-funded film in 2003 that she felt that she truly understood the role of crime syndicates in trafficking women and girls into the local sex industry. Sofi, the director of the Tanjung Pinang-based NGO, Sirih Besar, is a former journalist with an interest in women's and migrant worker issues. She, too, first learned of trafficking when she was invited to attend an ICMC seminar in 2003. In both cases, these activists were already aware of the difficulties sex workers and female overseas migrant workers faced, but these encounters gave them a new vocabulary. As Sofi observed:

> At that time I didn't understand the term trafficking. I only knew that a lot of women were being sold in Kepri, because it involved migrant workers. I used to 'borrow' domestic workers and they always arrived in a mess.[14] That's how

it started. But it was only when the ICMC people told me that it was trafficking that I began organizing. I established the NGO in December 2004 and by
May 2005 we were registered.

(Interview, November 2006)

When ICMC called for proposals for SIGHT, Sita, the director of Kemala Bintan,
had never heard of the term trafficking. Like Sofi, her only experience with trafficking involved a 'borrowed' domestic worker (in this case, by her landlady) who
was hunted down by the police and returned to the company when she ran away:

I didn't know what trafficking was and I had no experience running an NGO.
It was only after I was awarded the project that it was explained to me that
trafficking involved the moving of people from one place to another for financial purposes involving exploitation or deceit.

(Interview, November 2006)

Devi, another journalist, co-founded an NGO that did research for the provincial
government on trafficking. She first heard of the term when attending an information session at Forum 182, the NGO network established with CTP funding
(Interview, November 2006).

It is striking that although Tanjung Pinang was also home to a large internationally focused sex industry all these anti-trafficking NGOs focused primarily on
migrant labour. As Sofi commented, ICMC taught her that:

Trafficking is not just about the sale of women. Trafficking also occurs when
there is movement of people with false documents for the purposes of exploitation. Migrant workers are exploited, for example, if they can't pray and they
are forced to wash the dog and they don't get their wages – that's exploitation.
If that's made worse by the fact that they were tricked or enticed to become
a domestic worker, then we have a process and an objective and that makes
it trafficking.

(Interview, December 2006)

Devi's understanding of the links between the state labour migration programme
and trafficking were also clearly informed by the approach taken by Solidaritas
Perempuan and others, as recorded in the CTP and ATP reports. This included
their emphasis on possible state engagement in labour trafficking:

In Tanjung Pinang, trafficking is synonymous with migrant workers. Migrant
workers aren't trafficked if they are fully aware of what they're getting into;
have full control over their circumstances; know exactly where they're going,
what they'll be doing and how much they'll get paid; and can work without
any kind of pressure. But no-one's really in that kind of situation. They're
trapped in an illusion that all their economic woes will be solved if they can
get work and so they pay an illegal passport agent and go overseas. That's

why smuggling is also really a form of trafficking. If workers really know what they're doing, they'll go through legal channels. But even then, there's a chance that they'll be trafficked, because the agents promise more than they'll deliver. That's the great irony of it – the government is also a trafficker.

(Interview, November 2006)

Along with IOM training, the CTP was also fundamental in reshaping the strategies (and to some extent the views) of more experienced NGO activists involved in HIV-AIDS prevention in Batam, although those activists are sometimes reluctant to recognize the extent to which their understandings and practices have been transformed. When asked about human trafficking in 2004, Irwan, then with the Mothercare Development Foundation (Yayasan Pembinaan Asuhan Bunda, YPAB) and now the director of Setara Kita, acknowledged there were some cases of trafficking in the islands. However, he strongly emphasized that, with the exception of underage girls, most sex workers had previous experience and had entered the industry voluntarily.[15] At that time, he made no connection at all between trafficking and Batam's role as an international transit site for labour migrants.

Six years later, Irwan readily used the term trafficking to describe victims of exploitation in both the sex industry and among returning labour migrants. Irwan remained dismissive of claims by some NGOs that *all* sex workers are victims of trafficking – arguing that, ultimately, NGOs should be talking about lack of legal recognition of the sex industry and the need for basic standards to keep sex workers safe from exploitation. With regard to migrant workers, however, he said that although it did not initially appear to him that they had been trafficked, once he started to record their stories he realized that they had not only been exploited, but had been subject to a 'means' (*cara*) and 'process' (*proses*) – in this case recruitment and training – which meant that they were victims of trafficking. Irwan explained that he had adopted the anti-trafficking framework in part because it has currency in the islands, and NGOs using it have more success getting donors and the local government on board. This reality has had implications for both his discourse and practice. At the discursive level, he chooses to use the term 'trafficking' to talk about people he wishes to help even though he knows that they do not meet all three key elements of the UN Trafficking Protocol, namely process, means and purpose. Intellectually, he feels that the discursive act of labelling a migrant worker as a 'victim of trafficking' has the effect of highlighting the exploitation faced by workers in host countries. In terms of practice, he knows that government officials can be convinced to buy a plane ticket for a victim of trafficking, often not asking for details about the victim's circumstances, but would never fund the individual repatriation of a failed migrant worker.

Irwan and Sofi experienced similar dilemmas in their dealings with the IOM, which was much less committed to a focus on labour trafficking than the Solidarity Center or ICMC. IOM funding was crucial for all the NGOs involved in the Solidarity Center/ICMC projects, because it was the primary agency interested in victim repatriation. However, despite the inclusion of labour trafficking in IOM definitions, NGOs found it difficult to get approval for repatriation for abused migrant workers, which the IOM described as having 'thin' (*tipis*) cases of trafficking. This anomaly was partly because of the IOM's historical emphasis on trafficking for sexual exploitation, but also partly because it insisted on the rigid application of its victim identification checklist. Both Irwan and Sofi found that the checklist did not accommodate the 'grey areas' associated with labour trafficking, particularly in relation to issues of consent. This prompted them to lobby for modification of the IOM checklist, but also, as Sofi put it, to 'emphasize some facts and omit others to make migrant worker cases look "thicker" (*lebih tebal*)'.

Eventually, however, Irwan and Sofi began to question the implications of using the 'process, means, purpose' based definition of trafficking. The realities they experienced on the ground demonstrated not only that many labour migrants experienced exploitation, but that most of these workers did not fit the check-box approach promoted by the IOM and other international donors responsible for funding counter-trafficking programmes. As a consequence, over time, for these activists, the term 'trafficking' came to represent the inability of people to extricate themselves from exploitative circumstances regardless of whether or not they initially sought to enter them. They began to argue that as long as the outcome was exploitation, a migrant worker could be considered a victim of trafficking and they increasingly felt that the bureaucratic hurdles put in place by the IOM simply acted to constrain their capacity to assist those who needed their help.

It is important to note that this framing of labour trafficking/labour migration was not the only view expressed by the NGOs involved in the Solidarity/ICMC projects. Sita, the director of Kemala Bintan, felt that the problem with identifying labour migrants as victims of trafficking was that it absolved the government of responsibility in addressing the endemic problems associated with the national labour export programme:

> Really, it's just about the processes of obtaining passports and work visas. Matters for the Departments of Manpower and Immigration. If they sorted themselves out, there wouldn't be the same level of exploitation. Labelling them victims of trafficking diverts attention from the labour migration system.
>
> (Interview, November 2006)

While Sita's position was actually in line with many of the messages in the SIGHT project report, she ran into trouble with both ICMC and the IOM when she announced that she thought that repatriation was a problematic strategy because it did not take into account the circumstances that prompted migrants to seek work abroad. As Sita's unwillingness to view labour exploitation as labour trafficking could not be resolved, she chose to dissolve Kemala Bintan rather than apply for further funding (Interview, November 2006).

These tussles between local NGOs and international donors over the definitions employed to identify and assist victims of trafficking were not simply about access to funding, although funding is not an inconsequential issue for small NGOs located in Indonesia's periphery, which have few sources of revenue and assistance. For the last several years, the inability of both the national government and international donors to address labour exploitation in host countries, coupled with the absence of funding for programmes focused on migrant labour rights, has meant that anti-trafficking initiatives have provided the only means available to assist returning migrant workers. More importantly, however, NGO activists' experiences in the field have convinced them that labour migration is an inherently exploitative phenomenon that requires sustained attention. At first, they had wholeheartedly embraced the concept of trafficking, which offered them a way to understand and deal with the human tragedies they encountered all too regularly in their work. But as time passed, they came to believe that the concept of trafficking was too narrow to effectively deal with the issues faced by migrant workers because it identifies 'victims' in an essentially arbitrary fashion, and because the realities facing migrant workers did not match the donor agencies' definitions and programmes. In short, while the component elements of the trafficking definition – process, means, purpose – made sense on paper, they did not accommodate the full range of positive and negative experiences encountered by labour migrants.

Conclusion

NGO activists report that there has not been sufficient funding for counter-trafficking activities in the Riau Islands since the end of the ATP project and the withdrawal of IOM funding. The provincial government provides some incidental support for counter-trafficking programmes run by NGOs, local offices of the Ministries of Welfare and Women's Empowerment Bureau continue to provide shelter for victims of trafficking, and the police pay on results for information that leads to arrests in a trafficking case.[16] But in the absence of continued foreign funding, NGO activities on human trafficking have been drastically curtailed. As a consequence, most new NGOs and some established players have disappeared. Kemala Bintan failed to survive beyond the SIGHT project. Local activists report that YMKK became inactive after the SIGHT project was completed, although its head, Lola Wagner, remains in high demand with international groups and works with UNIFEM Singapore. The church shelters continued to do their low-profile work, joined by a Singaporean-funded shelter for domestic workers operating under the name of Pondok Madonna. Of those that remain, Setara Kita continues to work on human trafficking in Batam, as well as on its primary long-term programme for children, while in Tanjung Pinang Sirih Besar continues to leverage its close relationship with local government to attract funding for its work in the deportation holding centre. In Tanjung Balai Karimun, Kaseh Puan has returned to HIV-AIDS work, having been resuscitated from a state of near-collapse by ATP funding. These organizations have been joined by a new NGO called the Anti-Trafficking Movement (Gerakan Anti-Trafficking, GAT), which monitors labour-sending companies in Batam and identifies trafficking cases in the flows of irregular migrants returning through unofficial routes to Batam.[17] Along with Sirih Besar and Setara Kita, GAT and another NGO called the Association of the Friends of Indonesia's Children (Perhimpunan Rekan Anak Indonesia, PRAI) sit on the provincial anti-trafficking taskforce.

As is clear from the account presented in this chapter, the discursive and resourcing shifts associated with the rise of the anti-trafficking framework have dramatically changed the activist landscape around issues concerning working-class women and their mobility, displacing other kinds of activist agendas and shaping the activities of the remaining local NGOs in this Indonesian periphery. International organizations and donor agencies actively sought to use existing NGOs working with sex workers and/or active in the fields of HIV-AIDS prevention and reproductive and sexual health to pursue their anti-trafficking agendas because they provided a seemingly 'ready-made' means of disseminating the international anti-trafficking agenda. Both experienced activists as well as relative newcomers to the NGO scene responded favourably to the opportunity to become actively involved in the Solidarity Center/ICMC projects. With little prior understanding or knowledge about human trafficking, their understanding of it was shaped almost entirely by the definitions contained in Solidarity Centre/ICMC and IOM training manuals and checklists.

NGOs in the Riau Islands concerned with migrant labour initially embraced the Trafficking Framework promoted by the Solidarity Center and ICMC, not least because it provided a much-needed explanation for the issues faced by prospective and returnee migrant workers. However, local activists discovered that the broad scope of the Solidarity Center/ICMC Trafficking Framework was not matched by an equally broad definition of who could be considered an eligible recipient of IOM repatriation support. Many became frustrated by the seemingly arbitrary boundaries used to distinguish between documented labour migrants, victims of trafficking and smuggled migrants when they found that donor agencies were reluctant to assist migrant workers who did not easily fit the framework's definition of victims. This led some to question the relevance of the anti-trafficking framework to their work.

The experience in the Riau Islands reflects the mixed legacy of the Solidarity Centre/ICMC projects in Indonesia. At the national level they were pivotal in shaping the National Plan of Action and the Anti-trafficking Law, and in raising the profile of human trafficking amongst policy-makers, regulators and policing authorities. At the local level, they facilitated the creation of local government counter-trafficking programmes, built capacity within local police and immigration agencies, and facilitated joint anti-trafficking efforts between local authorities and local NGOs. These efforts played a significant role in developing Indonesia's anti-trafficking infrastructure and capacity and contributed to the US decision to take Indonesia off the Tier 2 Watch List in 2007. However, it is at the discursive level that the Solidarity Centre/ICMC projects have had their most enduring effect. One of the most notable features of the Indonesian anti-trafficking landscape is the relatively minor position accorded to the issue of trafficking for sexual exploitation. The fact that labour trafficking has come to occupy a central place in counter-trafficking efforts is due in no small part to its positioning within the Solidarity Center/ICMC reports and training manuals, and particularly the weight it has been accorded in the project's Trafficking Framework.

As this chapter has shown, in the Riau Islands at least, the framing of labour trafficking within the interlinked Solidarity Center/ICMC projects had a significant impact on the way in which NGO activists came to understand both trafficking and labour migration. The practical consequences of this framing are manifold. Prior to the implementation of the CTP, there were few organizations in the Riau Islands working on labour migration issues and those that were in operation were run by Christian charities. Following the CTP, a range of new anti-trafficking NGOs began to take on board issues facing labour migrants. Much of this work focused on direct assistance in the form of reception, short-term housing and repatriation – crucial tasks that local authorities have been unable or reluctant to address.

However, ultimately, the decade-long programme has not resulted in significant improvements in the experiences of overseas migrant workers. The discursive shifts in the way that Indonesia's labour export programme has been understood have also shaped a critique of the government's response to labour exploitation. The inherent problems with the formal labour export system continue to encourage grey migration and migrant smuggling, and migrant workers continue to face labour exploitation regardless of their immigration status in host countries. Given the strong focus of the Solidarity Center/ICMC initiatives on migrant labour, this stark reality begs the question whether the anti-trafficking framework can ever adequately address the problems faced by low-skilled overseas migrant workers.

Notes

1 Initially ranked in Tier 3 in 2001, Indonesia was upgraded to Tier 2 in 2002, a position it maintained until 2006 when it was placed in the Tier 2 Watch List before recovering its Tier 2 ranking the following year.

2 The chapter draws on interviews with key actors in Jakarta, including representatives of ICMC, the Solidarity Center and several major migrant labour NGOs, conducted between 2001 and 2010 and during fieldwork in the Riau Islands in 2004–8 and 2010, in which interviews were conducted with all the NGOs involved in Solidarity Center/ ICMC projects. The bulk of the data was collected as part of a project entitled *In the Shadow of Singapore: The Limits of Transnationalism in Insular Riau*, funded by Australian Research Council Discovery Project Grant DP0557368. An earlier version of parts of this chapter was presented at the 5th Euroseas Conference, University L'Orientale, Naples, 12–15 September 2007. We would like to thank Wayne Palmer for his assistance with follow-up interviews in the Riau Islands in 2010.

3 For details about the sex industry in the Riau Islands, see Ford and Lyons (2008).

4 In the 1990s, two church-funded Christian NGOs provided services to migrant workers.

5 This same report made a series of sensationalist claims about the sexual exploitation of all Indonesian female migrant workers, the majority of whom they claimed face sexual abuse and forced prostitution at the hands of recruitment brokers, agents and employers (Dzuhayatin and Silawati 2002: 17–18).

6 For information on the IOM's Indonesian programmes, see http://www.iom.or.id/. For details of the IOM's work with the Ministry of Women's Empowerment on the draft of the national anti-trafficking law and at the local level, see the chapter by Wayne Palmer in this volume.

7 Terres Des Hommes Netherlands replaced the Ford Foundation as YMKK's main funding source in 2006 and this signalled a move away from reproductive health to counter-trafficking. TDH's programme director saw support for YMKK and other NGOs

with existing reproductive health or HIV programmes as important because they became 'entry points' for engaging in counter-trafficking (Lindquist and Piper 2007: 149).

8 This description of the programme and its implementation process draws on this report and on supplementary data from an interview conducted with Ruth Rosenberg and Rebecca Surtees at ICMC's Jakarta office in July 2003 and in interviews with Rudy Porter and Jamie Davis from the Solidarity Center, conducted in 2008 and 2010.

9 Project staff were subsequently also involved in the initial drafting of the 2007 anti-trafficking law, during which time an ICMC Project Officer assisted a team from seven different ministries, representatives from the provinces and several experts.

10 According to the Solidarity Center/ICMC report, parliament introduced its own draft because progress in the Ministry for Women's Empowerment on the bill was slow, but there were no significant differences between the drafts. For an alternative narrative of the bill's evolution, see the chapter by Wayne Palmer in this volume.

11 Kaseh Puan had participated in the initial CTP survey but did not receive funding under the CTP small grants scheme.

12 This was one of two changes – organ harvesting also appeared in the 'Goal' column.

13 This last category includes offshore fishing platforms and other forms of overseas migrant labour.

14 It is common practice in the Riau Islands for agents to send intending migrant domestic workers for 'training' in local homes.

15 When interviewed in 2010, Irwan claimed that his interest in human trafficking pre-dated the UN Trafficking Protocol, having begun when he was working on HIV-AIDS prevention with YMKK. This statement stands in contrast to the 2004 interview, conducted when Irwan was working for YPAB, when trafficking was only mentioned once in the course of a two-hour interview, and then only when prompted.

16 According to a senior police officer, in 2010 the fee stood at Rp.500,000 (Interview, April 2010).

17 For details of GAT's border 'policing' activities, see Ford and Lyons (2011).

References

ACILS and ICMC (2004) *Assisting Victims of Human Trafficking in the Indonesian Legal Process: A Manual for Service Providers*, Jakarta: American Center for International Labor Solidarity and International Catholic Migration Commission.

Agustinanto, F. (2003) 'Riau', in Rosenberg, R. (ed.) *Trafficking of Women and Children in Indonesia*, Jakarta: International Catholic Migration Commission and the American Center for International Labor Solidarity, pp. 178–82.

Ditmore, M. (2005) 'Trafficking in lives: How ideology shapes policy', in Kempadoo, K., Sanghera, J. and Pattanaik, B. (eds) *Trafficking and Prostitution Reconsidered: New Perspectives on Migration, Sex Work, and Human Rights*, Boulder, CO: Paradigm Publishers, pp. 107–26.

Doezema, J. (2005) 'Now you see her, now you don't: Sex workers at the UN trafficking protocol negotiation', *Social and Legal Studies*, 14 (1): 61–89.

Dzuhayatin, S. and Silawati, H. (2002) 'Indonesia: Migration and trafficking in women', in Raymond, J. G., D'Cunha, J., Dzuhayatin, S. R., Hynes, H. P., Rodriguez, Z. R. and Santos, A. (eds) *A Comparative Study of Women Trafficked in the Migration Process: Patterns, Profiles and Health Consequences of Sexual Exploitation in Five Countries* (Indonesia, the Philippines, Thailand, Venezuela and the United States), North Amherst, MA: Coalition Against Trafficking in Women, pp. 16–21.

Ford, M. and Lyons, L. (2008) 'Making the best of what you've got: Sex work and class mobility in the Riau Islands', in Ford, M. and Parker, L. (eds) *Women and Work in Indonesia*, London and New York: Routledge, pp. 173–94.

—— (2011) 'Outsourcing border security: NGO involvement in the monitoring and assistance of Indonesian nationals returning illegally by sea', paper presented at the Addressing Maritime Safety Threats in Southeast Asia Workshop, Brisbane, 23–4 May.

Lindquist, J. (2008) 'Navigating landscapes of exception in Southeast Asia: A commentary on Aihwa Ong's "Scales of exception: experiments with knowledge and sheer life in tropical Southeast Asia"', *Singapore Journal of Tropical Geography*, 29 (2): 133–6.

Lindquist, J. and Piper, N. (2007) 'From HIV prevention to counter-trafficking: Discursive shifts and institutional continuities in South-East Asia', in Lee, M. (ed.) *Human Trafficking*, Cullompton, Devon: Willan Publishing, pp. 139–58.

Lyons, L. and Ford, M. (2007) 'Where internal and international migration intersect: Mobility and the formation of multi-ethnic communities in the Riau Islands transit zone', *International Journal on Multicultural Societies*, 9 (2): 236–63.

—— (2010) '"Where are your victims?" How sexual health advocacy came to be counter-trafficking in Indonesia's Riau Islands', *International Feminist Journal of Politics*, 12 (2): 255–64.

Misra, N. (2003) 'The National Plan of Action', in Rosenberg, R. (ed.) *Trafficking of Women and Children in Indonesia*, Jakarta: International Catholic Migration Commission and the American Center for International Labor Solidarity, pp. 219–23.

Republic of Indonesia (2005) *The Elimination of Trafficking in Persons in Indonesia, 2004–2005*, Jakarta: Coordinating Ministry For People's Welfare.

Rosenberg, R. (2003a) 'Overview', in Rosenberg, R. (ed.) *Trafficking of Women and Children in Indonesia*, Jakarta: International Catholic Migration Commission and the American Center for International Labor Solidarity, pp. 11–33.

—— (ed.) (2003b) *Trafficking of Women and Children in Indonesia*, Jakarta: International Catholic Migration Commission and the American Center for International Labor Solidarity.

—— (2006) *Anti-Trafficking Technical Assistance: Indonesia Analysis of United States Government Funded Anti-Trafficking Activities, February 6–February 21, 2006*, Washington, DC: United States Agency for International Development.

Solidarity Center/ICMC (2006) *Final Narrative Report: Strengthening the Initiative of Government and Others Against Human Trafficking (SIGHT), September 20, 2004–November 30, 2006*, Jakarta: American Center for International Labor Solidarity and International Catholic Migration Commission.

—— (2009) *Final Program Report: Anti-Trafficking in Persons in Indonesia (ATP), A Project of the Solidarity Center, ICMC and USAID, March 8, 2007–September 30, 2009*, Jakarta: American Center for International Labor Solidarity and International Catholic Migration Commission.

Sugiarti, K., Davis, J. and Dasgupta, A. (eds) (2006) *When They Were Sold: Trafficking of Women and Girls in 15 Provinces of Indonesia*, Jakarta: International Catholic Migration Commission and American Center for International Labor Solidarity.

Wahyuningrum, S. (2007) 'The politics of trafficking in Indonesia: Gender, national rhetorics and power', Unpublished MA thesis, Mahidol University, Bangkok.

5 A trafficking 'not-spot' in a China–Vietnam border town

Zhang Juan

In April 2009, a bittersweet love story set in the China–Vietnam border town of Hekou hit major cinemas across China. *Red River* tells the tale of Ah Tao, a 17-year-old innocent Vietnamese girl, and a middle-aged Chinese hustler, Ah Xia. The film's main protagonist, Ah Tao, was persuaded to work in the massage parlour-cum-brothel that her aunt had opened in Hekou. Like her aunt, she crossed the Red River and entered Hekou in China's Yunnan province illegally by boat. She worked in her aunt's parlour as a cleaner and a masseuse for a while until she was enticed by Ah Xia to work in his street-side mobile karaoke stall singing duets with Chinese customers, who would ogle at her youthful beauty. Ah Tao and Ah Xia gradually fall in love but are then parted by circumstances.

In many ways, Ah Tao's story is just another tale about the struggles that a Vietnamese migrant worker faces when living in a Chinese border town: she leaves home in search of wealth and opportunity in a foreign country and ends up in undesirable jobs, her dreams unsatisfied. However, her story could also be framed within the discourse of human trafficking. The 'rumour of trafficking' (Wong 2005) has loomed large along China's borders, especially those regions adjacent to Vietnam, Laos and Myanmar, since the early 2000s (see *People's Daily* 2004; Ma 2009; Richburg 2009). Anecdotes about uneducated young women from rural areas being duped, abducted and coerced into selling sex, being sold as wives to disabled Chinese men, or being enslaved and exploited as factory workers are spread by word of mouth and sensational news reports (Marshall 1999; Tran 2006; *China Daily* 2010). Typically, these anecdotes fashion the tale of a trafficked victim, often depicted as a naïve village girl, who crosses the border into China without a legal travel document such as a passport or an authorized entry and exit permit, thereby falling prey to human traffickers. These human traffickers are rumoured to 'hunt' for their victims in Chinese towns and villages, as well as at railway and bus stations in the border regions. They usually work alone in environments with which they are familiar. Lured by their glib language and false promises, young village girls follow the traffickers and embark on a journey of no return. Ah Tao thus appears to fall right into the neatly defined category of 'trafficked victim'. But instead *Red River* highlights her tale of love and cross-border aspirations.

As Molland (this volume) points out, in order for an anti-trafficking programme to have a tangible effect, trafficking 'hotspots' must be discursively constructed prior to the fashioning of specific steps to combat trafficking in that particular space. In other words, specific geographic locations perceived to be prone to human trafficking must be first isolated, selected and targeted regardless of whether 'real trafficking' takes place in these 'high risk' locations. Rural areas with high levels of poverty and out-bound mobility are often identified as hotspots (see Sharma 2003; Zhao 2003; Samarasinghe 2008; also see Eilenberg in this volume). Molland (this volume) criticizes the underlying assumptions that guide the current anti-trafficking framework, which identifies target groups (both 'perpetrators' and 'victims'), trends of mobility and migration, observable trafficking locations and enduring routes for human transportation. The ways in which certain localities are marked out illustrate how well-intended intervention programmes can become a self-serving pursuit detached from social reality.

However, the construction of hotspots paints only half of the picture. Using Hekou as an example, I sketch out the less visible, but equally powerful, construction of a trafficking 'not-spot', showing why particular border towns are not identified as 'high risk' locations even when all symptoms of trafficking are unmistakably manifest. These deliberate absences and silences sometimes speak more to the contentious nature of the anti-trafficking hyper-discourse because these are the moments that mark its limits. In short, despite the high profile of anti-trafficking initiatives, at the local level they are often de-prioritized in favour of development efforts that bring tangible benefits to the local economy. Thus while the anti-trafficking framework remains discursively relevant along the China–Vietnam border, flexible translations and interpretations of this framework often render it more rhetorical than pragmatic.[1]

From battlefield to Special Economic Zone

The town of Hekou sits right at the point where the Nanxi River and the Red River merge, and China and Vietnam meet (Figure 5.1). The county in which it is situated shares a 193-kilometre international border with Lao Cai province in northern Vietnam. Before the formation of state borders, these two rivers were frequently crossed by people living and doing business on both sides. Merchants from Hong Kong, Macau, Hai Phong and Ha Noi went to Lao Cai to set up trading companies. Chinese traders from Guangdong and Guangxi provinces settled in Hekou to explore lucrative opportunities. By the early twentieth century, Hekou had gained its fame as a 'Little Hong Kong' because regional trade had brought with it great prosperity. Local residents of the same ethnic background and kinship networks traversed the frontier frequently and freely. Marriage between the Chinese and Vietnamese was a common practice (Grillot 2010). However, from the 1940s onwards, Hekou was devastated by successive waves of military violence and political chaos that swept across both China and Vietnam. Then, following separate declarations of independence, the Chinese and Vietnamese states demarcated national boundaries as part of their nation-building and modernization projects. Laws and regulations about border-crossing were enforced by government bodies to solidify the sanctity of sovereign nation-states. Marriage between Chinese and

Figure 5.1 The Vietnam–China borderlands

Vietnamese was discouraged by local authorities as a 'backward' minority custom that might jeopardize state efforts to monitor and control flows across the newly defined international border.

In the 1950s and 1960s, private crossings for economic purposes were considered decadent capitalist practices by both states. Economic exchanges at the border were stigmatized, and trade – the major lifeline that had sustained the everyday needs of ordinary borderlanders – was suspended. By the late 1970s, the ideological insecurity of both states had escalated into cross-border hostility, culminating in a brief war in 1979 followed by ten years of political stalemate accompanied by repeated small-scale skirmishes in the border region. International border crossings were shut down, and borderlanders were deterred from crossing by undercover police patrols, the fear of densely planted landmines on both sides of the borderline and the lack of material resources to be exchanged. The border opened again in 1989, when Deng Xiaoping marked out a special economic zone (SEZ) at the edge of China's southern territory. In 1992, Hekou was declared one of five 'open border towns' (*kou'an kaifang chengshi*), and cross-border trade in Hekou again began to prosper. Bilateral trade at the state level as well as cross-border trade and tourism carried out by privately owned companies became central pillars of the local economy. In 2007 border trade in Hekou generated over 8.5 billion yuan, the highest of all Yunnan's border ports (Ministry of Commerce of China 2008).[2]

By the end of 2009, a new road bridge, the Red River Bridge, between Hekou and Lao Cai was completed as part of the well-funded Greater Mekong Subregions (GMS) Kunming-Hai Phong Economic Corridor road network. This bridge is the third bridge to cross this particular section of the China–Vietnam border. This new bridge connected two newly designated free trade zones in Hekou and Lao Cai, facilitating the flow of heavy vehicles. These two free trade zones within the border SEZ are distinct spaces marked out by the politics of 'exception' (Ong 2006). Various economic and political concessions are granted to different practices within these special zones.

Before the Red River Bridge was even completed, hotels and restaurants, massage parlours and karaoke bars, private clinics and a brand new tourist (sex) 'market' were already being built. By early 2009 they had been leased and occupied by keen entrepreneurs preparing for the arrival of traders, workers, long-distance truck drivers and other groups of potential clients. Locals were unanimous about the positive effect of the third bridge. For example, a fruit trader, Mr Liu, observed that with the bridge and the highway between Lao Cai and Kunming, and the construction of the Trans-Asian Railway underway (over the old French-built Dianyue Railway tracks), Hekou would truly become a conduit through which China could conquer the Southeast Asian market. A battlefield in the past, Hekou today has been transformed into a land of opportunities and desire. Thousands of traders, peddlers, tourists, truck drivers, workers and migrants cross the Hekou border on a daily basis, rendering this crossing one of the busiest in the region (*Yunnan Daily* 2009).

While the fluid movement of people and capital across the border brings about unprecedented prospects for economic growth, unsettling memories of war and unrest coupled with new threats posed by transnational crime and disease justify practices of border control. Meanwhile, local borderland authorities find ways to provide productive subjects with an easy passage, while seeking to prevent less privileged individuals from entering legally. Over the years, the number of 'illegal' immigrants living in Hekou has increased markedly because of rapid economic development in the frontier. It is estimated that over 70 per cent of the Vietnamese working in Hekou are 'illegitimate aliens' who crossed the border by boat, including tens of thousands of undocumented Vietnamese women, many of them under the age of 18, who travel into China via rivers and secret passageways each year (UNICEF 2004; McGivering 2006; Tran 2006). Although it is difficult to know for sure how many 'illegal entries' occur, officials working in the Hekou Customs estimate that numbers range from a few dozen to a few hundred per day.

Local authorities in Hekou are well aware of the constant movements but turn a blind eye to most of these transgressions. They remain able to perform control and regulation when such needs arise while also capitalizing on 'illegal' cross-border flows. As in the Indonesian borderlands of West Kalimantan, where Indonesian border police and the military are economically dependent on 'illegal' cross-border activities (Eilenberg in this volume), in Hekou, local authorities seek to benefit from these moving bodies for the economic value they generate.

Loose women, not lost women

In the China–Vietnam frontier, young Vietnamese women who illegally cross the border to solicit business in the sex sector constitute a special group. Their exotic and erotic bodies are a constant attraction for Chinese men who seek pleasure at the border. But their illegal status also marks them as the easy target of disciplinary action. Since the reopening of the Hekou border in the early 1990s, this small town has gradually developed a reputation as a 'men's paradise and women's goldmine' (*nanren de tiantang, nuren de jinkuang*). Every weekend Hekou's main streets are congested with sedans from Yunnan and other provinces. These sedans carry Chinese men to Hekou in search of a good time. They are known locally as 'artillerymen' (*paobing*), for they come in 'troops' just to 'bang' the Vietnamese women who work in the sex market.[3] The sexual engagements these men have with Vietnamese women represent a unique 'borderland' experience where one can indulge in exotic intimacy unavailable in most inland cities in China.

Local borderlanders in Hekou share a common view: no one would want to come to this place if it were not so 'open' (*kaifang*). China's popular economic reform motto *kaifang gaohuo* (open up, to 'make alive') in this case has acquired a double meaning. The term *kaifang* does not only mean 'open up the market'. It connotes more liberal attitudes, especially with regard to sex. In other words, the term *kaifang* denotes sexual promiscuity. *Gaohuo* is a political economic phrase which literally means to 'make alive', or to invigorate the economy through flexible strategies enabled by a free market. But in vernacular Chinese the verb *gao* has a wide range of meanings. It could mean to make, to perform, to enable, to humour, depending on the context of usage. In its most crude form, *gao* also means to have sexual intercourse, or 'to bang'. Therefore in Hekou's local context, when people teasingly use the term *gaohuo jingji*, it means not just 'to invigorate the economy', but that the liveliness of the economy is all about the 'banging'. In this way, the reform principle of *kaifang gaohuo* has become a potent discursive framework within which the usually surreptitious business of commercial sex becomes forthright and legitimized.

Although it is never officially acknowledged or denied as a legitimate component of the local economy, sex is amongst the most lucrative of businesses in Hekou. According to local borderlanders, the sex sector is at least a multimillion yuan industry. A 2003 study reported that there were up to 2,000 mobile sex workers (mostly Vietnamese and a small number of Chinese) in Hekou at a time when the small town's urban population was less than 100,000 (He 2003: 13). In 2006, when the local county government carried out sexually transmitted infections (STIs) and HIV-AIDS prevention campaigns with funds from the central government, the British Council and UNICEF, it was reported that 600–700 Vietnamese 'service girls' (*fuwu xiaojie*) were permanently based in Vietnamese Street (Hekou Yao Nationality Autonomous County Government 2006).

While these figures are indicative rather than factual, they point to the fact that Hekou's sex sector is an intrinsic part of locally licit business activity. The sex industry provides a means of livelihood for the families of sex workers, as well as ample employment opportunities in a chain of allied businesses including hotels, restaurants, convenience stores, private clinics, karaoke bars, foot massage clinics and spas. It also supports the operation of long-distance transport businesses linking Hekou to other parts of Yunnan.

Whether long-term settlers, or short-term drifters, almost all of the Vietnamese sex workers soliciting on Vietnamese Street came to China without proper documentation such as legal border entry and exit papers, passports, or local work and residence permits. They are in effect illegal workers and residents in Hekou. However, to work in a hair salon-cum-brothel, or to rent a shop at the market to start their own businesses, these women do not have to worry about legal paperwork or official procedures. A mere two to four yuan monthly residence fee and a one-off 40 yuan processing fee payable to the management of the tourist markets is sufficient for these women to stay as long as they like.[4] As the amount charged is insignificant, some locals argue that these payments are merely a gesture: after all, these women attract many Chinese tourists to the markets and make a substantial contribution to the local economy. The Lao Cai local government, across the border, is believed to be involved in this scheme as well. It tacitly allows Vietnamese women to leave the country without documentation because the customers they attract in Hekou are also vital to the survival of Lao Cai's tourism industry. When Chinese men travel to the border for sexual pleasure, many of them go on a day tour in Lao Cai.[5] An active, mobile and open border is therefore key to creating an economic win-win situation for both towns.

The financial rewards for sex work are considerable. The average monthly household income in Vietnam's rural border regions is around 200–300 yuan. This amount can be earned with just one night's service in Hekou. In one account of the sex industry in Hekou, a young Vietnamese woman called Ah Yue described making money in Hekou as 'really easy' (He 2003: 33). Whereas she could make at most 50 yuan a month at home in Vietnam working on the farm, in Hekou, she could usually earn 100 to 150 yuan a day, sometimes even 300 yuan a night if the customer was generous. According to several Hekou local tour agents, who also work as middlemen, young and pretty girls can easily earn up to 2–3 million yuan during their time as sex workers. They can then 'retire' when they reach their mid- or late-twenties and go back home to start anew – buy a house, get married or start a business. Many choose to stay in China and run their own parlours and recruit young girls from their home villages. Others marry Chinese men and migrate to other parts of the country.

The Vietnamese women who cross into China embrace the same aspirations as the Ghanaian sex workers described by Anarfi (1998), who migrate to Côte d'Ivoire in the hope of gaining enough capital to buy a house or to start a business. These young women see sex work as a means to accumulate capital for later economic independence rather than a desperate act to lift themselves out of dire poverty (Doezema 2000). Although most of them do not enjoy working in the sex sector, they see it as a fast and relatively effortless source of income (Kempadoo 1998). In the words of Vanh, a young woman from Yen Bai province in northern Vietnam:

At home I often helped my parents with farm work and household chores. Despite all our hard work, we still had a meagre standard of living. I wanted to contribute to my family financially, so I dropped out of school and followed a friend to Hekou for employment. Since I couldn't run a shop or buy things to sell because I had no money, I had to work day and night in the Vietnamese restaurants and food stalls. These jobs never seemed to make my dreams come true. From my conversations with other Vietnamese girls, I learnt that the only way to make good money was to sell our bodies. That's how I came to work here.

(Cited in He 2003: 34)

In the spirit of opening up the border economy, the 'opening' of the body for business seems to be a flexible strategy that women can adopt to explore new possibilities (Farrer 2008) and to 'optimize' their limited 'capital' (Zheng 2009). Under the umbrella of *kaifang gaohuo*, the 'opening' of the body is legitimized and deemed as an intrinsic aspect of the overall economic liberalization process. The business of sex, therefore, is not so much considered a side-effect of capitalism or the commodification of the body, but more of a market experiment. This could be one of the reasons why local borderlanders often perceive Vietnamese sex workers in Hekou as capable and scheming gold diggers rather than as innocent country girls tricked into sexual exploitation. These young women embody entrepreneurial traits, such as their aggressive soliciting styles, bargaining capabilities and their apt use of 'personal assets' in the form of their youthful and seductive bodies. To borrow Doezema's (2000) intriguing phrase, then, Vietnamese sex workers in Hekou are by and large considered to be 'loose women' rather than 'lost women'.

During my field research in Hekou, many Chinese tourists and a number of businessmen told me that one of their most exciting experiences in the border town was when they visited Vietnamese Street. These Chinese men claimed that they were 'chased' and 'pursued' by pretty and young Vietnamese women who 'begged' to sleep with them. For these Chinese men, whose experience of buying sex in other parts of China was secretive or embarrassing, as prostitution still is strictly illegal, this play of open pursuit opened up new realms of pleasure.[6] The saucy tales of Vietnamese Street tickled the fantasies of the Chinese as they heard about how men were 'captured' as they passed by a massage shop and 'forced into action'. Many enjoyed being surrounded by young girls, touching, hustling, air-kissing and flirting. Some described how the Vietnamese girls were aggressive, flirtatious, predatory, and at times almost too masculine, in their style of soliciting. For example, a middle-aged trader Mr Sun who came to Hekou frequently for business and leisure told me:

You see those Vietnamese girls in the sex market, they are so young, and they act as if they don't know anything, just want to make enough money to make a living. But I am telling you, they are the most deceptive. They try to seduce you when you go inside the market, calling you 'elder brother' or 'my darling', and touching you, kissing you, making promises that they are skilful (in bed) and cheap. What they really want is to get all your money! They try to confuse your mind with their flesh and then rob all your money away.

Mr Sun's view was widely shared among the more than 30 businessmen and tourists in Hekou that I talked to. Chinese men in Hekou regard these women as 'entrepreneurs' produced by the newly opened borderland market. For them, Vietnamese Street is a place of exotic engagement and far from a place of innocence. Therefore, women working in Vietnamese Street are not harmless, chaste creatures either. The men's perceptions of these women portray them as manipulative opportunists who set traps for men who fall prey to their sexual play. They also render these women as an exception to the typical narratives of innocent, virginal victims in the global sex trafficking discourse.

Producing a trafficking 'not-spot'

The constant influx of Vietnamese women into Hekou's commercial sex market is essential in attracting curious Chinese tourists and keeping affluent businessmen entertained. To a large extent, the borderland tourism sector is closely intertwined with the sex industry. For this reason alone, it is impractical for Hekou's local government to exercise closer surveillance and to more closely police cross-border movements, even if it had the resources and capacity. At the same time, paradoxically, the local government has been forced to add its voice to the international anti-trafficking chorus in order to obtain funding and development support from both international and national organizations. In order to do so, it must demonstrate that it is attuned to the interests of international development agendas and that it is willing to address human trafficking.

In the face of these competing pressures, it is hardly surprising that the local government continues to tacitly permit the illegal entrance of young Vietnamese women to sell sex and/or other services in China, while at the same time signing bilateral communiqués that attest to its commitment to the anti-trafficking agenda and launching a few rescue missions to 'save' and repatriate the occasional estranged Vietnamese victim. This paradox stems from a context where China's borders with Southeast Asia have become more 'porous' and 'permeable' (Chin and Zhang 2007; Blanchard 2010; Deng 2010), leaving the state vulnerable to increasing incidents of arms trade, illicit drug trade, smuggling, money laundering, illegal migration, and in recent years human trafficking. Although Yunnan remains one of China's poorest provinces, it is relatively well off compared to bordering regions in countries like Myanmar, Laos and Vietnam. In addition, rural men who find it difficult to get married, due to a severe sex ratio imbalance and the growing cost of weddings, are willing to buy foreign brides as a cheaper and easier option (Zhao 2003). This spatial-economic unevenness and the long international border have created the conditions for it to be identified as a hotspot for domestic and cross-border trafficking (Richburg 2009).

The fact that human trafficking has increasingly become a hot topic in China, especially in its frontier zones, is undeniable. The 2008 Strategic Information Response Network (SIREN) report, authored by the United Nations Inter-Agency Project on Human Trafficking (UNIAP), indicates that from 1989 to 1999 over 8,000 Vietnamese women entered China via Guangxi province and became wives of Chinese men. The report claims that most of them were victims of trafficking (UNIAP 2008a). According to Le Hong Loan, the chief of the rights promotion and child protection section of the United Nations Children's Fund (UNICEF) Vietnam, at least 22,000 women have been trafficked to China to be wives, sex workers or house maids since 1991, and only 8,000 have been successfully repatriated (UNICEF 2008).[7]

In 2000, Yunnan joined the International Labour Organization's (ILO) 'International Program on the Elimination of Child Labour' and the 'Mekong Sub-Regional Project to Combat Trafficking in Children and Women' (IPEC-TICW) to collaborate with five other GMS countries in anti-trafficking projects. Since 2001, UNICEF China has worked with the Chinese law enforcement agency and women's rights agencies as well as their counterparts in Vietnam, Laos and Myanmar to increase cross-border collaboration on anti-trafficking initiatives. One such collaboration was the first United Against Trafficking campaign launched by China and Vietnam in the border towns of Dongxin (Guangxi, China) and Mong Cai (Vietnam) in 2004, as a joint effort to combat trafficking in women and children. Six border region anti-trafficking cooperation and liaison offices and women's safe houses were established in border towns including Dongxing and Pingxiang (bordering Vietnam in Guangxi), Jingxi and Ruili (bordering Myanmar in Yunnan), as well as Longchuan and Hekou (bordering Vietnam in Yunnan) with funding from UNICEF and the Chinese central government (UNICEF 2004). UNICEF even organized and paid for a six-month Vietnamese language programme for Chinese border police in Guangxi so that they could carry out 'rescue missions'.

These well-funded programmes seemed to have produced tangible results. From 2005 to 2006, according to a UNICEF report (2008), the Chinese and Vietnamese police launched two special anti-trafficking actions and saved hundreds of victims. In December 2007, China signed the Coordinated Mekong Ministerial Initiative against Trafficking (COMMIT) Joint Declaration with Cambodia, Laos, Myanmar, Thailand and Vietnam to further extend cross-border collaborations. In 2008, the first official publication on China's anti-trafficking commitment was published by the State Council. The China National Plan of Action on Combating Trafficking in Women and Children (2008–2012) (hereafter Plan of Action) declares that the Chinese Government has acted consistently to combat human trafficking and will actively expand the provision of education, assistance and aftercare for women and children at risk (State Council of China 2007).[8] The Plan of Action also pledges to strengthen relations with relevant international organizations and to utilize multilateral police cooperation.

These grand gestures create the general impression that China has indeed generated a rather impressive résumé in recent years with regard to its anti-trafficking efforts and commitments. However, it is not difficult to detect the heavy influence of international agencies in China's actions. Organizations such as the ILO, UNICEF, the United States Agency for International Development (USAID), the Department for International Development (DFID) of the United Kingdom, and the Asian Development Bank (ADB) are pushing every step of the way, encouraging China to get on board and conform to the international conventions. For example, the 2008 annual report of the Congressional-Executive Commission on China, a commission created by the US Congress in 2000 to monitor human rights and the development of the rule of law in China, lists amongst its recommendations efforts to 'urge Chinese government officials to sign and ratify the Trafficking in Persons Protocol, to revise the government's definition of trafficking and reform its anti-trafficking laws to align with international standards', to 'fund research on trafficking-related issues in China', and to 'support bilateral exchanges between U.S. and Chinese law enforcement officials and civil society organizations that work on trafficking' (Congressional-Executive Commission on China 2008: 17). In the same year, the ILO (2008) claimed that prior to its intervention, local authorities in Yunnan only focused on law enforcement and rescue missions but not on prevention measures, but that 'these stereotypes are now being broken down and the approaches are changing', that 'a broader definition of trafficking is now accepted . . . and a more comprehensive approach to the problem is underway'. Clearly, the ILO is actively altering how trafficking is understood locally through its multi-million dollar projects.

As a result, internationally accredited anti-trafficking interventions such as awareness raising campaigns, income-generating education projects, and micro-credit loans have been implemented in identified trafficking hotspots, usually 'source' communities marked by poverty and ignorance. In most cases, anti-trafficking interventions in these communities are poverty reduction programmes in disguise.[9] Similarly, in Yunnan, local anti-trafficking endeavours are guided by the presumption that trafficking and underdevelopment are always linked (ILO-IPEC 2002: 21). Anti-traffickers in China tune into the logic of international organizations, and identify high-risk target zones as the poor, remote areas where ethnic minorities live (Li 2003: 52).

While international organizations insert themselves more visibly in China's anti-trafficking endeavours, various national and local agencies embrace the funds and technical assistance (mostly poverty-reduction or development-related) that come with these organizations. Since the early 2000s, the ILO has injected funds provided by DFID and the UN's Human Security Fund into anti-trafficking endeavours in the GMS region (ILO 2009). UNIAP also plans to devote nine million dollars to GMS and a fair share of this amount will go to Yunnan via the COMMIT framework (UNIAP 2009). As a member of the GMS, Yunnan is a recipient of several ADB development loans for the construction of provincial roads and a cross-border transportation corridor (ADB 2009a, 2009b). Most of these loans invariably include trafficking prevention components (ADB 2009c).

In the case of Hekou, the local government has vowed to take a stance against trafficking as one of the six border region anti-trafficking liaison centres and a beneficiary of ADB, UNICEF and USAID development funds. In 2008, the Hekou County Bureau of Justice published and distributed over 2,000 copies of a trafficking prevention manual and booklets on 'effective ways of self-protection' in the border region (Hekou Bureau of Justice 2008). In December 2008, Wu Xiaoyong, the deputy chief of the Public Security Bureau in Honghe prefecture (where Hekou is located) signed a communiqué on combating trafficking in women and children in the China–Vietnam border regions with the Public Security Bureau in Lao Cai. Both parties renewed their anti-trafficking commitments and promised intensive bilateral collaboration in the years to come (*Yunnan People's Daily* 2009b). In early 2009, the Hekou border police proudly announced that a total of six cross-border trafficking cases were solved successfully in 2008. Six trafficked victims, all young Vietnamese women forced into prostitution, were 'saved' and repatriated to their respective home towns (*Yunnan People's Daily* 2009a).

These kinds of public gestures and stories of success raise curious questions: if the local government in Hekou has taken such a firm stance on human trafficking and is working overtime to produce tangible results, why is Hekou's most famous sex market, Vietnamese Street, never targeted? The heart and soul of Hekou's tourism industry lies on Vietnamese Street. Among thousands of young Vietnamese women selling sex in Hekou, most of whom have crossed the border illegally into China, why have only six been rescued? What makes Vietnamese Street a trafficking 'not-spot', and why are the sex workers on that street not worth saving?

The presence and absence of the anti-trafficking discourse at the local level is the product of a strategy in which keeping the trafficking narrative alive is as important as keeping it subdued. The space in between presence and absence is where flexible management takes place. During my field research in Hekou, local government officials and businessmen alike keep on stressing how Hekou is a safe border and an ideal destination for trade and travel. They claimed that this place simply does not fit the profile of a typical trafficking hotspot identified by international experts. Hekou is a highly modernized town and the hub of regional commodity exchange. In addition, in comparison to the China–Myanmar and China–Laos borders, this border is relatively clean from the illicit drug trade and arms trade. The Vietnamese women who work in the 'leisure and entertainment' (*xiuxian yule*) sector have routine STI and HIV-AIDS check-ups funded by the central government and international organizations to ensure that they are clear from any contagious diseases. In other words, what Hekou offers is clean, economical pleasure that has become part of the tourism and business experience. Tales of trafficking would simply not be in Hekou's local interests.

To achieve this ideal image, local authorities implicitly manipulate the terms and concepts which are used to represent the social landscape. The terminological equivalent of 'human trafficking' in China is *renkou guaimai*, which literally means 'human abduction and sale'. Article 240 of the 1997 Criminal Law Code categorically states that 'trafficking is the abduction, kidnap, purchase, transportation, transfer of women and children for the purpose of *selling the victim*' (emphasis added).[10] This is drastically different from the definition in the UN Trafficking Protocol, which clearly identifies exploitation as the marker of trafficking. This discrepancy creates room for Chinese anti-traffickers to manoeuvre. A situation where a person is deceived or abducted without being sold is not considered a legitimate trafficking case under Chinese Criminal Law.[11]

As the global trafficking discourse starts to take hold, the Chinese 'indigenous' notion of human trafficking has evolved in accordance with international practice. Evaluations of what constitutes a trafficking case now occur in a rather flexible way. Chinese authorities use the UN Trafficking Protocol to determine whether 'internationally recognized' trafficking has taken place, or simply refer to the Chinese law if a narrower scope on what is deemed trafficking seems to be apt. The manipulation of key concepts in part explains why most of the sex workers in Hekou's Vietnamese Street are not perceived to be victims of trafficking. While almost all women working in Vietnamese Street would meet the definition of 'trafficked victim' under the UN Trafficking Protocol, since actual selling and purchasing of women is rare in the markets, under Chinese Criminal Law, trafficking is not prevalent there.[12]

Keeping Vietnamese Street out of the reach of the law is essential in maintaining the liveliness of Hekou's local businesses. Social reality is skewed in order to maximize that malleable space and to make it work better for local economic and developmental interests. In this way, Vietnamese Street becomes a 'space of exception' (Ong 2006), which is not confined by the political normativity determined by China's legal framework, nor touched by relevant international conventions. It is made into a pure and simple tourist market in an 'opening' border town, rather than a risky, dangerous space where crime abounds, or a poor underdeveloped 'source community' where trafficking takes place. Moreover, as Doezema has pointed out, 'a woman's "virtue" is at the heart of state laws and practices against "trafficking"' (Doezema 2000: 43). Because their lack of 'virtue', Vietnamese women in Hekou are not considered to be eligible for targeting and inclusion in the discursive construction of trafficking in women along the China–Vietnam border. As the Hekou county government carves up specific social spaces for flexible cross-border interactions, what happens within that space is treated as an exception to political and sovereign normativity. With this underlying framework, sex trade in Hekou is all about business, leisure and pleasure, and is less concerned with the global hyperbole of morality and security surrounding human trafficking.

What we see in Hekou is a highly complex social reality where sex work continues without being associated with human trafficking, and certain public gestures have to be made in order for China to be recognized by the international community as a compliant member and an eligible receiver of continuous financial and technical support. This is how anti-trafficking promises come to stay mostly on the lips and rarely get translated into action, as the local authorities and other local players shift between the exercise of sovereign power and the fashioning of particular social-spatial imageries in order to accommodate their competing priorities. This paradox has indeed revealed how contentious the framework of human trafficking could be at the level of local practice.

Conclusion

In this chapter, I have sketched out how the politics of making exceptions play out in the production of a trafficking 'not-spot' in the China–Vietnam borderland. In the case of Hekou, the public discourse on cross-border trafficking is constantly adjusted to both denounce its immorality and criminality while diffusing the implications of that same discourse for everyday life. Vietnamese Street thus is a salient example of how a potential trafficking hotspot is conveniently overlooked by local agents even as anti-trafficking narratives gather strength on China's frontiers. In other words, the sex markets in Hekou must be operated as a space of exception – as a 'not-spot' – in order for it to be excluded from national and international legal frameworks and to continue to generate profits without ringing alarm bells about breaches of human rights.

Hekou's trafficking 'not-spot' is produced by market incentives and a strategy of making exceptions. In order to achieve optimal results, local authorities in Hekou must maintain an ambivalent presence of both the trafficking and anti-trafficking rhetoric. The central and local authorities in China make public alliances with powerful international donors and other stakeholders because anti-trafficking requirements are a package deal with international development assistance. Driven by this motivation, Hekou positions itself to be identified as a 'key' place for anti-trafficking liaison and educational intervention (i.e. an ideal location to set up an anti-trafficking liaison office) in order to secure continuous political and financial support from the state and international organizations. It cannot afford to be identified as a high-risk hotspot that signals warning and undesirability to potential traders, investors and visitors.

Also noteworthy is the way in which the Chinese deliberately project a particular image of the Vietnamese women who sell sex in Hekou. These women are perceived as capable, seductive, deceptive and predatory whores rather than victims of an unfortunate destiny. The agency of these Vietnamese women is not deprived or erased, but recognized as an apt embodiment of liberalization due to economic reform in the borderland. This skewed recognition of agency has robbed the Vietnamese of the possibility of being identified as victims of sexual and labour exploitation by giving them the merit of being entrepreneurial for meeting a market demand.

Hekou's borderlanders make liberal references to the reform principle of *kaifang gaohuo* and constantly modify and negotiate the meanings and appropriateness of their practices. In the spirit of 'opening up', borderlanders are keen to preserve easy passages for Vietnamese women to cross into China as they bring tangible benefits to the border economy. In the meantime, performances of making pledges, carrying out rescues and repatriations of 'trafficked victims' have to be made to show that Hekou is on the same stage with everybody else as China 'opens' itself to comply with the international order. The ambiguous nature of the anti-trafficking discourse allows a space of flexibility for Hekou's borderlanders to benefit from both articulation and deliberate silence. As local authorities continue to showcase their efforts in signing anti-trafficking agreements, raising awareness and rescuing 'victims' along the China–Vietnam border, more Vietnamese women will carry on traversing this border to live and work in Hekou through easy passages and secret crossings, and tourists, businessmen and investors from inland China will also keep on visiting the border to indulge in the fantasy and experience of exotic intimacies.

Notes

1 Ethnographic field research for this chapter was carried out in Yunnan, China and Lao Cai, Vietnam from January 2007 to April 2008. I wish to thank Macquarie University in Sydney, the Vietnam Academy of Social Sciences in Hanoi, the Department of Culture and Information in Lao Cai, and the Asia Research Institute in Singapore for their generous support and cooperation. My gratitude also goes to Lenore Lyons, Michele Ford, Chris Lyttleton, Caroline Grillot, Sverre Molland, Vicente Reyes and Rosemary Wiss for their comments and suggestions of earlier drafts of this chapter. All names of informants and places mentioned in this chapter are pseudonyms except for those that have already been identified in media.

2 The average exchange rate in the border area in 2007 was $US 1 dollar equivalent to 8.1 yuan.

3 See Williams *et al.* (2008) for a discussion of similar militarized language used by Singaporean sex tourists who cross the border into Indonesia.

4 The residence fee varies from person to person depending on her personal relationship with the shop and the market management.

5 Commercial sex is also available across the border in Lao Cai, but it is more individualized and operates in a more discreet fashion. Visitors in Lao Cai need to engage a middleman (a pimp, a hotel employee or a local business partner) to access commercial sex. Most Chinese men who cross the border in group tours and stay in Lao Cai for no more than two days find it far less convenient to have sex there than in Hekou. This may in part explain why a sex market that is similar to Vietnamese Street is absent in Lao Cai.

6 From the 1950s to the 1960s in China, prostitution was regarded as a crime. Prostitutes were arrested and sent to labour camps for re-education. In 1958, the Chinese central government even announced that prostitution in China had been completely eradicated, which served as a symbol of China's transformation into a modern nation (Hershatter 1997). Until today, China has not given up this abolitionist stance regarding prostitution. A number of laws were published over the years to ban prostitution. For detailed accounts on how prostitution as an industry developed in response to these changes of law, see Jeffreys (2004), Pan (1999) and Zheng (2008).

7 The accuracy of these trafficking figures is debatable. Even the ILO/IPEC report admits that it is impossible to say with certainty how much trafficking actually takes place because many cases go unreported.

8 UNIAP (2008b) acknowledges that in 2006, over 2,000 trafficking cases in China were solved (although data on actual prosecutions is not published). Over 3,000 legal aid agencies were established nationwide, the majority (97 per cent) of which were at prefectural and county levels.

9 For a discussion of these issues in Laos see Molland (this volume).

10 People's Republic of China Criminal Law 1979 was revisited at the Eighth National People's Congress, Fifth session on 14 March 1997.

11 But if other forms of violence have occurred in the process, such as rape, sexual abuse, physical injury and fraud, offenders will be penalized according to other codes of the Criminal Law.

12 All the victims of the six rescues carried out in 2008 by the Hekou border police were invariably identified as sold into entertainment venues for prostitution.

References

ADB (2009a) 'GMS: Kunming-Hai Phong Economic Corridor'. ADB Online. Available at http://www.adb.org/Projects/project.asp?id=33307 (accessed 23 August 2009).

—— (2009b) 'Western Yunnan roads development II project'. ADB Online. Available at http://www.adb.org/Projects/project.asp?id=40626 (accessed 23 August 2009).

——(2009c) 'Loan projects addressing anti-trafficking concerns, 2002–2007'. ADB Online. Available at http://www.adb.org/Human-Trafficking/Loan-Projects.asp (accessed 23 August 2009).

Anarfi, J. K. (1998) 'Ghanaian women and prostitution in Cote d'Ivoire', in Kempadoo, K. and Doezema, J. (eds) *Global Sex Workers: Rights, Resistance and Redefinition*, New York and London: Routledge, pp. 104–13.

Blanchard, B. (2010) 'China casts nervous eye at erstwhile ally Myanmar'. Online. 25 January. Available at http://www.asiaone.com/News/Latest+News/Asia/Story/A1Story20100125-194184.html (accessed 16 August 2010).

Chin, Ko-lin and Zhang, S. X. (2007) *The Chinese Connection: Cross-Border Drug Trafficking Between Myanmar and China*, Washington, DC: U.S. Department of Justice.

China Daily (2010) 'Women from Laos, Vietnam and Myanmar increasingly marrying to Yunnan'. *China's Daily Online*. 27 May. Available at http://en.kunming.cn/index/content/2010-05/27/content_2169085.htm (accessed 14 August 2010).

Congressional-Executive Commission on China (2008) 'The Congressional-Executive Commission on China annual report 2008'. Online. Available at http://www. purdue. edu/crcs/itemResources/CECC/CECCannRpt2008.pdf (accessed 15 August 2010).

Deng, Jingyin (2010) 'Hordes of illegal workers crossing China's borders'. *Global Times Online*. 12 July. Available at http://china.globaltimes.cn/society/2010-07/550401.html (accessed 20 August 2010).

Doezema, J. (2000) 'Loose women or lost women? The re-emergence of the myth of white slavery in contemporary discourses of trafficking in women', *Gender Issues*, 18 (1): 38–54.

Farrer, J. (2008) 'Play and power in Chinese nightlife spaces', *China: An International Journal*, 6 (1): 1–17.

Grillot, C. (2010) *Volées, envolées, convolées: vendues, en fuite, ou re-socialisées, les 'fiancées' vietnamiennes en Chine*, Paris: Connaissances et Savoirs.

He, Zhixiong (2003) 'Migration and the sex industry in the Hekou-Lao Cai border region between Yunnan and Vietnam', in Darwin, M., Wattie, A. M. and Yuarsi, S. E. (eds) *Living on the Edges: Cross-Border Mobility and Sexual Exploitation in the Greater Southeast Asia Sub-region*, Yogyakarta: Gadjah Mada University, pp. 1–44.

Hekou Bureau of Justice (2008) 'Hekou qianghua fazhi xuanchuan jiaoyu'. Yunnan People's Government Online. Available at <http://hhhk.xxgk.yn.gov.cn/canton_model1/newsview.aspx? id=88864> (accessed 11 August 2009).

Hekou Yao Nationality Autonomous County Government (2006) 'Bianjing diqu yule changsuo fuwu xiaojie aizibing/xingbing yufang kongzhi xuanchuan jiaoyu', *Weisheng Ruankexue (Soft Science of Health)*, 20 (1): 61.

Hershatter, G. (1997) *Dangerous Pleasures: Prostitution and Modernity in Twentieth-Century Shanghai*, Berkeley: University of California Press.

ILO (2008) 'Preventing human trafficking in the GMS–China'. ILO Online. 29 October. Available at http://www.ilo.org/public/english/region/asro/bangkok/child/trafficking/wherewework-chinadetail.htm#top (accessed 16 August 2010).

—— (2009) 'The Mekong Sub-region project to combat trafficking in children and women

(ILO-TICW)'. ILO Online. Available at http://www.ilo.org/dyn/migpractice/migmain. showPractice?p_lang=en&p_practice_id=59 (accessed 22 October 2009).

ILO/IPEC (2002) 'Yunnan Province, China – situation of trafficking in children and women: A rapid assessment'. ILO Online. Available at http://www.ilo.org/wcmsp5/groups/public/---asia/---ro-bangkok/documents/publica tion/wcms_bk_pb_12_en.pdf (accessed 23 August 2009).

Jeffreys, E. (2004) *China, Sex and Prostitution*, London and New York: Routledge.

Kempadoo, K. (1998) 'The migrant tightrope: Experiences from the Caribbean', in Kempadoo, K. and Doezema, J. (eds) *Global Sex Workers: Rights, Resistance and Redefinition*, New York and London: Routledge, pp. 124–38.

Li, Qiaoping (2003) 'Zhongyue shuangbian yufang kuaguo guaimai funu er'tong gongzuo shishi qingkuang ji xiangguan wenti', *Dongnanya zongheng*, 6: 49–52.

Ma, Guihua (2009) 'Smashing the snakeheads'. *China Daily Online*. 2 November. Available at http://www.chinadaily.com.cn/life/2009-11/02/content_8881359.htm (accessed 15 August 2010).

Marshall, S. (1999), 'Vietnamese women are kidnapped and later sold in China as brides', *Wall Street Journal*, 3 August.

McGivering, J. (2006) 'Vietnam-China trafficking on rise'. BBC News Online. 24 January. Available at http://news.bbc.co.uk/2/hi/asia-pacific/4643110.stm (accessed 15 August 2010).

Ministry of Commerce of China (2008) 'Yunnan Hekou kouan duiwai maoyi zaichuang xingao'. Ministry of Commerce of China Online. 5 February. Available at http://kmtb. mofcom.gov.cn/aarticle/g/ 200802/20080205381470.html (accessed 3 March 2008).

Ong, A. (2006) *Neoliberalism as Exception: Mutations in Citizenship and Sovereignty*, Durham, NC and London: Duke University Press.

Pan, Suiming (1999) *Cunzai yu huangmiu: Zhongguo dixia xingchanye kaocha*, Beijing: Qunyan.

People's Daily (2004) 'China, Vietnam launch anti-trafficking campaign'. *People's Daily Online*. 4 June. Available at http://english.peopledaily.com.cn/200406/04/eng20040604_145303.html (accessed 10 August 2010).

Richburg, K. (2009) 'Chinese border town emerges as new front line in fight against human trafficking'. *Washington Post Online*. 26 December Available at http://www.washingtonpost.com/wp-dyn/content/article/2009/12/25/AR2009122 501841.html (accessed 14 August 2010).

Samarasinghe, V. (2008) *Female Sex Trafficking in Asia: The Resilience of Patriarchy in a Changing World*, London and New York: Routledge.

Sharma, N. (2003) 'Travel agency: A critique of anti-trafficking campaigns', *Refuge*, 21 (3): 53–65.

State Council of China (2007) *China National Plan of Action on Combating Trafficking in Women and Children (2008–2012)*. Online. Available at http://www.humantrafficking.org/publications/612 (accessed 23 August 2009).

Tran, Dinh Thanh Lam (2006) 'No red lights for trafficking women to China'. IPS News Online. 10 February. Available at http://ipsnews.org/news.asp?idnews=32113 (accessed 14 August 2010).

UNIAP (2008a) 'SIREN trafficking data sheet – China'. UNIAP Online. Available at http://www.no-trafficking.org/reports_docs/china/CHINA%20SIREN%20data%20sheet%20Sept%202008.doc (accessed 23 August 2009).

—— (2008b) 'Counter-trafficking action being taken in China'. UNIAP Online. Available at http://www.no-trafficking.org/china_action.html (accessed 23 August 2009).

—— (2009) 'UNIAP on human trafficking in the Greater Mekong Sub-region'. UNIAP Online. Available at http://www.no-trafficking.org/reports_docs/UNIAP%20MTE%20Report%20-%20Executive%20Summary (accessed 11 October 2009).

UNICEF (2004) 'China and Vietnam extend cross-border cooperation on anti-trafficking to launch of joint communication campaign'. UNICEF Online. Available at http://www.unicef.org/china/media_920.html (accessed 12 October 2009).

—— (2008) 'China, Vietnam join hands to fight cross-border trafficking of women'. UNICEF Online. Available at http://www.unicef.org/infobycountry/ china_2530.html (accessed 23 August 2009).

United Nations (2000) *Protocol to Prevent, Suppress and Punish Trafficking in Persons, Especially Women and Children.* United Nations Online. Available at http://www.uncjin.org/Documents/Conventions/dcatoc/final_documents_2/convention_%20traff_eng.pdf (accessed 23 August 2009).

Williams, S., Lyons, L. and Ford, M. (2008) 'It's about bang for your buck, bro: Singaporean men's online conversations about sex in Batam, Indonesia', *Asian Studies Review*, 32 (1), 77–97.

Wong, D. (2005) 'The rumour of trafficking: Border controls, illegal migration, and the sovereignty of the nation-state', in Abraham, I. and van Schendel, W. (eds) *Illicit Flows and Criminal Things: States, Borders and the Other Side of Globalisation*, Indianapolis: Indiana University Press, pp. 69–99.

Yunnan Daily (2009) '2008 nian Hekou lüyou shouci tupo baiwan renci'. *Yunnan Daily Online*. 20 January. Available at http://yn.yunnan.cn/html/2009-01/20/content_207336.htm (accessed 22 February 2009).

Yunnan People's Daily (2009a) 'Hekou bianfang jiancha chenggong jiejiu beiguai yüeji shaonü'. *Yunnan People's Daily Online*. 10 February. Available at http://www.yunnanpeople.com.cn/honghe/hhxw/200902/3654.html (accessed 12 May 2009).

—— (2009b) 'Dianyue lianshou, zhongdian daji kuaguo guaimai'. *Yunnan People's Daily Online*. 29 October. Available http://www.yunnan.com.cn/2008page/society/html/2009-10/29/content_958800.htm (accessed 11 November 2009).

Zhao, G. M. (2003) 'Trafficking of women for marriage in China', *Criminal Justice*, 3 (1): 83–102.

Zheng, Tiantian (2008) 'Anti-trafficking campaign and karaoke bar hostesses in China', *Wagadu*, 5: 73–92.

—— (2009) *Red Lights: The Lives of Sex Workers in Postsocialist China*, Minneapolis: University of Minnesota Press.

6 Territorial sovereignty and trafficking in the Indonesia–Malaysia borderlands

Michael Eilenberg

During a 2005 visit to the West Kalimantan border, Indonesian President Susilo Bambang Yudhoyono announced a series of large-scale development initiatives planned along the nation's border with East Malaysia. This renewed focus on the border was the result of a combination of factors including the economic interests of national and international plantation companies, issues of territorial sovereignty and security, and rising pressure from the international community and neighbouring countries to deal with undocumented labour migration and contraband smuggling. In the words of the President:

> For this [plan] to develop, we need to develop a road running parallel to the border. We must close down all [unauthorized border crossings] that often are employed for the undertakings of illegal activities. If this plan goes well tens or even hundreds of thousands of people could be employed in the border area.
>
> (Cited in PKB 2005)

As noted by the President in his speech, these initiatives were expected to make the local border population less dependent on wage labour in East Malaysia and thereby become more attached to their own nation-state.[1] In other words, the development of labour intensive industries and the expansion of infrastructure along the entire length of the Kalimantan border would enable the Indonesian state to establish production zones that could not only compete with and attract investment from Malaysia, but would also keep Indonesian workers at home.

The Indonesian state has often questioned the national loyalty of the border population because of their engagement in so-called illegal cross-border activities. Various forces such as shared ethnicity and the lack of genuine development initiatives have shaped these engagements. Decades of cross-border interaction have in no small part nurtured a strong attachment to neighbouring East Malaysia. For many borderlanders their connections over the border are often stronger than those with their own nation, a fact that recently led to debates over their citizenship status (*Harian Berkat* 2009). The expansion and contraction of border surveillance over time has further nurtured borderland autonomy in which formal state laws often are perceived as colliding with local livelihood practices. At times 'illegal' cross-border flows, including workers, have been hardly noticed or simply ignored by various public authorities. However, a sudden shift in administration can lead to a criminalization of these flows and crossings, as is the case in the most recent attempt to reclaim the borderlands.

The same year that the President visited the West Kalimantan border, the Coordinating Ministry for Social Welfare released a report on the elimination of human trafficking in Indonesia which stated that the extreme porosity of the border between Kalimantan and East Malaysia was an obvious hindrance to combating human traffickers and claimed that there was a dire need for increased border controls in the area (Menko Kesra 2005: 22). The issues of migrant illegality and trafficking have also appeared prominently in press statements about the changing border regime (*Suara Karya* 2005; *Equator News* 2007b; *Jakarta Post* 2008a, 2008b; *Media Indonesia* 2008; *Jakarta Globe* 2009a). Indeed, Indonesia's central government has increasingly seen underdevelopment and poor infrastructure along the border with East Malaysia, together with the rise in undocumented labour migration and smuggling, as a problem of national security. According to this view, development and national security along its territorial borders go hand in hand and consequently border development has become a priority of successive governments.

This chapter aims to explore the role that counter-trafficking initiatives have played in attempts by the Indonesian state to reclaim authority along its territorial borders.[2] Drawing on data collected through personal interviews with government officials and community members in 2002–2003 and 2007, and analysis of government reports and newspaper clippings covering the period from 2002 to 2009, it documents how increased criminalization and the prevention of unauthorized flows of cross-border labour migrants have come to the forefront of national rhetoric concerning border development, territorial sovereignty and security. The chapter argues that the anti-trafficking discourse has had unintended negative consequences along a border where the mundane practices of undocumented labour migration are often not distinguished from the more exploitative practices of human trafficking.

Irregular migration as a matter of national security

The West Kalimantan borderland (see Figure 6.1) has long been a source of anxiety for state authorities. Border populations are seen as potentially subversive subjects who ruinously adhere to various illegal practices in pursuit of their daily livelihoods. The border zone, dividing two separate nation-states with their different administrative, regulatory and economic regimes, generates structures of opportunity that provides fertile ground for activities deemed illegal by one or both states to flourish.

Since Independence, the level of regulatory state authority along the border has waxed and waned with changes in government administrations and policies. State control has sometimes been strong, such as during the period of Confrontation between Malaysia and Indonesia in the 1960s and the communist counter-insurgency that raged in the decade to follow. As a consequence, the border was

Figure 6.1 The West Kalimantan–Sarawak border

officially closed for several years. The tense situation led to heightened militarization on both sides of the border and the borderland functioned as a security buffer
zone. During this period, cross-border migration was extremely difficult and dangerous. After the armed confrontations and eradication of communist insurgents,
it again became possible to cross the border, a development which set the stage
for large-scale resource exploitation. However, although many of the former high-
ranking army personnel who carried out the fight against the communists were
granted large timber concessions along the border by President Suharto's New
Order regime, these undertakings – carried out in the name of national security and
development – generated few local jobs.

   In 1994 President Suharto introduced a security and prosperity approach (Keppres 1994). This decree stated that border development was imperative for the
upholding of national security. The idea at that time was to create a buffer zone
along the border solely under the authority of the military. In reality, the decree
was used to justify large-scale resource extraction in the border region by the
military in tandem with Suharto's business cronies. During this period, resource
exploitation as well as infrastructural and other kinds of development initiatives
were stalled. This meant that transport was time-consuming, unreliable, and often
interrupted or made impossible by seasonally restricted roads and waterways.
Stalled by remoteness from the provincial economic centre in Pontianak, cross-
border trade and labour migration again became crucial for the local economy.

The scale and volume of cross-border migration has risen dramatically since the 1997 economic crisis and the fall of Suharto in 1998, as the presence of central government and military authority at the margins of the state was largely reduced or became non-existent. However, after nearly a decade of increased local autonomy, the pendulum moved back because of renewed government interest in stretches of lightly populated land suitable for both large-scale agricultural development projects but also defence and security. The 1994 Presidential Decree initially introduced by Suharto has come to play a vital role in recent government border plans and is repeatedly mentioned in various government reports. The concept of security and prosperity is used in today's rhetoric of border development and the 'safety belt' (*sabuk pengaman*) is to be composed of oil palm and rubber plantations rather than dense and difficult to manage forest.

The concept of an Indonesian–Malaysian agricultural corridor was first suggested as a suitable border strategy in a 2001 publication from the National Agency for the Assessment and Application of Technology (Hamid *et al.* 2001). Then, on 14 October 2003, a meeting was held in East Kalimantan between the Indonesian Government and officials from the Malaysian states of Sabah and Sarawak. The main topic was cross-border trade and development of a spatial plan for the border area between the two countries. In a report prepared for the meeting it was stated that the main spatial policy was: 'To boost the development of [the] border area as an Indonesian "front line" to Malaysia' (DJPR 2003). A month later, in November 2003, the National Development Planning Agency, Bappenas, released the first official report on a strategy and model for developing the border areas of Kalimantan (Bappenas 2003). One of the main concerns highlighted in these government reports was again the un-restricted flow of labour migrants prompted by under-development and lack of border policing.

In May 2005, the Minister of Agriculture, Anton Apriantono, announced the formation of an oil palm plantation corridor to span the entire length of the 2,000 kilometre-long border with Malaysia. He claimed that the initiative would create more than half a million jobs, attract foreign exchange, strengthen the border against neighbouring Malaysia, and reduce the prosperity gap between people living along the border and those in Malaysia (*Pontianak Post* 2005; *Jakarta Post* 2005b). Besides creating jobs for local populations, the government expected to move unemployed workers from densely populated provinces of Indonesia into the sparsely populated border area as part of a large transmigration project.[3] However, its ultimate mission, as quoted in a 2006 report on the key management plan of the country's borders, was to create a: 'Secure, Orderly, and Advanced Territory' (Bappenas 2006a). According to the report 'secure' (*aman*) means creating security conditions that can be controlled and are conducive for business and free from illegal activities; 'orderly' (*tertib*) means that all economic activities, social and cultural at the border are based on (state) law and regulation; and 'advanced' (*maju*) refers to increased economic welfare of local communities (Bappenas 2006a: 41).

The combination of security, order and advancement became buzzwords in the national discourse on border development. Among other things, the Middle-Term

National Development Plan for 2005 to 2009 (Rencana Pembangunan Jangka Menengah 2005–2009, RPJM) stressed the eradication of illegal cross-border movement and smuggling as a means of securing and maintaining order in border areas of Indonesia. As stated in Chapter Five on 'Enhancing Security and Order, and Overcoming Crime', the aim of the government is to 'secure the border areas of Indonesia by securing cross-border activities' (Perpres 2005a). The aims of 'The Program of Development of Border Areas' are:

> Maintaining the territorial integrity of the Republic of Indonesia, through the affirmation of the sovereignty of the NKRI (Unitary State of the Republic of Indonesia); [. . .] to enhance nationalism among the [border] communities; and to ensure the supremacy of law and legal regulations with regard to violations that are occurring in border areas.
>
> (Perpres 2005a)

Yet despite these initiatives and other attempts to develop a master plan for the border region, the various government bodies involved in the process have been largely crippled as there is no official law or decree that specifies what exactly makes up the border region and what is the division of labour between different levels of government (*Jakarta Post* 2009b). Successive Indonesian administrations since the presidency of Megawati Sukarnoputri have discussed the content of a National Border Law that is to determine the levels of government and departments that will be responsible for the future management of Indonesia's border regions (*Equator News* 2007c). Both the governments of Megawati and Susilo Bambang Yudhoyono drafted laws on the spatial planning of the Kalimantan border area that stipulated the main priorities for the border. However, these drafts never received the presidential signature and therefore never materialized as formal laws; thus the actual steps towards developing the border area have been repeatedly postponed. Besides the administrative hurdles, one often mentioned reason for government reluctance to implement development initiatives is the immediate need for law and order on the border (Keppres 2003; Perpres 2005b).

Feeding into the discourse of law and order, the military immediately embraced the opportunity to regain authority along the border that was partly lost after the fall of Suharto. High-ranking military spokespersons promptly expressed their strong support for the government's plans. In March 2006 on an inspection tour of the East Kalimantan border the Commander-in-Chief of the National Armed Forces (TNI) Djoko Suyanto, announced that he was in favour of the planned border development:

> We support the development of border areas in the aim to improve the welfare of the people, in addition to this there are strategic goals related to aspects of security to be considered. We will continue to build defence posts along the border in the years 2006, 2007, 2008 and 2009 until the issue of [economic] disparity in the border area is completely solved.
>
> (Cited in *Berita TNI* 2006)

Riding high on the rhetoric of security and a general public demand for stronger territorial defence against Malaysia, the military have pushed to reassert state sovereignty through coercive force by establishing permanent military control posts with military battalions to secure 'peace' in the border area and prevent unauthorized border crossings (*Jakarta Post* 2005a; *Antara* 2007; *Equator News* 2009). The lawless borderland was seen as an obvious entry point for foreign terrorists and therefore in dire need of military protection. It was even suggested that a unit of the police special anti-terror corps (Detasemen Khusus, Densus 88 Anti-Terror) should help patrol the border (*Equator News* 2005).[4]

Starting in late 2006, several hundred soldiers were dispatched to the area to support the undermanned border military, and 31 control posts or camps were erected along the West Kalimantan border with barbed wire and shooting ranges each manned by one heavily armed company (30–40 persons) who patrol the borderline on a regular basis.[5] Additionally 24 posts are planned just a few kilometres away from Putussibau, the Kapuas Hulu district capital; a large military camp with room for one battalion from the regional command in Pontianak has been erected; and a large military airbase is planned (*Equator News* 2008). This growing presence of state authority in the form of border militarization is, as described above, largely an outcome of the perceived loss of national sovereignty and major public, regional and global pressure to eradicate so-called illegal flows of humans, contraband and terrorism. It was within these debates on border development and sovereignty that the concept of counter-trafficking as a security measure began to develop.[6]

The emergence of the anti-trafficking discourse

The influx of undocumented Indonesian labour migrants across the border has for long been an issue of tension between the Indonesian and Malaysian authorities (Liow 2003).[7] The Sarawak authorities have repeatedly accused the Indonesian authorities of ignoring the undocumented flows of migrants, which has supposedly led to increased crime rates in Malaysia. Since 2002, the Malaysian Government has initiated several programmes of mass expulsion and repatriation of illegal Indonesian workers, resulting in more persistent and aggressive raids on labour camps in Sarawak and throughout the country (Ford 2006; Eilenberg and Wadley 2009). In the first ten months of 2008 alone, the National Agency for Placement and Protection of Indonesian Overseas Workers estimates that the Sarawak authorities deported approximately 2,000 illegal Indonesian workers across the border to West Kalimantan (BNP2TKI 2008).

But the spectre of human trafficking and other illegal border activities has forced Malaysia and Indonesia into dialogue.[8] During the 37th General Border Committee (GBC) meeting in December 2008 both the Indonesian Defence Minister and the Malaysian Prime Minister highlighted the need for increased bilateral ties in regard to border security, emphasizing that the current economic situation and the difficult living conditions along the border might give rise to an increase in illegal activities like human trafficking (*Bernama* 2008). The Malaysian Prime Minister Abdullah Ahmad Badawi was quoted saying:

To improve cooperation and handle the poverty issue, we need to intensify the collaborated efforts of our intelligence agencies and help eradicate criminals, smugglers and human traffickers.

(Jakarta Post 2008c)

The Indonesian Defence Minister, Juwono Sudarsono used similar wording when discussing this and related issues:

Efforts to deal with non-traditional security threats and challenges such as smuggling, terrorism, illegal logging, illegal fishing and human trafficking – which have been discussed many times at Southeast Asian regional forums – need to be strengthened at this bilateral level as well.

(Jakarta Post 2008c)

The intense focus on human trafficking at the highest levels feeds and reflects growing levels of media coverage of the issue. Human trafficking is increasingly making the headlines in national and provincial newspapers and, in line with government rhetoric, it is often portrayed as a major security problem and obstacle for border development *(Pontianak Post* 2007, 2009a, 2009b, 2009d; *Jakarta Globe* 2009b; *Jakarta Post* 2009c, 2009d). Among these reports, a steady increase in the number of trafficking cases reported by the police and other government authorities in the West Kalimantan borderlands has been noted *(Pontianak Post* 2009c).

Most cases of organized human trafficking reported in the national news media and government take place in demarcated 'hotspots' (see Molland in this volume) along the border such as the border crossing points at Entikong (Sanggau district) and Aruk (Sambas district) in West Kalimantan. In 2010 the head of the provincial police announced that West Kalimantan ranked second highest out of 12 regions experiencing human trafficking, with a total of 722 cases or 19.33 per cent. This ranking is slightly better than West Java with 850 cases. He further highlighted the Entikong crossing as experiencing the majority of human trafficking cases because of its accessible location and more developed infrastructure *(Equator News* 2010). The increasing visibility of trafficking in the province in part reflects the readiness of the provincial government to employ the anti-trafficking discourse. When West Kalimantan governor Usman Jafar issued the first regional decree on the prevention and eradication of the trafficking of women and children in 2007, the decree argued that the province was especially prone and vulnerable to acts of trafficking because of its shared border with Malaysia (Perda 2007).

This official commitment to eradicate human trafficking was enthusiastically embraced by the current governor Cornelis MH, who replaced Usman Jafar in January 2008. Cornelis subsequently received an invitation from the United Nations to participate in a May 2008 roundtable discussion on the issue of human trafficking at the UN headquarters in Geneva *(Antara* 2008). After his return from Geneva, he released several regulations and provincial decisions on anti-trafficking (Kepgub 2009, 2010; Perda 2010). These various decrees, along with statements by the governor, readily linked the lack of border control with an increase in human trafficking (BP2AMKB 2010).

Human trafficking takes many different forms along the West Kalimantan border. While many forced undocumented migrant workers are deployed within the domestic sector, the plantation and factory sectors make up the largest share of the reported trafficking cases. These modes have increasingly been recognized in definitions, along with baby selling, mail-order brides and sex work (Sugiarti *et al.* 2006: 210–11). The broadening of trafficking categories (some of which were previously seen as licit activities) and the popularity of the anti-trafficking discourse have resulted in a steady increase of reported cases, but have also led to confusion regarding what constitutes trafficking and what does not (see Ford and Lyons in this volume). Furthermore, trafficking data is more or less solely derived from the more accessible border crossings like Entikong and Aruk, which are relatively close to the provincial capital where human rights NGOs (international and national) are most active (BP2AMKB 2010).

It is also here that the discourse of anti-trafficking is strongest. Several high-profile national NGOs like Shelter Aisyiah[9] and Anak Bangsa provide temporary shelter in recovery centres and various kind of assistance (legal and medical services, rehabilitation and reintegration) to trafficked persons at the Entikong border crossing and both organizations collaborate with and receive funds from the International Organization for Migration (IOM). Other NGOs like the Legal Aid Foundation of the Indonesian Women's Association for Justice (Yayasan Lembaga Bantuan Hukum Perempuan Indonesia untuk Keadilan, YLBH-APIK), the Institute for Legal Aid and Family Consultations (Lembaga Konsultasi Bantuan Hukum dan Keluarga, LKBH-PEKA) and Pancur Kasih raise awareness about and provide services for trafficking victims in the major cities of Pontianak and Singkawang (USAID 2006).

On the ground, the actual servicing and handling of trafficking victims is more or less solely managed by these NGOs although some coordination is carried out with local government authorities. Yet while capacity-building programmes and technical assistance involve service providers and local government, the relationship between them is not without problems. A report written by the International Catholic Migration Commission and the American Center for International Labor Solidarity in 2006 on trafficking in 15 provinces of Indonesia mentions that local government authorities in the Sanggau district (where the Entikong border crossing is located) were frustrated by service providers, which refused to help persons whom the local authorities regarded as trafficked but the service providers did not (Sugiarti *et al.* 2006: 213).[10] These skirmishes between government actors and service providers are the result of the haste with which the anti-trafficking discourse is being implemented and demonstrate the lack of a coordinated and systematic approach to dealing with trafficking. In short, despite the issuing of several decrees on anti-trafficking by the provincial government, local governments still lack the capacity to detect trafficking victims and provide services for them.

While most NGOs report a growth in trafficking cases, actual statistical data on trafficking are still very limited and vague as there are divergent perceptions of what constitutes a 'trafficked person' among the various NGOs working in the province. Different perceptions of trafficking, differing data sources and a lack of capacity make it very difficult to get any exact figures. Anak Bangsa recorded 160 cases of human trafficking for the period January to June 2009 at Entikong, reporting that the large majority of victims were not from West Kalimantan but various parts of Java and only 20 per cent were adult males (*Republika* 2009). With even fewer cases reported at Aruk, it is plausible to suggest that the numbers of trafficked victims in other more difficult to access border crossings would be fairly low.

In the more marginal border areas like Kapaus Hulu, where the abovementioned NGOs are largely absent, the discourse of trafficking is weak and often much less nuanced (*Borneo Tribune* 2009). When the term is used it is often difficult to distinguish it from other kinds of illegal cross-border movements and trade. Over-whemingly, also, it is associated with the military's rhetoric of border security and lawlessness and is seen by local borderlanders as yet another top-down concept applied by central and regional state authorities to delimit and regulate their cross-border movements. But while the term 'human trafficking' (*trafiking* or *perdagangan manusia*) seldom appears in everyday conversation, the direct consequences of counter-trafficking initiatives are being felt among borderland communities, as undocumented labour migration becomes increasingly criminalized in these borderlands. Moreover, counter-trafficking is having a disproportionate effect on borderlanders, who are much less likely to be victims of trafficking but get caught up in the counter-trafficking net.

Different kinds of labour migrants

Officially it is illegal to cross the border with the intention of working in Sarawak, except at the official crossing in Entikong. For a long time local authorities ignored locals who cross the more remote part of the border without any official documents, as official resources are few and corruption is widespread (Tirtosudarmo 2002; Eilenberg and Wadley 2009). But as the anti-trafficking framework gains traction in more remote areas of the province, previously largely unrestricted, relatively benign and rather mundane acts of undocumented labour migration are no longer distinguished from the more severe acts of organized human trafficking and exploitation carried out by criminal syndicates. As a result, borderlanders report that the number of cases of arrests and harassment by border police and the military is drastically intensifying. As a consequence, borderlanders' access to cross-border employment is shrinking, with severe economic consequences for local livelihoods.

Local livelihood strategies have historically been based on the advantages that the fluidity of the border presented. Centuries of unhindered labour migration into Sarawak have provided a steady cash income for borderlands that historically have been deprived of national and provincial economic development. The borderland's proximity to major political and economic centres in Sarawak and its remoteness from its own provincial capital has resulted in close networks of trade, migration and kinship across the border. While the border is seen by administrators as a rugged wilderness full of geographical obstacles, to locals it is a land of low-lying hills and river plains that offer few physical barriers to cross-border flows. Where the state sees an inhospitable landscape, borderlanders see centuries of well-worn trade routes.

Borderland populations strategically apply their long-term and intricate networks of cross-border kin relations to cross the border and find work (Eilenberg and Wadley 2009). As one borderlander commented, referring to his close relationship with his Sarawak family, 'We are still of one descent.' Encouraged by increasing economic differences between the two countries and the lack of reliable and well-paid waged jobs in the borderland, growing numbers of borderlanders seek temporary employment in Sarawak.[11] As a consequence, labour migration has become a large part of the informal borderland economy, and the wages earned provide a substantial source of cash income for borderland households.[12] As the Indonesian and the Malaysian authorities increase surveillance along their territorial borders, however, it becomes increasingly difficult to carry on these long-term practices.

Large numbers of non-borderland Indonesian migrants also cross from this region into Sarawak to find work in the large oil palm plantations stretching along the Sarawak side of the border.[13] Informal labour brokers or middlemen (*calo*) mediate the labour experiences of these migrants. The *calo* often work in tandem with Malaysian plantation companies and provide travel documents like passports, ID cards and visas for a hefty fee. A common strategy among the *calo* is to assist the migrants entering Malaysia on a short-term Social Visa that later can be converted into a work permit. The jobs in the plantation sector are generally lower paid and working conditions dire, with long working hours and poor safety records (Idrus 2008). Here labour migrants are usually housed in small settlements within the oil palm plantations isolated from surrounding communities and the prying eyes of the Malaysian authorities. Not having the advantage of close-knit ethnic relations to mediate work relations, they are extremely vulnerable to exploitation by unscrupulous labour syndicates. Not allowed to leave the plantation perimeter to purchase everyday commodities or socialize, these workers are extremely dependent on the goodwill of the plantation owners, to whom they often end up being financially indebted.[14] While many of these migrant workers start out as voluntary migrants they easily end up in a system of debt bondage with threats of arrest and deportation hanging over their head.

By contrast, local labour migrants tend to work within the construction and service industry in jobs secured by Sarawak kin, whose ability to secure reasonable working conditions and salaries is based on decades of labour migration and mutual trust between the worker and Sarawak employers. In addition, these networks supply much-needed official documents, like identity cards and birth certificates, which ensure higher salaries and more security, as migrants are less vulnerable during police raids and less likely to face jail time and expulsion across the border.[15] These local labour migrants are far less likely to be exploited than the more vulnerable non-borderland Indonesian migrants, who are dependent on the *calo*.

Borderlanders cross illegally into Sarawak because there have historically been few other workable alternatives. According to the 1967 Basic Agreement between Malaysia and Indonesia, inhabitants living in the immediate area on either side of the border are to be allowed to cross it for short social visits (Agustiar 2000). To be able to do so, however, they need an official border-crossing pass (*Pas Lintas Batas*), locally known as a Red Letter (*Surat Merah*). Applying for such a pass is time consuming and expensive and the pass does not allow the taking up of employment. Because of these constraints, most borderlanders prefer crossing the border illegally. This poses few obstacles as they have an intimate knowledge of the border area and can blend into the Sarawak population almost seamlessly.

For many years, the only officially recognized border-crossing point where non-border residents could pass and international trade was allowed in West Kalimantan was the Entikong (Indonesia) and Tebedu (Sarawak) Cross-Border Inspection Post (*Pos Pemeriksaan Lintas Batas*, PPLB) situated in the district of Sanggau. This official entry and exit point was opened in 1989 and is fully staffed by immigration and custom authorities (Fariastuti 2002). The PPLB at Entikong is also used by legal labour migrants from other parts of Indonesia who enter Malaysia using the services of officially licensed human resource recruitment agencies and work on short-term contracts (Fariastuti 2002). Besides the official crossing in Entikong there are Cross-Border Posts (*Pos Lintas Batas*, PLB) at Aruk (Sambas district), Jagoi Babang (Bengkayang district), Jasa (Sintang district) and Nanga Badau (Kapuas Hulu district) where borderlanders are allowed to cross for the purpose of short temporary social visits. These crossing points also attract large numbers of outside migrants from other parts of the province and Indonesia who use the PLBs as 'illegal' gateways into Sarawak. In addition to these designated routes, there are estimated to be more than 60 small unofficial back-roads or *jalan tikus* (literally mouse paths) that connect 55 villages in West Kalimantan with 32 villages in Sarawak (BP2AMKB 2010). The borderlanders themselves mostly use these small *jalan tikus* as entering Sarawak though these require intimate knowledge of local geography.

When borderlanders cross the border without official documents in order to take up work in Sarawak they do not see themselves as criminals breaking the law. On the contrary, from their perspective cross-border labour migration is a licit and deep-rooted practice developed over centuries that has become an integral part of the local economy. They argue that economically and politically marginalized border communities have been forced to develop their own cross-border livelihood strategies because the Indonesian state has not yet managed to develop the borderland and overcome the economic disparities between communities on either site of the border. As a labour migrant from the borderland pragmatically declared: 'If the government can't provide us with local economic opportunities we will provide for ourselves and continue working in Sarawak, breaking the law or not' (Interview, April 2007).

However, the perceived legitimacy of entering Sarawak through unauthorized entry points like Nanga Badau only extends to borderlanders themselves. According to borderlanders, labour migrants from other parts of Indonesia are interlopers who do not possess the historical and cultural right to cross the border in search of work. Local animosity towards 'outside' migrants is further inflamed by increasing competition for jobs. Borderlanders also argue that these outsiders are prone to criminality and violence and often blame the 'low morals' of these outsiders for Malaysia's increasingly punitive response to labour migrants in Sarawak.[16] The recent global financial crisis and consequent pressure on regional labour markets in both Indonesia and Malaysia have put extra strain on local borderlanders and Indonesian labour migrants in general (*Jakarta Post* 2008d). While the previous economic crisis of 1997–98 had modest negative effect on the immediate borderland population due to their intimate cross-border links and more or less unrestricted access to the border, the current economic crisis has been felt much more broadly as a result of the amplified focus on border security between Indonesia and Malaysia. But whatever their status, undocumented labour migrants crossing the West Kalimantan–Sarawak border have increasingly been criminalized as 'illegals'.

Initial steps have been taken to upgrade the Nanga Badau Cross-Border Post into a Cross-Border Inspection Post similar to the one in Entikong. In 2006 as part of the spatial planning of the Kalimantan-Sarawak-Sabah border region (KASABA), the central and provincial government selected five border entry points in West Kalimantan which would be developed into economic growth centres in order to prevent illegal flows. One was to be situated at the Nanga Badau border crossing in the Kapuas Hulu district, which was highlighted as a priority one area in special need of development initiatives (Bappenas 2006b: 33; *Equator News* 2007a).[17] Customs and immigration buildings have been constructed and a gate erected. However, the designation of Nanga Badau as an official Cross-Border Inspection Post has previously been repeatedly postponed by central and provincial government (*Kompas* 2002; *Sinar Harapan* 2003; *Pontianak Post* 2004; *Equator News* 2006). There are several reasons why this border point has not yet been officially opened. According to one border inhabitant:

> The reason why the Nanga Badau gateway is not [officially] opened yet is because then every cross-border transaction can continue to be declared illegal, and when illegal it becomes the game of government institutions and the security apparatus for collecting unofficial taxes. Every person who goes into Sarawak is asked to pay 50 Malaysian Ringgit when they return to various officials [military and police]. If the border gate becomes official there will be no more unofficial taxes. If this gate is not [officially] opened soon it means that the central government wishes the border area to remain lawless.
>
> (Interview, March 2007)

Given the obvious link between cross-border activities and illegality, it is difficult to assess the extent to which state agents and local officials are involved in illegal cross-border labour migration beyond simply facilitating and collecting fees on their side of the border. However, it is an open secret in the border area that the police and the military are economically dependent upon so-called 'illegal' activities. Their collection of under-the-table 'taxes' on various contraband goods and the movement of people is widespread (*Jakarta Post* 2008e). It is also sustained:

the very same officials that today levy charges on labour migrants were deeply engaged in the collection of 'timber taxes' during the heyday of cross-border timber trafficking (1999–2005).

Although the local Women's Empowerment Bureau in the Kapuas Hulu district has received tip-offs about the existence of trafficking in the district, there is no concrete data on trafficking related cases at the Nanga Badau crossing (*Borneo Tribune* 2009). Compared to the thousands of voluntary undocumented labour migrants who cross this border every month the number of forced crossings appears to be very small. Despite the small number and fairly restricted geographical spread of trafficking cases, media reports on the potential for trafficking commonly depict trafficking as a threat which affects the entire length of the border. But such reports seem to be largely unsubstantiated and based on sporadic rumours. Undocumented border crossings across the West Kalimantan border takes many different forms, some more benign than others. It is here argued that the more benign acts of voluntary cross-border labour migration far outnumber the acts of organized human trafficking. However, for policy-makers, NGOs and law officials, acts of organized human trafficking and more benign voluntary acts of undocumented labour migration often blur together, as the distinction between the various categories are not clear-cut and up for interpretation.

Conclusion

As these manifestations of the anti-trafficking discourse in the West Kalimantan borderland suggest, globally powerful concepts have been readily employed by Indonesian state authorities in the construction of a security discourse designed to prevent the unauthorized flows of people across their porous land border with Malaysia, and in doing so shore up the territorial sovereignty of both countries.

The main ideal or motive behind counter-trafficking measures in Indonesia, as depicted by the Coordinating Ministry for Social Welfare and relevant international organizations, is to prevent the widespread exploitation and abuse of Indonesian migrant workers, especially vulnerable groups like women and children (Menko Kesra 2005; Sugiarti *et al.* 2006; USAID 2006; Ford and Lyons in this volume). While organized human trafficking and forced labour as described above certainly occur along the length of West Kalimantan's border with Sarawak, such acts are far less common than crossings made by undocumented voluntary labour migrants. However, it is these undocumented migrant workers who suffer most, as they become caught up in the thrust to reassert territorial sovereignty and implement rigid security through the guise of counter-trafficking regimes.

The increased tendency to deal with undocumented labour migration under the heading of 'trafficking' has deeply affected the ability of Indonesian migrant workers, and especially borderlanders, to cross the border and attain much-needed cash income through employment in Sarawak. In part, this response is driven by international pressure on the Indonesian Government to address human trafficking. Increased military patrolling of the border and the harsh treatment meted out to labour migrants have been justified by reference to the global discourse of anti-trafficking. However, in rural West Kalimantan, Indonesian state authorities' adoption of anti-trafficking measures has been as much a strategy to legitimize a stronger Indonesian state presence along the border with Malaysia and display its sovereign power as an attempt to prevent human trafficking.

This return to the rhetoric of security has a dual purpose, as it did during the New Order regime of Suharto. First, it seeks to reclaim the image of a strong unified state whose power is solidified at the border, hereby countering the strong media and popular criticism of the state as being weak and unable to police its territorial borders. Second, besides being a territorial delimiter, the border is also perceived as a resource frontier in need of colonization, in the sense that the adjoining borderlands still contains large patches of what in government policy narratives are designated 'waste' or 'idle' lands to be readily exploited for agricultural development. As mentioned in the quotation by President Susilo Bambang Yudhoyono at the beginning of this chapter, one purpose of these grand development plans is to domesticate the border population by eradicating poverty, discouraging borderlanders' economic and social orientation towards East Malaysia, and increasing their sense of national consciousness. But despite promises of hundreds of thousands of local jobs, the borderland is still largely devoid of employment opportunities. For now, then, the state security and development discourse – as exemplified through anti-trafficking initiatives – only has a negative impact on local livelihood strategies.

Notes

1 Various kinds of plantation developments such as oil palm were identified as suitable initiatives (Potter 2009).
2 This chapter is based on field research conducted during multiple visits to the West Kalimantan borderlands, funded by grants from Aarhus University (2002–3) and the Danish Research Council for Development Research (2007). The conclusions drawn in this chapter are those of the author and not the funding institutions.
3 In August 2005, the Minister of Forestry addressed a letter to the Minister of Agriculture concerning oil palm plantations in the border area and requested that the Agricultural Ministry remember that large parts of the border area were set aside for conservation purposes and forestry cultivation. In October 2005, the Minister of Agriculture accepted that only 180,000 ha (not 1.8 million ha) along the border were actually suitable for oil palm plantations (Wakker 2006) and in December the Directorate General of Spatial Planning acknowledged the need to reconsider the environmental impact when developing spatial planning for the Kalimantan border (DJPR 2005). Despite not being implemented in its original grand form, an Indonesian–Malaysian agricultural corridor along the border is still on the government agenda (Departemen Pertanian 2009).
4 Statements by high ranking military generals, as well as the military's past and current business interests, indicate that there is more at stake for the military than security issues. Several commentators claim that the military build-up in the border area is more about reclaiming a share of the revenues lost during the early days of decentralization from further timber harvesting and oil palm plantations than dealing with illegal activities threatening national security (Wakker 2006; WALHI 2007).
5 These Tentara Lintas Batas (border soldiers) are locally known as the LIBAS (*Pontianak Post* 2006).
6 The link between discourses of security and migration (read human trafficking) is by no means limited to the Indonesian–Malaysian border. Throughout Asia discourses of

anti-trafficking and illegal migration are used by nation-states to justify securitization policies, see for example (Curley 2008).

7 Several recent incidents of mistreatment or abuse of Indonesian migrant workers by their Malaysian employers have accentuated this tension (*Jakarta Globe* 2009c).

8 Undocumented labour migration is just one of many border issues. Indonesia and Malaysia have for long been disputing their shared sea and land borders, nearly leading to open conflict. For example at the 14th summit of the Association of Southeast Asian Nations (ASEAN) in April 2009 one of the main discussions was related to issues of border security especially disputes between Indonesia and Malaysia (*Jakarta Post* 2009a).

9 Aisyiah is the women's wing of the large Muhammadiyah organization and their aid to trafficking victims involves a focus on Islamic values.

10 For details of the projects run nationally and in other borderlands by the American Center for International Labor Solidarity and the International Catholic Migration Commission, see Ford and Lyons in this volume.

11 The estimated per capita income in the West Kalimantan border areas is approximately US\$300–400 per annum, while across the border in Sarawak, Malaysia it is US\$4,000–7,000 per annum (*Jakarta Post* 2009e).

12 For a discussion of other kinds of illegal cross-border activities such as contraband smuggling, see Wadley and Eilenberg (2005, 2006).

13 Other labour migrants end up in the service or entertainment industry or are employed as domestic workers.

14 For details of similar arrangements along other parts of the Kalimantan border, see Idrus (2010).

15 This pattern of kinship-mediated labour migration is by no means unique to this part of the border. Similar configurations can be seen among borderland populations along the entire length of this Indonesian–Malaysia land border (Bala 2001; Ardhana *et al.* 2004; Amster 2005; Eghenter 2007; Ishikawa 2010) and elsewhere in Southeast Asia (Horstmann 2006; Klanarong 2009).

16 The authorities' tougher handling of undocumented migrants and their Malaysian mediators has resulted in Sarawak borderlanders becoming more cautious and less willing to help their ethnic kin in Kalimantan to find jobs. If found guilty of assisting illegal migrants, Malaysian citizens can expect to be fined MYR 50,000 for each person assisted and caned six times in public or jailed for up to five years. Undocumented labour migrants can expect fines up to MYR 10,000 (*Jakarta Post* 2004).

17 Five economic growth centres were also selected in the neighbouring province of East Kalimantan.

References

Agustiar, M. (2000) 'Indonesian workers in Sarawak: The direction of the daily commuting workers via the Entikong-Tebedu border post', in Leigh, M. (ed.) *Language, Management and Tourism. Borneo 2000. Proceedings of the Sixth Biennial Borneo Research Conference*, Kuching University Malaysia.

Amster, M. (2005) 'Cross-border marriage in the Kelabit Highlands of Borneo', *Anthropological Forum*, 15 (2): 131–50.

Antara (2007) 'Indonesia-Malaysia bangun 40 pos perbatasan', 15 June.

—— (2008) 'PBB undang Gubernur Kalbar terkait human trafficking', 5 May.

Ardhana, I. K., Langub, J. and Chew, D. (2004) 'Borders of kinship and ethnicity: Cross-border relations between the Kelalan Valley, Sarawak, and the Bawan Valley, East Kalimantan', *Borneo Research Bulletin*, 35: 144–79.

Bala, P. (2001) 'Interethnic ties along the Kalimantan-Sarawak border: The Kelabit and Lun Berian in the Kelabit-Kerayan highlands', *Borneo Research Bulletin,* 32: 103–11.

Bappenas (2003) *Strategi dan Model Pengembangan Wilayah Perbatasan Kalimantan,* Jakarta: Kementerian Perencanaan Pembangunan Nasional, Badan Perencanaan Pembangunan Nasional.

—— (2006a) *Buku Utama Rencana Induk Pengelolaan Perbatasan Negara,* Jakarta: Kementerian Perencanaan Pembangunan Nasional, Badan Perencanaan Pembangunan Nasional.

—— (2006b) *Rencana Induk Pengelolaan Perbatasan Negara: Buku Rinci di Provinsi Kalimantan Barat (Draft Akhir),* Jakarta: Kementerian Perencanaan Pembangunan Nasional, Badan Perencanaan Pembangunan Nasional.

Berita TNI (2006) 'Panglima TNI: Tidak ada alasan tolak pembangunan perbatasan', 23 March.

Bernama (2008) 'Malaysia-Indonesia agree to step up border security to check cross border crimes', 11 December.

BNP2TKI (2008) *2.038 TKI Ilegal Dideportasi dari Sarawak ke Entikong,* Jakarta: Badan Nasional Penempatan dan Perlindungan Tenaga Kerja Indonesia, BNP2TKI.

Borneo Tribune (2009) 'Perbatasan rentan trafficking', 23 November.

BP2AMKB (2010) *Perdagangan Orang Terutama Perempuan & Anak di Kalimantan Barat,* Pontianak: Badan Pemberdayaan Perempuan, Anak, Masyarakat dan Keluarga Berencana, Provinsi Kalimantan Barat.

Curley, Melissa and Wong Siu-Lun (2008) *Security and Migration in Asia: The Dynamics of Securitization,* Routledge: New York.

Departemen Pertanian (2009) *Pedoman Teknis Pengendalian Lahan Pertanian di Wilayah Perbatasan,* Jakarta: Direktorat Pengelolaan Lahan, Direktorat Jenderal Pengelolaan Lahan Dan Air, Departemen Pertanian.

DJPR (2003) *Spatial Policy and Development of the Kalimantan-Sarawak-Sabah Border Area,* Jakarta: Direktorat Jenderal Penataan Ruang, Departmen Pemukian dan Prasana Wilayah.

—— (2005) *Strategi Perwujudan Rencana Tata Ruang Pulau Kalimantan Dalam Rangka Menunjang Pelaksanaan Program Heart of Borneo,* Jakarta: Direktorat Jenderal Penataan Ruang.

Eghenter, C. (2007) 'Of negotiable boundaries and fixed lines in Borneo: Practices and views of the border in the Apo Kayan Region of East Kalimantan', *Moussons,* 11: 133–50.

Eilenberg, M. and Wadley, R. L. (2009) 'Borderland livelihood strategies: The socio-economic significance of ethnicity in cross-border labour migration, West Kalimantan, Indonesia', *Asia Pacific Viewpoint,* 50 (1): 58–73.

Equator News (2005) 'Jalan tikus perbatasan pun diintai Densus 88', 15 November.

—— (2006) 'M'Sia masih ogah buka PLB Badau', 18 September.

—— (2007a) 'Badau dipersiapkan jadi kawasan agropolitan', 20 November.

—— (2007b) 'Bangun industri mega di perbatasan', 21 February.

—— (2007c) 'Keppres perbatasan masih dibahas', 25 February.

—— (2008) 'Kesepakatan pembangunan Lanud Putussibau diteken', 7 August.

—— (2009) 'TNI siap amankan perbatasan', 24 March.

—— (2010) 'Entikong jalur paling rawan trafficking', 21 June.

Fariastuti (2002) 'Mobility of people and goods across the border of West Kalimantan and Sarawak', *Antropologi Indonesia,* 67: 94–104.

Ford, M. (2006) 'After Nunukan: The regulation of Indonesian migration to Malaysia', in

Kaur, A. and Metcalf, I. (eds) *Mobility, Labour Migration and Border Controls in Asia*, Hampshire: Palgrave Macmillan, pp. 228–47.

Hamid, Mukti, S. H. and Widianto, T. (2001) *Kawasan Perbatasan Kalimantan: Permasalahan dan Konsep Pengembangan*, Jakarta: Pusat Pengkajian Kebijakan Teknologi Pengembangan Wilayah – BPPT.

Harian Berkat (2009) 'Puring Kencana bergabung Malaysia?', 6 March.

Horstmann, A. (2006) 'Deconstructing citizenship from the border: Dual ethnic minorities and local reworking of citizenship at the Thailand-Malaysian frontier', in Horstmann, A. and Wadley, R. L. (eds) *Centering the Margin: Agency and Narrative in Southeast Asian Borderlands*, New York: Berghahn Books, pp. 155–76.

Idrus, N. (2008) 'Makkunrai passimokolo': Bugis migrant women workers in Malaysia', in Ford, M. and Parker, L. (eds) *Women and Work in Indonesia*, New York: Routledge, pp. 155–73.

—— (2010) 'Passports optional', *Inside Indonesia*, 100, April–June.

Ishikawa, N. (2010) *Between Frontiers: Nation and Identity in a Southeast Asian Borderland*, Ohio: Ohio University Press.

Jakarta Globe (2009a) 'Plan to develop Kalimantan border proposed', 4 February.

—— (2009b) 'Sex traders use violence, kidnapping', 23 January.

—— (2009c) 'The misery of Indonesia's migrant workers', 19 August.

Jakarta Post (2004) 'Delicate problems in Indonesia-Malaysia ties', 31 May.

—— (2005a) 'Military wants battalions in border areas', 8 August.

—— (2005b) 'Government plans world's largest oil palm plantation', 18 June.

—— (2008a) 'Economic development key to RI border improvements', 28 February.

—— (2008b) 'President calls for better border area', 8 September.

—— (2008c) 'RI, M'sia sign deal on border control', 12 December.

—— (2008d) 'Malaysia to hire less Indonesians as it slips into economic slowdown', 5 December.

—— (2008e) 'Weak security sees smuggling along RI-Malaysia borders', 25 February.

—— (2009a) 'ASEAN gears up to build security community', 2 March.

—— (2009b) 'Development stalls along border areas as government offices struggle with management', 29 May.

—— (2009c) 'Nine women fall victim to human trafficking in West Kalimantan', 21 February.

—— (2009d) 'Pontianak court sentences free human trafficking suspects', 25 February.

—— (2009e) 'Most people along border areas "live in poverty"', 17 February.

Kepgub (2009) *Pembentukan Pusat Pelayanan Terpadu Pemberdayaan Perempuan dan Anak (P2TP2A)*, Pontianak: Keputusan Gubernur Kalimantan Barat No. 370.

—— (2010) *Pembentukan Tim Koordinasi Penanggulangan, Penempatan, dan Perlindungan Tenaga Kerja Indonesia (TKI) Bermasalah di Luar Negeri Provinsi Kalimantan Barat*, Pontianak: Keputusan Gubernur Kalimantan Barat No. 22.

Keppres (1994) *Badan Pengendali Pembangunan Kawasan Perbatasan*, Jakarta: Keputusan Presiden Republik Indonesia No. 44.

—— (2003) *Penataan Ruang Kawasan Perbatasan Kalimantan, Sarawak Dan Sabah. Keputusan President Republik Indonesia, Draf Ke-7*, Jakarta: Direktorat Jenderal Penataan Ruang.

Klanarong, N. (2009) 'Border crossing of Muslim women in southern-border provinces of Thailand', *Asia Pacific Viewpoint*, 50 (1): 74–87.

Kompas (2002) 'Pos lintas batas Badau dibangun', 22 April.

Liow, J. (2003) 'Malaysia's illegal Indonesian migrant labour problem: In search of solutions', *Contemporary Southeast Asia: A Journal of International & Strategic Affairs*, 25 (1): 44–64.

Media Indonesia (2008) 'Wilayah perbatasan: Kebutuhan hidup dan nasionalisme', 2 June.

Menko Kesra (2005) *Penghapusan Perdagangan Orang di Indonesia Tahun 2004–2005*, Jakarta, Kementerian Koordinator Bidang Kesejahteraan Rakyat.

Perda (2007) *Pencegahan dan Pemberantasan Perdagangan Orang Terutama Perempuan dan Anak*, Pontianak: Peraturan Daerah Provinsi Kalimantan Barat No. 7.

—— (2010) *Rencana Aksi Daerah Penghapusan Perdagangan Perempuan dan Anak*, Pontianak: Peraturan Daerah Provinsi Kalimantan Barat No. 5.

Perpres (2005a) *Rencana Pembangunan Jangka Menengah 2005–2009*, Jakarta: Peraturan Presiden Republik Indonesia, Perpres, No. 7.

—— (2005b) *Rencana Tata Ruang Kawasan Perbatasan Negara di Kalimantan*, Jakarta: Peraturan President Republik Indonesia, Draft KE-14, Direktorat Jenderal Penataan Ruang.

PKB (2005) 'Jumpa pers bersama president RI, Susilo Bambang Yudhoyono', *Berita Pemerintah Kalimantan Barat*, 24 June.

Pontianak Post (2004) 'PLB dibuka, illegal logging kian menggila difasilitasi oleh pengusaha Malaysia', 24 June.

—— (2005) 'Buka lahan sawit sepanjang perbatasan: Strategi baru amankan batas Malaysia-Kalimantan', 10 May.

—— (2006) 'TNI tempatkan 600 personil: Jaga sepanjang perbatasan Kalbar', 2 August.

—— (2007) 'TNI AD kaji skuadron heli di perbatasan', 7 March.

—— (2009a) 'Kalbar urutan tiga potensi trafficking', 22 January.

—— (2009b) 'Pengamanan perbatasan', 1 December.

—— (2009c) 'Polres Sanggau ungkap 33 kasus trafficking', 6 April.

—— (2009d) 'Trafficking dan KDRT masih tinggi', 27 February.

Potter, L. (2009) 'Resource periphery, corridor, heartland: Contesting land use in the Kalimantan/Malaysia borderlands', *Asia Pacific Viewpoint*, 50 (1): 88–106.

Republika (2009) 'Kasus trafficking lewat Entikong turun 40 persen', 7 June.

Sinar Harapan (2003) 'PPLB Badau dirampungkan tahun 2004', 12 May.

Suara Karya (2005) 'Pemerintah akan bangun perbatasan', 23 June.

Sugiarti, K., Davis, J. and Dasgupta, A. (eds) (2006) *When They Were Sold: Trafficking of Women and Girls in 15 Provinces of Indonesia*, International Catholic Migration Commission/American Center for International Labor Solidarity, Jakarta.

Tirtosudarmo, R. (2002) 'West Kalimantan as "Border area": A political-demography perspective', *Antropologi Indonesia*, special volume: 1–14.

USAID (2006) *Anti-Trafficking Technical Assistance: Indonesian Analysis of United States Government Funded Anti-Trafficking Activities*, Washington, DC: United States Agency for International Development (USAID), 6–21 February.

Wadley, R. L. and Eilenberg, M. (2005) 'Autonomy, identity, and "illegal" logging in the borderland of West Kalimantan, Indonesia', *Asia Pacific Journal of Anthropology*, 6 (1): 19–34.

—— (2006) 'Vigilantes and gangsters in the borderland of West Kalimantan, Indonesia', in Horstmann, A. (ed.) *State, People and Borders in Southeast Asia*: A Special Issue of the *Kyoto Review of Southeast Asia*, 7: 1–24.

Wakker, E. (2006) *The Kalimantan Border Oil Palm Mega-Project*, Amsterdam, AIDEnvironment.

WALHI (2007) 'There is still military in the forest', *Indonesian Forum for Environment (WALHI)*, 27 June.

7 Exploitation and escape

Journeys across the Burma–Thailand frontier

Nicholas Farrelly

Along the Burma–Thailand border, through official channels or via countless informal paths, efforts to escape from the difficulties of life in Burma are ongoing.[1] In many individual stories, obvious push factors such as war and poverty are combined with the groaning boredom, educational void and incessant petty hassles that dictate life for Burma's non-elite citizens. Those who flee these familiar hardships are confronted by a new language, culture and economy. Few receive a warm welcome on the Thai side of the border and most find they are forced to survive at the bottom of a stark social and political hierarchy, often under conditions far from the comfortable life that they may have originally imagined. As *bama* (Thai for Burmese) they are generally regarded as a dispensable and temporary imposition.[2]

Every Thai city and many Thai towns and villages now host parts of this Burmese population – a semi-regulated labour force undertaking the dirty, dangerous and demeaning jobs that few Thais actively seek out. Thailand has now accumulated around two million Burmese migrants (Caouette and Pack 2002: 1), although nobody can be sure of the precise number.[3] In Burma's Shan, Karenni, Karen and Mon States, as well as the Kachin State and the Burman-majority Divisions/Regions, countless families have stories of migration: of chance, fortune and, sometimes, calamity. Their individual agency and aspirations combine in a collective search for futures outside the economic and political stalemates that have festered under Myanmar Government military rule.[4]

The scale of this collective migration, the most extensive in mainland Southeast Asia, has attracted significant and consistent scholarly attention from a range of disciplines. Studies of migrant health (Leiter *et al.* 2006; Voravit 2008), and particularly HIV-AIDS (Kriengkrai 2002; Mullany *et al.* 2003; Ford and Aphichat 2007; Saether *et al.* 2007), but also mental health (Cardozo *et al.* 2004), have predominated. There are many studies that dwell on the particular circumstances of refugees living along the Burma–Thailand border (e.g. Dudley 1999; Brees 2008; Oh and van der Stouwe 2008). Other contributions focus explicitly on labour (Darunee 2001; Pim 2001; Arnold and Hewison 2005), with some examining the perennial topic of the sex industry, particularly in the context of human trafficking (Pimpawun *et al.* 2006). On the emotive issue of human trafficking, the most valuable analyses, such as Feingold (2005), challenge prevailing expectations of migrant lifestyles, choices and risks, and also of opportunism and victimhood. Such critical exploration serves to highlight the interaction of regulatory apparatuses and migrant aspirations. However, there have been only very general efforts to examine how human trafficking interacts with the much broader context of large-scale, semi-regulated migration among scholars of the Burma–Thailand border region.

Human trafficking occurs despite frameworks of law and policy which are designed to limit opportunities for the exploitation of migrants.[5] Through a range of national legal instruments, and with international support, the Governments of Thailand and Myanmar have come to publicly embrace opportunities to implement counter-trafficking measures. But not every Burmese migrant is trafficked, nor are all trafficked migrants exploited. It is thus possible to suggest that the human trafficking counter-measures of the Thai and Myanmar Governments are misaligned with the continuum of migration outcomes that constitutes the realities of such large-scale migration. It is the ambiguous interaction of migrant categorizations, economic imperatives and anti-trafficking policies that shapes my analysis.

As Larsen (2010: 1) argues, human trafficking 'occurs within the context of high levels of people movement (particularly undocumented), which are primarily driven by the desire for greater economic opportunity and a better quality of life'. These are precisely the circumstances for the majority of Burmese in Thailand, whose migration outcomes usefully illustrate the continuum of exploitation and escape that best explains the interlocking categories of opportunistic labour migrant and victim of trafficking. This is a continuum that ranges from occasional migrant successes (those who escape); to the countless stories of ordinary labouring hardships and personal toil; to those relatively rare cases where Burmese experience genuine human rights abuses and where prosecutable forms of exploitation occur.

This chapter seeks to interrogate the potency of the global anti-trafficking framework as it applies to the Burma–Thailand border region. First, I explore issues of context and categories with respect to the journeys that migrants make across the border and describe the routinization of Burmese migrant journeys, in order to demonstrate that what motivates vast numbers of semi-regulated Burmese migrants to Thailand is the chance to escape their limited opportunities at home. I then examine how Thai and Myanmar Governments have sought to manage the 'problem' of cross-border trafficking and migration in this wider context of the regional political economy. By doing so, I show how laws for managing the continuum of cross-border movements and exploitative labour practices are designed to deal with some criminal activities without threatening the flow of cheap labour.

The chapter argues that while some migrants undoubtedly experience the kinds of exploitation targeted by national and international counter-trafficking efforts, there are in fact many cases where clear distinctions between migration and trafficking are impossible to maintain. Indeed, as Leiter *et al.* (2006: 96) have asserted, 'cross-border migration from Burma to Thailand is best understood in the context of the many Burmese heading to Thailand as refugees, asylum or voluntary, irregular migrants, with trafficking across borders being 'frequent'. This suggests that, rather than being uncritically labelled as ...ces of human trafficking, Burmese migrant experiences are best plotted (and re-plotted) on a continuum that recognizes the fact that their opportunities are limited not so much by egregious exploitation as by the haphazard regulation of regional labour flows.

Making the journey: context and categories

Almost 20 years ago human rights advocates identified human trafficking across the Burma–Thailand border as 'a modern form of slavery' (Asia Watch and the Women's Rights Project 1993: cover). Their observations, which highlighted the most horrific examples of abuse, set the tone for much subsequent commentary on trafficking in Southeast Asia.[6] Criminal enterprises do profit from the exploitation of migrants who seek better opportunities in Thailand. However, as Molland (2010: 213, 225) has argued in his critique of counter-trafficking discourses as they relate to the Laos–Thailand border region, 'the distinction between trafficking and voluntary migration, which is so important to anti-trafficking programs, does not resonate easily' in situations where facilitators of cross-border labour markets are heterogeneous, and their actions motivated by social practice as well as profit. As this suggests, much of what is described as 'human trafficking' simply does not exhibit all the characteristics that the term implies, among them 'that labour migration is non-consensual; that borders are significant in shaping labour migration flows; and that trafficking is operated by organised crime groups' (Molland 2010: 213).

This is not to underplay the injustices, inequities and exploitation experienced by so many Burmese in Thailand.[7] The life of the migrant worker involves a level of vulnerability that would not be accepted in any other part of Thai society. However, it is equally important to recognize that those who find themselves vulnerable have the capacity to formulate strategies – through trafficking and other migration networks – to make relatively smooth transitions to employment, albeit usually illegal, in Thailand. Talking to migrants, it becomes clear that their ultimate goal may even lie elsewhere, with some travelling onwards to Malaysia or Singapore, or further afield. A lucky minority will receive valuable endorsements to travel, study or work in Western democracies, particularly in desirable English-speaking countries like the United States, United Kingdom or Australia. In many of these cases, human trafficking networks, with varying degrees of sophistication, will help to facilitate their journeys.

Those migrants who are able – through happenstance, or perhaps preparedness, savvy and resilience – to escape from Burma without experiencing grave exploitation are often frustrated by poor pay and conditions and commonly describe their lives in Thailand as 'tough', 'boring', 'fine enough', 'crazy' or 'problematic'. While they grumble, most recognize that such conditions are not the equivalent of slavery. Without seeking to trivialize the dangers and exploitation that some face, it is the prospects of an imagined 'better life' that inspires those who are prepared to risk their savings and survival for a chance to work in Thailand. Some have dramatic explanations – their home village may have been attacked by the Myanmar armed forces or they may have been explicitly targeted for political persecution – but for most migrants the justifications for leaving Burma are more mundane. The immediate goal is often to merely escape the familiar challenges that they have faced in one of Asia's least developed countries.[8] The choice is often stark: deadening under-employment in Burma, military conscription or domestic labour migration to Burma's few sites of large-scale employment, such as Naypyidaw, Yangon or the mines of the north. As a result, many make their journeys even after reports of difficulties filter back to aspiring migrants at home.

These primarily economic migrants are variously described as 'legal migrants', 'undocumented labour', 'refugees', 'illegal workers', 'asylum seekers', 'stateless peoples' and 'victims of trafficking'. There is confusion about precisely which categories deserve priority. Overlapping and blurred boundaries between those who are 'trafficked', 'smuggled' or who travel 'independently' intersect with those between migrant workers, refugees and the many other kinds of people who find themselves crossing the Burma–Thailand frontier.[9] So while an individual may consider herself to be an economic migrant, in the sense that her key ambition is to find well-remunerated employment in Thailand, she may have recently survived as an internally displaced person in Burma and possess a personal story of well-founded fear of political persecution that would meet the criteria for a strong refugee claim. If this Burmese migrant is then smuggled to Bangkok by a family friend who takes her to work in a factory with poor conditions and bad pay, has she been 'trafficked'? What if she finds work in Thailand's commercial sex industry?

Some commentators on Burma–Thailand border dynamics address this complexity by establishing a distinction between 'immigrant workers' and 'political refugees' (Supang and Ratchada 2010: 303). This distinction is problematic because the Thai and Myanmar Governments are not signatories to the 1951 United Nations Convention Relating to the Status of Refugees. Burmese may be processed and identified as refugees by the UNHCR in one of the camps along the Thai side of the border. But since refugee claims often take years to be processed, many who may otherwise make a claim for asylum opt instead to seek out employment in Thailand. Banki and Lang (2008: 59–60) argue that it is unwise to distinguish Burmese in Thailand based on their supposed political or economic status. They claim that 'there is value in analysing displaced populations as a single entity with separate but interrelated parts'. And those parts, whether publicly presented as 'political' or 'economic', are intimately linked to a much broader set of realities in the Burma–Thailand borderlands. More detailed discussions of migrant journeys to Thailand, and the resulting opportunities for work, may be one way to help blur the unhelpful distinctions that some still prefer to make.

Routine journeys, ordinary work

Journeys between Burma and Thailand are often quick and seamless; opportunities for unregulated crossings between the two countries are entirely commonplace. As

Clarke (2009: 1069) explains, '[c]rossing the border is more like moving from one town into another, rather than crossing an international frontier'. The routinization of the Burma–Thailand migration system has ensured that it is now a simple journey between the countries. The Burma–Thailand border meanders for over 2,000 kilometres and there are many places where crossings occur. Well-developed routes from the rest of Burma into Mon and Karen States and Taninthayi Division, and then into Thailand, operate alongside the more northerly routes through the Shan State. Burmese routinely cross the border, even on a daily basis, for work or to access services like health care.

The most significant gateways for Burmese migrant workers are the Thai towns of Ranong, Three Pagodas Pass, Mae Sot and Mae Sai (Figure 7.1). The stately border posts at Tachilek-Mae Sai and Myawaddy-Mae Sot are prestige sites for both the Myanmar and Thai Governments. These sprawling urban centres signify long-term government efforts to control the Burma–Thailand border region. In both cases, they are built adjacent to zones of significant civil conflict and, in the case of Myawaddy-Mae Sot, fighting between ethnic Karen armies and Myanmar Government forces is on-going. The border posts in these sensitive areas are marked by all of the pomp and status of major regional centres, with full complements of township-level political, economic and cultural institutions. Notwithstanding the significant investments in the surveillance of the immediate vicinity of the official border checkpoints, large numbers of Burmese cross illegally each day. At the bridge between Mae Sai and Tachilek, children are particularly brazen in their circumvention of border formalities. They are joined by all manner of smugglers, migrants and other opportunists. Those who are prepared to take a small risk can easily get around the physical border fortifications. In the dry season, illegal border hopping between Tachilek and Mae Sai is even more straightforward as the modest stream which flows between Burma and Thailand can be crossed on foot. The Thai soldiers, security agents and police stationed at the various crossings are generally unconcerned by flows of undocumented human traffic.

However, the simplicity of an undocumented cross-border incursion is not the only factor that a prospective migrant needs to consider. If their goal is to journey past the immediate border region, perhaps to cities like Chiang Mai or Bangkok, then more attention to organization is required. For some migrants, fees may need to be paid to get to Thailand or, more importantly, to travel onwards to places of employment. For amounts ranging from 2,000 to 15,000 baht[10] it is possible to enlist the assistance of brokers and middlemen, often working in collaboration with both the Myanmar military and relevant local armed groups, and then with Thai authorities or influential elements (*phu mi ittiphon*) who can facilitate transportation and the 'permissions' required to travel the chosen migration route. The goal for some migrants might be a big city where they can attempt to disappear, but in other cases it will be the factories of the east, the farms of the central plains, or the brothels, fishing fleets, rubber plantations and resorts of the south. There are also those migrants from Burma who have ambitions to travel to Malaysia and Singapore or beyond. For those who cannot afford to pay the fees, the costs of any journey could prove higher with subsequent demands for the repayment of large

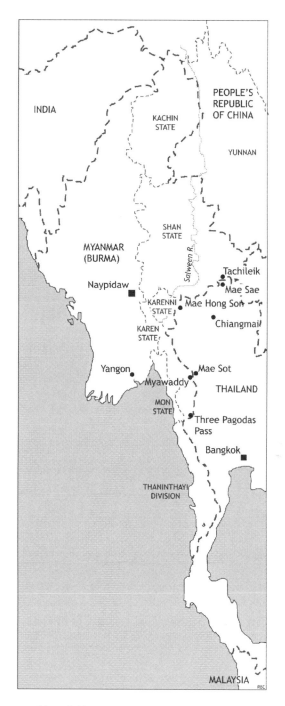

Figure 7.1 Burma and its neighbours

'debts' calculated, reportedly, on a judgement about the earning potential of the migrant. Such a debt may be a factor of the perceived profitability associated with a migrant's labour or it may, instead, be an arbitrary amount designed to guarantee their bondage.

Even those who pay their own way across the border are not guaranteed a successful journey. Stories abound of migrants being arrested by the Thai authorities immediately after purchasing their onwards transport. One young migrant told me of his disgust at being rounded up after paying 8,000 baht to a broker who promised to find him work in Bangkok. He only made it '500 metres from the bridge into Thailand' before the Thai police arrested him. He was promptly deported back to Burma and, even years later, the ignominy of the arrest was an obvious source of frustration. He later returned to Thailand and made enough money to start a small business in his home town. In his words, his initial arrest was just 'unlucky'. Such impressions are relatively common among migrants who identify the arbitrariness and confusion of law enforcement as a crucial, if sometimes unseen, component of their migrations and subsequent working lives.[11] To be arrested and deported is – as I have been told many times – 'inevitable' for the many Burmese who make the journey into Thailand.[12] Migrants on buses and trains are particularly susceptible to being targeted for arrest. The most effective brokers and facilitators have other conveyances – everything from mini-vans to river boats – for sneaking their human cargoes past the many Thai police checkpoints.

Once in Thailand migrants are put to work. The Thai economy reaps the most benefit from the energy and productivity of the Burmese who make the journey. According to one United Nations summary, in 1995 there were only 700,000 migrants in Thailand but by 2005 there were 1,773,349 (Martin 2007). From just over 2 per cent of the labour force the number of migrants rose to constitute 5 per cent in that ten-year period (Martin 2007). Many migrants are not accounted for by these official statistics. However, even conservative estimates of migrant productivity suggest that they contribute around US$8 billion to the economy, approximately 5 per cent of Thailand's gross domestic product (Martin 2007). As these figures suggest, Burmese migrants play an essential economic role. This is in part due to the scarcity of certain types of local labour. Burmese workers are employed to do the dirty, demeaning or dangerous work that most Thais have happily abandoned since the 1980s when a period of unprecedented prosperity began. They find work in construction, prostitution, hospitality, housekeeping, fishing, food processing, garment manufacturing and a range of other jobs. According to Myat Mon (2010: 41), 'fruit farms, flower farms (nurseries), rice farms and chicken producers in the northern region of Thailand are the most intensive users of migrant labour'. There would be significant problems if these workers were forced to abruptly depart. Houses would go uncleaned, fishing fleets unmanned and bridges unbuilt.

In any of these cases the remuneration migrants receive for their work in Thailand is many times more what they would earn in Burma.[13] But the economic roles performed by Burmese migrants have perversely reinforced a range of social, cultural and institutional barriers to their fuller integration. The experiences of exploited migrants in Thailand are often informed by 'underlying racism displayed by many Thais towards Burmese people' (Clarke 2009: 1071). Indeed, according to Myat Mon (2010: 40), they experience 'systematic exploitation in the workplace' that would not be tolerated if they were Thai. Burmese migrants have become 'the new urban poor' and many Thais have come 'to consider them undesirable' (Supang and Ratchada 2010: 319).

Burmese migrants are familiar with the gravest tales of exploitation and abuse. But instead of highlighting the exceptional elements of particular cross-border migrations and tragedies, most emphasize the routine journeys and supposedly ordinary experiences that come with crossing the border to Thailand. They point out that taking up the opportunities that migration offers requires certain skills, and it is an advantage to come from an area near the border. Those who live closest to the Burma–Thailand border even tend to grow up in explicitly multi-lingual environments, and this can be a day-to-day advantage during their time in Thailand.[14] Bilingualism, combined with social networks on both sides of the national frontier, can provide lucrative opportunities not available to those whose homes are far from border areas. In my conversations with experienced migrants, I have learned that access to information, higher levels of formal education, and connections to existing migrants who can help show the way all appear to mitigate the risks that migrants encounter. From these conversations, it is clear that they view the most vulnerable potential migrants as the young and the poor. Such perceptions reinforce the view that young women with no financial support are most 'at risk'. Some ethnic minorities, such as those who come with no prior exposure to the Thai language, are even more likely to face challenges in Thailand (Kajadpai 1997; Pornpimon 2005).

In general terms, however, crossing the border is not considered unduly hazardous. Rather than implying danger, the border between the two countries provides hitherto unforeseen economic opportunities and better personal security and community well-being for many migrants. Escaping Burma is an understandable ambition and the governments of the two countries have become comfortable with most migratory outcomes.

Controlling the 'problem' of human trafficking

The Thai and Myanmar Governments pay little heed to economic migrants unless they come to the attention of the authorities by virtue of their age, gender or some other perceived marker of their innate vulnerability to exploitation. Thai officials recount occasional horror stories but more often reflect on the humorous, even farcical, strategies that Burmese migrants employ to make the best of their limited opportunities. In these conversations it becomes clear that most migrants who are 'trafficked' will never become the subject of official concern.

In part, this is because of the sheer numbers of migrants who are part of various 'irregular migration' and 'trafficking' systems. Grundy-Warr (2004: 230) argues that '[b]y far the overwhelming notion of whole categories of migrants who do not become "regularized" within host state systems is that they constitute a "problem" to be prevented, managed, reduced or eliminated'. Controlling such 'problems' has tended to require greater planning and enforcement capabilities than the Thai and Myanmar Governments can muster. However, the lack of control is also the result of a lack of political will. In the case of Thailand, continued access to inexpensive labour motivates systemic oversights, and even criminal activity, when it comes to Burmese migrants. Indeed, influential networks – reputed to involve senior Thai military, police and political figures, working in conjunction with informal alliances of local gangsters, entrepreneurs and traders – are organized to prevent disruption by law enforcement. For the Myanmar Government, the 'problem' is different but no less profitable or desirable. Migrants who work in Thailand send home remittances that benefit the domestic economy, while officials in border areas have access to income streams from the 'taxes' levied on migrants. With these incentives in mind, the different but sometimes complementary concerns of the two countries can be productively described.

Thailand's response to migrant exploitation

In Thailand, migrants are still sometimes deemed a problem (*panha*) that requires management (*kan borihan*) and improvement (*kan prab pram*). This covers specific issues of concern like the narcotics trafficking undertaken by some migrants and less distinctive claims about amorphous social problems (*panha tang sangkom*). A humanitarian and human rights consciousness among sections of Thai society, including parts of the national bureaucracy, now supports advocacy on behalf of those who suffer most from the perceived abuses that come with crossing borders.[15] However, the standard response to these problems, which include human trafficking (*panha kan kha manut*) and refugees (*panha phu li pay*), has been to devote policing and other resources to disrupting the exploitation of some categories of migrants, particularly women and girls in Thailand's large sexual services industry. Thai activists continue to call for greater awareness of migrant rights and are particularly motivated to eradicate trafficking for the purpose of sexual exploitation.

International pressure has no doubt played a part in generating this response to what Thais now generally describe as 'labour exploitation' (*kod kee kud reed raeng ngan*). Thai authorities accept that some Burmese migrants are trafficked into Thailand under conditions that deserve their attention, or even criminal sanctions. At least a dozen Thai Government agencies are now tasked with managing the issue. Frontline Thai officials almost never fail to imply that many migrants are 'pitiable' (*na song san*) and deserve any compassion that Thailand can muster – though they are also quick to emphasize that the vast majority of migrants travel to Thailand willingly and that once they arrive in Chiang Mai or Bangkok they find life much more pleasant than at home in Burma, even if they are expected to repay a debt. The compassion voiced by some government figures is in part explained by their awareness of just how difficult (*raeng*, literally strong) conditions can be for certain migrants. Some Thai officials voice particular unease about what may happen to women or children who end up at the wrong end of the migration continuum, vulnerable to sexual or other degradations. Nonetheless, and often in the very same breath, Thai officials insist that many, if not the vast majority, of those who migrate from Burma to Thailand are not *technically* trafficked.

That technical assessment is a product of Thai uncertainty about how best to manage the countless undocumented migrants who have made Thailand their home. Since the 1980s, Thai Governments have endorsed inconsistent and incomplete regulatory and law enforcement efforts which swing, sometimes quite radically, between accommodation, classification, formalization, stigmatization and demonization of Burmese workers.[16] Over the years Thailand has steadily built a portfolio of legislative approaches to the exploitation of migrants. Some of the earliest laws used to protect trafficked persons include the Prostitution Prevention and Suppression Act 1996 and the Measures in Prevention and Suppression of Trafficking in Women and Children Act 1997. In both cases the emphasis was on the sexual exploitation of women and children. After a 2004 government directive described the need for a more comprehensive government response to human trafficking, a new legislative instrument, integrating international 'best practice', was prepared.

The Anti-Trafficking in Persons Act 2008 offers a new basis under Thai law for prosecuting those who exploit specific categories of people. Its text suggests that:

Whoever, for the purpose of exploitation, does any of the following acts:

(1) procuring, buying, selling, vending, bringing from or sending to, detaining or confining, harboring, or receiving any person, by means of the threat or use of force, abduction, fraud, deception, abuse of power, or of the giving money or benefits to achieve the consent of a person having control over another person in allowing the offender to exploit the person under his control; or

(2) procuring, buying, selling, vending, bringing from or sending to, detaining or confining, harboring, or receiving a child;

is guilty of trafficking in persons.

(Thai Government 2008: Chapter 1, Section 6)

The most stringent parts of the Act are focused on crimes against children, particularly any under 15 years of age. What this law and its stern penalties (up to 20 years' imprisonment and a fine of 400,000 baht) hide is the fact that abuses of power, and the economic relations that underpin them, have been intrinsic to Thailand's migrant labour-fuelled economy. In the face of the value of migrant labour, the enforcement of the law against human trafficking in Thailand remains a marginal activity.

Thailand was placed on the United States Government's Tier 2 Watch List in the 2010 Trafficking in Persons (TIP) Report. In reports from 2005–2009 it had been ranked as a Tier 2 country. The overall reason provided for this new, and sterner, judgement was that 'the [Thai] government's overall effort to address forced labor and forced prostitution of foreign migrants and Thai citizens did not make adequate progress' (US State Department 2010: 320). That report went on to suggest that:

> While corruption is believed to be widespread within the Thai law enforcement community, the government did not report investigations into any trafficking-related cases. Given the significant scope and magnitude of trafficking in Thailand, there were a low number of convictions for both sex and labor trafficking, and of victims identified among vulnerable populations.
>
> (US State Department 2010: 320)

The report notes the lack of attention to the involvement of corrupt government officials in trafficking and the low number of investigations, prosecutions and convictions under the 2008 Act, suggesting that Thailand could do much better in terms of investigating and successfully prosecuting crimes of human trafficking.[17]

From the perspective of Thai Government agencies one of the reasons for the low level of official activity under the 2008 Act is that a distinction is made between 'human trafficking', which implies exploitation, and 'people smuggling', which is considered to be a less egregious, even benign, form of facilitated mobility. For example, Thailand's Centre against International Human Trafficking highlights the particular distinction between what the Thais call human trafficking (*kan kha manut*) and the less serious issue of people smuggling (*kan lak lob khon phu yay tin than*).[18] According to that analysis, there are differences in terms of consent, purpose of movement, destination, recruitment, customer relationship, knowledge and control, profit and violence. For Thai officials, most Burmese migrants fit uneasily, if at all, into the national framework now applied to human trafficking. These ambiguities help explain Thailand's demotion to the Tier 2 Watch List.

A further challenge for Thai authorities is the wide range of Thai Government agencies that are involved in human trafficking counter-measures. From the Customs, Labour and Immigration departments, to the Border Patrol Police and various provincial-level policing and security agencies, to Thailand's military and intelligence services, no single government voice defines the response to Burmese migrants or human trafficking. In one case it was announced by the government that 'Immigration Police will lead 10 other government agencies responsible for national security and civilian intelligence services in stamping out illegal entry, unlawful employment and human trafficking' (Lubeigt 2007: 180).

Ultimately, as Clarke (2009: 1068) has argued, the enforcement of Thailand's Anti-Trafficking in Persons Act and other laws that deal with trafficking depends largely on local authorities. Yet the anti-trafficking framework and associated policy responses are even less well understood at the local level. Thai officials may sympathize with Burmese migrants who are exploited but they are well aware of why the use of brokers and facilitators is so widespread. In common with other parts of Southeast Asia, 'traffickers' are sometimes family friends or even relatives; categories of people that can be trusted (Molland in this volume). To facilitate their escape many migrants will rely on brokers and middlemen, family and friends, to get them across the border and into remunerated employment. For many Burmese migrants the notion that receiving assistance from family friends for migration could be criminal is difficult to fathom. Instead they have been habituated to see the involvement of such facilitators as a prudent, even essential, form of risk management. Dealing with a range of different political, cultural and economic systems means that expert knowledge on safe and successful migration may often be required. In a study of Shan migrant labourers in Thailand, Voravit Suwanvanichkij (2008) argues that there are many factors, such as 'misunderstanding, language barriers, discrimination, registration costs and other expenses' that have kept Shan migrants from becoming legally documented. But they have managed to find ways to travel to Thailand, to work and survive. Their negotiation of the semi-regulated migratory pathways means that their relative lack of legal documentation is only one part of the story.[19]

The lacklustre efforts of the Thai authorities to use their powers under the 2008 law are the most recent example of two strategic, but largely unspoken, judgements. The first, as noted earlier, is that Thailand needs the cheap labour that Burmese migrants can provide. As a result, Thai officials anticipate an on-going flow of migrants from Burma, some of whom will, they lament, be exploited by criminal or unscrupulous employers. The second strategic judgement is that Thailand does not have the resources to adequately monitor the large numbers of Burmese migrants who arrive in Thailand. The scale of the migration, and its contribution to Thai prosperity, justifies a level of ignorance about how many Burmese live in Thailand, and about exactly how or where they work.

Regulating escape from Burma

Strategic disinterest is also central to the Burmese Government's implementation of its counter-measures on human trafficking. McCabe (2008: 67) argues that '[t]he government of Burma has made little effort to limit human trafficking and restricts the information releases on human trafficking; therefore, the prevalence of human trafficking is unknown'. Burma has, since 2001, been classified by the United States in the bottom rung – a Tier 3 villain in global human trafficking terms. The 2010 TIP Report states that '[t]he government has yet to address the systemic political and economic problems that cause many Burmese to seek employment through both legal and illegal means in neighboring countries, where some become victims of trafficking' (US Department of State 2010: 96). It goes on to suggest that the 'most serious concern' is the rate of human trafficking for forced labour inside the country. The implication of this assessment is that those Burmese who escape to Thailand may, in fact, be avoiding the worst forms of labour exploitation.

Instead of focusing on domestic labour exploitation – which is within its power to mitigate – the Myanmar Government has instead emphasized its Anti-Trafficking in Persons Law, endorsed by the ruling State Peace and Development Council as Law No. 5/2005 and signed by Senior General Than Shwe. The law highlights the threat of the use of force or other forms of coercion – abduction, fraud, deception, abuse of power, and giving or receiving of money or benefit to obtain consent – as integral to the crime of human trafficking (Myanmar Information Committee 2005). It is, in key respects, very similar to Thailand's legislative instrument and reflects a shared international endowment of counter-trafficking regulations. According to a report in the *Myanmar Times*, since the 2005 establishment of the law 443 human trafficking cases have been identified, 1,158 offenders prosecuted, 1,028 trafficking victims rescued, and an additional 821 victims repatriated by other countries (Sann Oo and Yadanar Htun 2010). That report goes on to note that in 2008 a total of US$3 million was spent on anti-trafficking initiatives, split evenly between the Myanmar Government and United Nations agencies.

The fine details of Law No. 5/2005 give an indication of its limited ambitions. The law states that '[w]hoever is guilty of trafficking in persons *especially women, children and youth* shall, on conviction be punished with imprisonment for a term which may extend from a minimum of 10 years to a maximum of imprisonment for life and may also be liable to a fine' (Myanmar Information Committee 2005, emphasis added). It has also been reported that other laws deny passports to women under 26 who plan to travel outside the country without a chaperone (Feingold 2005). This regulation is a response, no doubt, to the large numbers of Burmese women who find themselves working in service, entertainment or sex industries in countries such as Thailand. These are the women who are, in general, most likely to be the target of international human trafficking counter-measures. That a Tier 3 country has sought to emphasize its compliance in this regard is illustrative of the strategic use of such legal provisions. It is pertinent that trafficking crimes against adult males are explicitly downgraded in importance with the minimum sentence for trafficking persons 'other than women, children and youth' being only five years, with a maximum of ten years.[20] The law thus explicitly prioritizes the rights of women, children and youth in ways that reproduce international discourses on trafficking, without necessarily acknowledging the reasons for the original insistence that women and children often need greater protection.

The 2010 TIP Report noted that '[i]n some areas, in particular international sex trafficking of women and girls, the Government of Burma is making significant efforts'. However, the report also strongly emphasized the government's continued use of forced labour, prompting Colonel Sit Aye, head of the Myanmar Police Force's Department Against Transnational Crime, to say that he was 'somewhat discouraged, as we feel that our efforts, the government and also the effort of UN agencies and international organisations, have not been well acknowledged' (Sann Oo and Yadanar Htun 2010).

As a result, according to Pedersen (2008: 223),

> even the most progressive officers . . . are . . . incensed by being singled out for criticism of their record on issues such as drugs and human trafficking, which they feel they have tried hard to address (even if their methods are crude and they lack capacity to launch an effective response).

The problem is that the government appears to limit the use of its human trafficking law to cultivating international endorsement. A Myanmar Government that was committed to protecting the rights of its migrant workers would implement laws to protect them from exploitation with significantly more vigour.

The Myanmar Government's unsuccessful efforts to deflect international opprobrium by attempting to disrupt trafficking inside Burma may, in fact, have empowered local authorities to insist on even more control over sensitive border-crossing activities. Caballero-Anthony (2008: 170), giving perhaps the kindest possible interpretation, argues that the government 'see[s] it as necessary to safeguard the security of Burmese migrants, especially those who are faced with labour exploitation by human traffickers who give false promises of finding local lucrative jobs in other countries'. Burmese migrants present a different interpretation of the motives that inform official regulation in the borderlands, noting that postings to the large border towns offer Myanmar Government officials, both military and civilian, benefit from access to non-salary income, especially generated from illegal activities like undocumented migration. While the protection of the vulnerable must rate as one of their priorities it is also likely that such sympathies are trumped by the need to supplement their very modest government salaries.

What is almost always ignored in government statements is that opportunities to migrate provide a welcome outlet for those Burmese who are frustrated with local economic and political conditions. Allowing these people to leave the country means not only that surplus workers are removed from Burmese society, but as Turnell *et al*. (2008: 18) note, remittances from Burmese migrant workers provide a potential means to improve Burma's economic situation. Since many migrants do send remittances to support the population of Burma that stays at home, they play a significant part in sharing the burden of the government's mismanagement of the economy. It is in the context of these remittances that efforts to reduce human trafficking meet a number of obstacles. Moreover, the fact that those fed up with life in Burma can leave is important from a political perspective, since if they were forced to stay then the government would probably face even more virulent domestic opposition. Allowing semi-regulated flows of labour across the border to Thailand, but also to other countries such as China, is one way that many of the most ambitious young Burmese are taken out of the political equation.[21] At the same time, however, their decision to leave Burma can make them appear suspicious to those who consider all foreign influences potentially treasonous.

Conclusion

Human trafficking along the Burma–Thailand border is inevitably mixed up with the substantial flows of other migrants across a relatively porous international frontier. Those who cross this border illegally, but with a voluntary and reasonably well-informed perspective on their prospects, far outnumber the relatively small number of people who are trafficked. Along a continuum of migration outcomes, where opportunities for exploitation and escape are what matter most, human trafficking marks one extreme. However, it must be considered as part of a portfolio of often unsatisfactory options for those escaping life in Burma and its hardships. Of course, life in Thailand can be difficult but, for many Burmese, it trumps the alternatives of economic decay, civil conflict and political hassles at home.

Meanwhile, both governments benefit from semi-regulated labour migration and have little will, even if they enjoyed the capacity, to end the human trafficking that takes place. Burmese migrants who escape to Thailand buttress the economies of both countries. Under these conditions it is understandable that the vast majority of undocumented or irregular migrant workers are largely ignored. Both countries appear comfortable with the existing level of Burmese migration to Thailand so long as the migrants work hard, avoid undue political agitation and blend anonymously into the background of mainland Southeast Asia's transborder society.

An enduring challenge is to identify and perhaps pre-empt the most egregious forms of exploitation without completely dismissing the functional, even productive, role that some 'traffickers' play in facilitating escape from Burma's economic and political quagmire. The goal of human rights and anti-trafficking campaigners is to focus attention on the egregious violations that occur. But, ultimately, counter-trafficking discourses serve to homogenize the aspirations of these migrants, who cross borders to take advantage of opportunities not available at home. In seeking to escape the hardships of life in Burma some become vulnerable to exploitation. It is an unsatisfactory set of circumstances that drives these migrants to try their luck in Thailand. However, prudent strategies of risk management may, in contravention of laws against human trafficking, require the engagement of facilitators and brokers to smooth the way.

Notes

1 This chapter benefits from field research undertaken in Thailand and Burma for periods of time over the past decade.
2 Burma's population consists of Burman and non-Burman peoples. The Burmans (*bama*) have come to dominate lowland Burma and form the core of the current Myanmar military government. Their majority status in the country is contrasted with the non-Burman ethnic minorities such as the Chin, Karen and Mon. While for the average Thai it is convenient to categorize these people as simply *bama*, for some 'Burmese' in Thailand it is their Shan or Karen ethnicity that is most important. For others, political or military affiliations are more important.
3 Estimates vary quite widely, partly as a product of different regimes of categorization. See for example Bodeker *et al.* (2005) and Brees (2008).
4 In this chapter I use 'Burma' for references to the country and 'Myanmar' for the government.
5 In recent years reports of abuse from former fishermen have become more common. The abuses suffered in that industry are now garnering increasing attention from Thailand's non-government sector. At the same time the regional anti-trafficking discourse has introduced assumptions about the gender or age of trafficked persons that militate against the full support of exploited fishermen.
6 An important example of this genre is from Burmese activist, Ko Myint Wai (2003).
7 Some Burmese migrants experience a relatively easy transition to life in Thailand. I

have occasionally met such migrants who told me they avoided the petty hassles, or more significant obstacles, faced by many of their peers. These individuals appear to be exceptional in key respects.

8 The Human Development Index ranks Burma (Myanmar) 138 out of 182 countries. In Asia only Pakistan, Nepal, Bangladesh, Timor-Leste and Afghanistan rank lower.

9 The difficulty of offering neat categorizations is an issue that has also been thoroughly examined in other Southeast Asian contexts. See for example Ford (2007) and Ford and Lyons (2011: 107–8).

10 This equates to between US$66 and US$495 at the rates prevailing in March 2011.

11 Caouette and Pack (2002: 28–9) collate a range of individual testimonies that highlight the challenges faced by migrants from Burma once they arrive in Thailand.

12 The classic, yet probably often apocryphal, description of a Burmese migrant's interaction with Thai authorities sees them asked to sing the national anthem. I have, on occasion, met current or former Burmese migrants who have belted out a passable version of the song. Some have even claimed that they have 'fooled' Thai authorities into convincing them that they were not Burmese after all.

13 Official wage rates across Thailand vary considerably. The minimum wage in Bangkok is 206 baht per day, and slightly lower in other high income provinces such as Nakorn Pratom, Nonthaburi, Pathum Thani, Samut Sakhon and Phuket. The minimum wage is lowest, just over 150 baht, in many part of the country including the Burma–Thailand border provinces of Tak and Mae Hong Son. Burmese working in the northern city of Chiang Mai can expect between 60–150 baht per day. In Burma, the average yearly wage is only a fraction of what can be enjoyed in Thailand. In Thailand even very low-paying positions in poor parts of the country pay more than twice what Burmese can expect in Burma.

14 The Shan, Kam Muang and Thai languages spoken, for instance, in the border conurbation of Tachilek-Mae Sai are all related.

15 In this region it is not only from Burma that migrants travel, or are trafficked. Thailand receives such illegal overland entrants from its near neighbours, such as Cambodia, Laos and China but also from countries that are more distant. There are many cases where even North Koreans have found their way into Thailand on the overland routes.

16 See Darunee 2001, for the best overview of these issues up to that time.

17 There were only eight confirmed convictions noted in the 2010 TIP Report.

18 Thailand has been somewhat inconsistent in its use of various terms for people smuggling and human trafficking. Relative nonchalance about people smuggling partly reflects the large numbers of Burmese workers, and others, who are brought into the country this way.

19 Ford and Lyons (2011) is especially relevant to this point about the semi-regulation, and official acceptance, of migration in peripheral areas of Southeast Asia.

20 Heavier sentences follow for those involved with 'organized criminal groups'.

21 Some migrants go on to become persistent critics of the military government that they left behind. The northern Thai city of Chiang Mai and the border town of Mae Sot, as two examples, are home to hundreds of exiles from Burma who now confront the Myanmar government with a range of resources and opportunities which they could not access at home. The comparative potency of exiled media organizations based in Thailand, which provide some of the best reporting on conditions inside Burma, are an example of strategic use of the extra political and social space that is available to some migrants.

References

Arnold, D. and Hewison, K. (2005) 'Exploitation in global supply chains: Burmese workers in Mae Sot', *Journal of Contemporary Asia*, 35 (3): 319–40.

Asia Watch and the Women's Rights Project (1993) *A Modern Form of Slavery: Trafficking of Burmese Women and Girls into Brothels in Thailand*, New York: Human Rights Watch.

Banki, S. and Lang, H. (2008) 'Protracted displacement on the Thai-Burmese border: The interrelated search for durable solutions', in Adelman, H. (ed.) *Protracted Displacement in Asia: No Place to Call Home*, London: Ashgate, pp. 59–81.

Beyrer, C. (2001) 'Shan women and girls and the sex industry in Southeast Asia: Political causes and human rights implications', *Social Science & Medicine*, 53 (4): 543–50.

Bodeker, G., Neumann, C., Lall, P. and Zaw Min Oo (2005) 'Traditional medicine use and healthworker training in a refugee setting at the Thai–Burma border', *Journal of Refugee Studies*, 18 (1): 76–99.

Brees, I. (2008) 'Refugee business: Strategies of work on the Thai–Burma border', *Journal of Refugee Studies*, 21 (3): 380–97.

Caballero-Anthony, M. (2008) 'Reflections on managing migration in Southeast Asia: Mitigating the unintended consequences of securitisation', in Curley, M. G. and Wong, S. (eds) *Security and Migration in Asia: The Dynamics of Securitisation*, Abingdon: Routledge, pp. 165–76.

Caouette, T. M. and Pack, M. E. (2002) *Pushing Past the Definitions: Migration from Burma to Thailand*, Refugees International and Open Society Institute.

Cardozo, B. L., Talley, L., Burton, A. and Crawford, C. (2004) 'Karenni refugees living in Thai–Burmese border camps: Traumatic experiences, mental health outcomes, and social functioning', *Social Science & Medicine*, 58 (12): 2637–44.

Cheah, P. Y., Khin Maung Lwin, Phaibun, L., Maelankiri, L., Parker, M., Day, N. P., White, N. J. and Nosten, F. (2010) 'Community engagement on the Thai-Burmese border: Rationales, experience and lessons learnt', *International Health*, 2: 123–9.

Clarke, M. (2009) 'Over the border and under the radar: Can illegal migrants be active citizens?' *Development Practice*, 19 (8): 1064–78.

Darunee Paisanpanichkul (2001) 'Burmese migrant workers in Thailand: Policy and protection', *Legal Issues on Burma Journal*, 10: 39–50.

Dudley, S. (1999) '"Traditional" culture and refugee welfare in north-west Thailand', *Forced Migration Review*, 6: 5–8.

Feingold, D. A. (2005) 'Human trafficking', *Foreign Policy*, 150: 26–32.

Ford, K. and Aphichat Chamrathrithirong (2007) 'Sexual partners and condom use of migrant workers in Thailand', *AIDS and Behavior*, 11 (6): 905–14.

Ford, M. (2007) *Advocacy Responses to Irregular Labour Migration in ASEAN: The Cases of Malaysia and Thailand*, Manila: Migrant Forum in Asia.

Ford, M. and Lyons, L. (2011) 'Travelling the *aspal* route: Grey labour migration through an Indonesian border town', in Aspinall, E. and van Klinken, G. (eds) *The State and Illegality in Indonesia*, Leiden: KITLV, pp. 107–22.

Grundy-Warr, C. (2004) 'The silence and violence of forced migration: The Myanmar-Thailand border', in Ananta, A. and Nuryidya Arifin, E. (eds) *International Migration in Southeast Asia*, Singapore: ISEAS Publications, pp. 228–72.

Kajadpai Burustpat (1997) *Chonklum noi sanchat bama*, Bangkok: Phraepitaya.

Ko, M. W. (2003) *Raeng ngan bamar: Jak raeng ngan tat su raeng ngan tuen*, Palalee Sakulto (translator), Bangkok: Committee for Democracy in Burma.

Kriengkrai Srithanaviboonchai, Choi, K. H., Griensven, F. van, Hudes, E. S., Surasing Visaruratana and Mandel, J. S. (2002) 'HIV-1 in ethnic Shan migrant workers in northern Thailand', *AIDS*, 16 (6): 929–31.

Larsen, J. J. (2010) 'Migration and people trafficking in Southeast Asia', Canberra: Australian Institute of Criminology.

Leiter, K., Voravit Suwanvanichkij, Tamm, I. Iacopino, V. and Beyrer, C. (2006) 'Human rights abuses and vulnerability to HIV/AIDS: The experiences of Burmese women in Thailand', *Health and Human Rights*, 9 (2): 88–111.

Lubeigt, G. (2007) 'Industrial zones in Burma and Burmese labour in Thailand', in Wilson, T. (ed.) *Myanmar: The State Community and the Environment*, Canberra: ANU E Press and Asia Pacific Press, pp. 159–88.

Martin, P. (2007) *The Contribution of Migrant Workers to Thailand: Towards Policy Development*, Bangkok: International Labour Organization.

McCabe, K. A. (2008) *The Trafficking of Persons: National and International Responses*, New York: Peter Lang.

Molland, S. (2010) 'The value of bodies: Deception, helping and profiteering in human trafficking along the Thai-Lao border', *Asian Studies Review*, 34 (2): 211–29.

Mullany, L. C., Maung, C. and Beyrer, C. (2003) 'HIV/AIDS knowledge, attitudes, and practices among Burmese migrant factory workers in Tak Province, Thailand', *AIDS Care*, 15 (1): 63–70.

Myanmar Information Committee (2005) 'Information sheet'. Online document. Available at: http://www.myanmar-information.net/infosheet/2005/050914.htm (accessed 18 November 2010).

Myat Mon (2010) 'Burmese labour migration into Thailand: Governance of migration and labour rights', *Journal of the Asia Pacific Economy*, 15 (1): 33–44.

Oh, S. A. and Stouwe, M. van der (2008) 'Education, diversity, and inclusion in Burmese refugee camps in Thailand', *Comparative Education Review*, 52 (4): 589–617.

Pedersen, M. (2008) *Promoting Human Rights in Burma: A Critique of Western Sanctions Policy*, Lanham, MD: Rowman & Littlefield Publishers.

Pim Koetsawang (2001) *In Search of Sunlight: Burmese Migrant Workers in Thailand*, Bangkok: Orchid Press.

Pimpawun Boonmongkon, Guest, P., Amporn Marddent, and Sanders, S. (2006) 'From trafficking to sex work: Burmese migrants in Thailand', in Blair, T. E. (ed.) *Living on the Edges: Cross-Border Mobility and Sexual Exploitation in the Greater Southeast Asia Sub-Region*, Nakhon Pathom: Southeast Asian Consortium on Gender, Sexuality and Health, pp. 158–223.

Pornpimon Trichot (2005) *Rai paen din: Sen tang jak bama su thai*, Bangkok: Mekong Studies Research Team, Asian Studies Centre, Chulalongkorn University.

Saether, S. T., Usawadee Chawphrae, Maw Maw Zaw, Keizer, C. and Wolffers, I. (2007) 'Migrants' access to antiretroviral therapy in Thailand', *Tropical Medicine & International Health*, 12 (8): 999–1008.

Sann Oo and Yadanar Htun (2010) 'US ignoring progress in human trafficking fight: Police force', *Myanmar Times*, 4 January.

Supang Chantavanich and Jayagupta, R. (2010) 'Immigration to Thailand: The case of migrant workers from Myanmar, Laos, and Cambodia', in Segal, U. A., Elliott, D. and Mayadas, N. S. (eds) *Immigration Worldwide: Politics, Practices, and Trends*, Oxford: Oxford University Press, pp. 303–20.

Thai Government (2008) 'The Anti-Trafficking in Persons Act B.E 2551'. Online document. Available at: http://www.baliprocess.net/files/Thailand/1.%20trafficking_in_persons_act_b.e%202551%20%28eng.%29.pdf (accessed 21 June 2011).

Turnell, S., Vicary, A. and Bradford, W. (2008) 'Migrant worker remittances and Burma: An economic analysis of survey results', Sydney: Burma Economic Watch, Macquarie University.

US Department of State (2010) *Trafficking in Persons Report*, Washington, DC: US Department of State, United States Government.

Voravit Suwanvanichkij (2008) 'Displacement and disease: The Shan exodus and infectious disease implications for Thailand', *Conflict and Health*, 2 (4): 1–5.

8 Discretion and the trafficking-like practices of the Indonesian state

Wayne Palmer

Observers of Indonesia's formal labour export programme claim that trafficking-like practices occur at each stage of the migration process. Many reports single out the actions of recruitment agents for particular attention. For example, the US Trafficking in Persons (TIP) Report states that Indonesia's licensed recruitment agents operate 'similarly to trafficking rings', noting that they 'routinely falsif[y] birth dates, including for children, in order to apply for passports and migrant worker documents' (US Department of State 2009: 159). The United States government also criticizes the fact that these agents keep female recruits in holding centres, sometimes for periods of many months, during which time they are not free to leave. In addition, agents allow women to finance migration through wage deductions after they have been deployed, a practice which the report argues creates situations of debt bondage and forced labour in the countries where they work. Not all of these practices contravene Indonesian law: indeed, post-deployment payment of recruitment fees and the use of holding centres are sanctioned by the state. However, it is clearly illegal to refuse recruits the right to leave those facilities and to falsify their personal data. Yet public officials responsible for monitoring the programme seldom refer evidence of illegality to law enforcement officers, choosing instead to ignore it.

The fact that the Government of Indonesia tolerates illegal behaviour by recruitment agents presents an interesting case for observers seeking to understand the role that states can play in addressing human trafficking. Accusations of state-sanctioned trafficking draw attention to the relationship between the state and illegality. As Heyman and Smart (1999: 1) have noted, 'While the state does not always conspire with crime, it is intriguing to inquire after the conditions under which governments and illegal practices enjoy some variety of symbiosis.' In the context of Indonesia's labour migration programme, the state tolerates illegal practices that help to meet the formal objectives of documenting migrant workers and maximizing deployments.

Close attention to bureaucratic processes reveals that while corruption is clearly a factor that persuades officials to ignore instances of illegality, they also do so as a way of exercising discretion. In Scott's (1997: 36) view, the 'appropriate and legitimate' use of discretion is essential for achieving 'good government'. Discretion allows the state to adapt to developments in ways that rigid rules and the strict enforcement of laws do not (Tremblay 1993: 329). However, as Rose-Ackerman

(1999) argues, improper discretionary regimes – such as instances where the extent of discretion is unknown, or where public officials act beyond the scope of their authority and fail to declare conflicts of interest – can compromise the integrity of public institutions. Many states respond by restricting discretion as part of anti-corruption initiatives. But, as Anechiarico (1996) observes, such efforts can reduce the dynamism of government, limiting the ability of public officials to take context into account when generating responses to particular cases.

This chapter examines the complex relationship between discretion and illegality through the study of an Indonesian Labour Attaché's actions when dealing with migrant workers and 'victims of trafficking'.[1] Labour Attachés are among the very few public officials responsible for enforcing Indonesia's labour recruitment and anti-trafficking laws overseas. They have limited access to established mechanisms for dealing with actions that contravene Indonesian laws, operating as they do within the borders of another country. In addition, their responses are partly guided by the priorities of the Ministry of Manpower, the institution with which they are affiliated in Indonesia. As a result, Labour Attachés in some locations are engaged in complex turf wars with colleagues from other ministries, particularly the Ministry of Foreign Affairs. Where this is the case, an extra layer of complexity is added to an already complicated environment for making decisions about how to best regulate the state migration programme. These factors have partly motivated Labour Attachés to ignore the principles of Indonesia's anti-trafficking framework when dealing with evidence of illegality within the migration processes of citizens working overseas. The following account of how Indonesia came to have anti-trafficking legislation, and how it has been operationalized by various parts of the state in relation to migrant workers, provides the necessary background for an understanding of why this is so.

Indonesia's anti-trafficking law

Indonesia passed Law No. 21/2007 on the Eradication of the Crime of Trafficking in Persons to 'provide a substantive and legal foundation on which to prosecute trafficking' as it is understood by international law (IOM 2009: 17–18). Prior to 2007, only the trade in women and male minors was punishable under the Indonesian Penal Code (Article 297), a situation symptomatic of wider trends in Southeast Asia, where anti-trafficking activities have tended to focus on women, children and sex workers (Piper 2005). Internationally, it has been recognized that victims of trafficking can 'include all people in vulnerable positions, including adult men' (IOM 2009: 17). Pointing to inadequacies in Indonesia's legal framework, lawmakers in the People's Representative Council argued that the state should seriously consider developing a more comprehensive definition of the crime since Indonesia is signatory to the UN Trafficking Protocol, citing Indonesia's obligation to translate the provisions into national law (Dewan Perwakilan Rakyat 2005a).

Analysis of parliamentary documents gives the impression that internal agitators have sought to close gaps in the law, which had allowed instances of trafficking to go unpunished, in an attempt to meet Indonesia's international obligations.

But in fact the drive to seriously consider a new framework came in response to external pressure. Indonesia was placed on Tier 3 of the TIP rankings in 2001 and 2002 for not complying with the minimum standards of the UN Protocol (US Department of State 2001, 2002). Tier 3 countries are subject to sanctions such as the termination of non-humanitarian aid and American opposition to support from international financial institutions (Lindquist and Piper 2007: 146–7; Lyons and Ford 2010: 255). In response, the legislature swiftly passed Law No. 23/2002 on the Protection of Children and the President issued Decree No. 88/2002 on the National Plan to Eradicate Trafficking in Women and Children (Dewan Perwakilan Rakyat 2006a: 323). Indonesia was promoted to Tier 2 for its 'significant effort' to comply (US Department of State 2003: 82). It maintained this position in two consecutive evaluations but was demoted to the Tier 2 Watch List in 2006 for failing 'to provide evidence of increasing efforts to combat trafficking' (US Department of State 2006: 140). The chair of the People's Representative Council reacted by requesting that the President immediately appoint a minister to represent the cabinet in efforts to formulate an anti-trafficking law (Dewan Perwakilan Rakyat 2006d). The bill was ready for the President to sign into law in time for it to be recorded in the 2007 TIP Report, which acknowledged Indonesia's 'significant effort' to comply (US Department of State 2007: 118), and Indonesia was removed from the Watch List.

The US Department of State's decision to apply pressure on Indonesia in 2006 was in part a protest against the fact that lawmakers had failed to pass a 'much-needed anti-trafficking law that [had] been under consideration for three years' (US Department of State 2006: 140). Although the drafting process began in 2002 as part of the National Plan of Action for the Eradication of Trafficking in Women and Children, a bill was not tabled in parliament until 2005. In that year, the draft was ranked thirty-fourth on the 2005–2009 five-year National Legislative agenda, but was raised to twenty-second in recognition of its relative importance compared to other bills. Formal deliberations on the draft did not commence for another year as a result of a struggle within the parliament's committee structure. The General Assembly had initially assigned responsibility for working on the bill to Commission III, which specializes in law, human rights and security, in recognition of the fact that trafficking is a crime that can have transnational dimensions. Commission VIII, which deals with religion, welfare and women's empowerment, lodged a formal protest, claiming that the anti-trafficking bill fell within its jurisdiction because of the widely accepted assumption that victims of trafficking are generally socio-economically disadvantaged women. The resolution resulted in the formation of a Special Committee (*panitia khusus*) made up of members from both commissions in December 2005.

An anti-trafficking bill had been registered with the People's Representative Council as early as July 2005. Despite claims to authorship by lawmakers in Commission VIII, who registered the draft as their initiative (Dewan Perwakilan Rakyat 2005a), the bill had been drafted by officials in the Ministry of Women's Empowerment in close cooperation with the International Organization for Migration (IOM).[2] Both groups of officials then worked together with civil society organizations such as the Pro-Women National Legislation Programme Network to bring the anti-trafficking bill to the attention of the legislature and garner the support of lawmakers from Commission VIII. The Ministry could have submitted the bill to parliament directly, but to do so would have required a cover letter from the President, which can be difficult to obtain. So the Ministry agreed that lawmakers in Commission VIII should claim authorship of the draft to expedite the process, using what bureaucrats refer to as the 'back door' to get bills tabled.[3] Lawmakers received praise for taking initiative, thereby helping to raise their public profiles, and the Ministry was able to ensure that the formal drafting process at least started with its preferred definition of trafficking.

The IOM's collaboration with the Ministry was part of a wider attempt to encourage Southeast Asian governments to adopt anti-trafficking legislation. The IOM has not always been able to achieve policy objectives in Indonesia through direct negotiations with the bureaucracy, which has resisted efforts by the IOM to even enlist the state as a member. In a compromise, the IOM signs cooperation agreements that give it a limited mandate to operate in Indonesian territory (Departemen Luar Negeri 2005: point 195). Indonesian officials who participated in the internal discussion hosted by the State Secretariat claim that membership was rejected because of the cost.[4] A former Ministry of Manpower employee and now senior official in the National Board for the Placement and Protection of Overseas Indonesian Workers claims that decision-makers were concerned that the IOM's definition of trafficking could be applied to the processes of the state migration programme. In any case, the IOM was able to participate in the process for creating anti-trafficking legislation via the parliamentary 'back door' even if the 'front door' was shut because of decision-makers' concerns.

The bill drafted by the IOM in conjunction with the Ministry of Women's Empowerment defined trafficking as a process which can end in exploitation. This part of the definition was retained in the version passed into law, albeit in a slightly modified form (Law 21/2007, Article 1).[5] As a result, practices that 'cause' individuals to become exploited may be treated as trafficking in Indonesia. This element of the trafficking law at least in part reflects the IOM's view that, since 'no person in the world would acquiesce to being exploited', anyone who is exploited must have been coerced at some point (IOM 2009: 26). The same concern underpins the US Department of State's understanding of 'labour trafficking', which it deems to be a form of forced labour extracted by employers who take 'advantage of gaps in law enforcement to exploit vulnerable workers' (US Department of State 2007: 18). These approaches to trafficking are expansions of the UN Anti-Trafficking Protocol, which interprets the crime more narrowly, asserting that there must be evidence that the process was carried out 'for the purpose of exploitation' before victimhood can be established (Article 3a). Critics like the IOM and the US Department of State argue that the UN definition leaves a grey area involving processes that end in exploitation, and in which coercion is not always identifiable. Informal interactions with – and indirect pressure by – these two institutions in Indonesia encouraged the state to identify exploitation as the key element of trafficking.

How the state sees trafficking in Indonesia

There is no widely accepted national understanding of what constitutes the criminal offence of human trafficking in Indonesia. As a result, different parts of the state have different interpretations of what factors make someone a victim of trafficking. Such fragmentation is characteristic of Indonesia, and true of states in the developing world more generally – a fact that has led van Klinken and Barker (2009: 2) to argue that any appearance of 'unity in the state' is an 'ideological image' promoted by the state itself which does not correspond to reality. In the case of human trafficking, the plurality of understandings is due in part to the fact that state institutions have adopted trafficking terminology to talk about particular situations and practices that they have a mandate to deal with. For these reasons, it is of importance to explore a variety of state positions on what trafficking is and who traffickers are before attempting to speak of a national response to the crime.

The Ministry of Women's Empowerment shares a similar understanding of trafficking with the IOM and the US Department of State and was thus only too happy to collaborate on the drafting of the bill. The Ministry's focus on exploitation is partly the product of a core institutional principle, which identifies all women as highly susceptible to abuse (Kementerian Pemberdayaan Perempuan dan Perlindungan Anak 2009). In its view, women face a higher risk of falling into abusive situations because they occupy weak positions in society. Ministry-supported research on women migrating for work through state-sanctioned channels argues that the system does not take account of the precarious position of women that can cause them to acquiesce to exploitation overseas (Naovalitha 2007: 34). Exploitation occurs partly because women are permitted to pay for the cost of recruitment through wage deductions. However, it is also prevalent because women are generally engaged in the informal sector, which is not covered by labour legislation in many destination countries (Ford and Piper 2007). Claims about migrant women's vulnerability feed into a more general position within the Ministry, namely that women are made vulnerable by the failure of states to guard them against practices that make it hard to resist economic, psychological or physical abuse. On this basis, the Ministry immediately classifies women who slip into exploitative work arrangements as a result of the migration process as victims of trafficking (Swasono 2006: xvii).

In the view of the Ministry of Justice and Human Rights, the state itself can contribute to trafficking – a possibility recognized in the UN Anti-Trafficking Protocol (Articles 12, 13 and 13b), but not in the anti-trafficking bill drafted by the Ministry of Women's Empowerment. In a special hearing, the Director-General for Immigration, whose division sits within the Ministry of Justice and Human Rights, argued that any anti-trafficking law should include sanctions for officials who facilitate the crime, pointing to the prevalence of state documents that misstate the names and dates of birth of bearers as incontrovertible evidence of state involvement in trafficking (Dewan Perwakilan Rakyat 2006c). Observers claim that corruption is responsible for the practice (IOM 2010), but the

Director-General also blames the magnitude of the problem on the inability of Indonesia's civil administration system to ensure that identity documents contain accurate data (Dewan Perwakilan Rakyat 2006c). It is common for Indonesian citizens to hold multiple national identity cards and for them to contain conflicting information (Ford and Lyons 2011). Immigration officials have complained to the National Police that it is difficult to reject passport applications using such documents partly because it implies an accusation against colleagues in other parts of the bureaucracy (Kepolisian Negara Republik Indonesia 2009). Evidence indicates that doing so in some locations has resulted in violent confrontations with local administrators.[6] Nevertheless, the Ministry has taken a formal stand against the inclusion of false data in state documents because the practice reduces its capacity to detect victims of trafficking before they leave the country.

By contrast, the Coordinating Ministry for Social Welfare, which coordinates the interdepartmental taskforce that processes and repatriates citizens deported from Malaysia, sees trafficking as a set of practices that denies migrant workers access to labour rights as defined under host law. Senior officials assert that practices that result in irregular migration status are said to be 'almost the same as trafficking' (personal correspondence, 26 June 2009). This is so, they say, because irregular migration status exposes migrant workers to the threat of arrest and detention by host authorities (Kementerian Koordinator Bidang Kesejahteraan Rakyat 2007), thus creating opportunities for employers to impose exploitative conditions on workers. The Ministry is particularly concerned that irregular migrants risk punishment by caning under the Malaysian Immigration Act 1959/63 (Article 3), a punishment referred to by Amnesty International (2010) as 'judiciary-sanctioned torture'. Taskforce reports adopt anti-trafficking language to describe activities understood to contribute to the scale of deportations and describe agents who facilitate labour migration using tourist visas as traffickers because their actions deliberately deprive people of legal rights that they might have otherwise enjoyed overseas and put them at risk of corporal punishment (Kementerian Koordinator Bidang Kesejahteraan Rakyat 2007, 2008).

The Ministry of Manpower and related state agencies also use the anti-trafficking discourse to frame non-procedural methods of recruiting and deploying migrant workers. It deems any facilitated labour migration that takes place without fulfilling the requirements of Law No. 39/2004 on the Placement and Protection of Indonesian Workers Overseas to be illegal. Licensed agents can be fined and imprisoned for misusing recruitment permission, or for deploying migrant workers who fall short of age and education requirements or who do not hold all the necessary documents, including competence certificates, insurance policies and employment contracts (Law 39/2004, Article 103). Government officials in the Ministry use the terms 'non-procedural labour migration' and 'trafficking' interchangeably to describe these practices. Moreover, the National Board for the Placement and Protection of Overseas Indonesian Workers, an institution which should coordinate with the Ministry when deciding policy, warns that non-procedural recruitment practices bear semblance to trafficking and that non-compliers could face sanctions under the anti-trafficking law (Badan Nasional

Penempatan dan Perlindungan Tenaga Kerja Indonesia 2008). This migration approach 'situates trafficking within the broader phenomenon of irregular migration' (Lindquist and Piper 2007: 139), and is a common starting point in Indonesia for the development of measures to prevent it.[7]

The National Police have shown sympathy for the approach adopted by the Ministry of Manpower. Former Chief of the National Police, Bambang Hendarso Danuri (2008), in a question and answer session with lawmakers in the lead up to his appointment, explains that illegal recruitment practices are often the first step into exploitative circumstances overseas. He argues that more enforcement in this area should help to prevent trafficking, probably based on his experience serving as Head of the Provincial Police in North Sumatra, which is a popular transit site for Malaysia-bound migrant workers from neighbouring provinces and islands deeper within Indonesian territory. The TIP Reports are critical of attempts to prevent trafficking that 'fail to distinguish illegal migration from trafficking' (US Department of State 2005: 12). But a senior police officer posted in the Indonesian Embassy in Malaysia claims that the concern should only apply in destination countries, where victims of trafficking could end up being treated as unlawful migrants. By contrast, he suggests that prevention efforts that conflate the two categories in sending countries can prevent both trafficking in persons and illegal labour migration (Interview with Police Attaché in Kuala Lumpur, 23 June 2010).

The National Police signed a memorandum of cooperation with the Ministry of Manpower in 2007 in which they agreed to lend law enforcement tools to thwart deployments that do not 'meet the administrative, documentary and procedural requirements' of the recruitment law (Departemen Tenaga Kerja dan Transmigrasi and Kepolisian Negara Republik Indonesia 2007: 6). Under this arrangement, the police should coordinate with the Ministry in order to determine which law best applies (Departemen Tenaga Kerja dan Transmigrasi and Kepolisian Negara Republik Indonesia 2007: 7(1)). Recruiters who by-pass the official system, particularly those without licences from the Ministry of Manpower, are generally charged under the anti-trafficking law. The Ministry recommends this course of action partly because the maximum system of fines and imprisonment is more severe for trafficking than for non-procedural recruitment. Moreover, the Ministry does not have mechanisms with which to level internal sanctions against unlicensed recruiters, who by definition operate outside the labour export programme and are beyond the coercive reach of its apparatus.

But Ministry of Manpower staff identify the National Police as a major obstacle to the application of Law No. 39/2004 on the Placement and Protection of Indonesian Workers Overseas to licensed agents and choose not to involve them in many investigations. Law No. 8/1981 on the Procedure of Criminal Law requires officials to report evidence of crime, but allows investigations to be carried out internally with the aid of civil servant investigators (Penyidik Pegawai Nasional Sipil) (Articles 1(1), 6 and 108(3)). Police argue that the mechanism allows public institutions to cut them out of the investigation process altogether (Interview with Police Attaché in Kuala Lumpur, 23 June 2010). Instead, the Ministry of Manpower prefers to use a system of administrative sanctions, including warning letters, moratoria on the right to deploy workers and the revocation of recruitment licences (PER-05/MEN/III/2005, Article 3(1a-c)), to address evidence of illegality that involves licensed recruiters. Officials in the Ministry of Manpower boast that these sanctions make it possible to reprimand agents that the legal system fails to convict because of inadequate evidence or because police, public prosecutors and judges have been paid off.[8] When asked to give input on the necessity of an anti-trafficking law, for example, the Director-General for the Placement and Protection of Overseas Indonesian Workers argued that their system of sanctions was an adequate method with which to discipline errant recruiters (Dewan Perwakilan Rakyat 2006c: 601–2). However, licensed agents and their associations often accuse the Ministry of inconsistent and unpredictable behaviour (Interview with the General-Secretary of the Association of Indonesian Manpower Suppliers, 13 October 2009).

Responding to trafficking overseas

While anti-trafficking laws passed in Indonesia attempt to deal with situations that occur in other countries, they are of little practical use to embassy staff abroad. The Ministry of Foreign Affairs is responsible for guiding Indonesian embassies in their responses to trafficking and holds technical coordination meetings in which officials explain the procedure for handling cases of trafficking to consular staff. According to Ministry protocol, embassies should make use of host state mechanisms when victims and perpetrators fall outside the jurisdiction of Indonesian law enforcement institutions, and should report cases where traffickers are located in Indonesia to the Ministry of Foreign Affairs for follow-up at home. Moreover, the Ministry forbids missions to use any criteria other than citizenship in deciding how to handle trafficking cases involving their citizens (Departemen Luar Negeri 2009: slide 9-10).

In practice, systems for handling trafficking cases in embassies are decidedly more varied. In countries with large communities of blue collar and informal sector migrant workers, Indonesian missions operate a dual system for providing services to that group and to other citizens. In Kuala Lumpur, for example, Indonesians involved in crime but who are not migrant workers meet directly with the Police Attaché who then liaises with host state law enforcement institutions. By contrast, migrant workers must first undergo an interview in the Labour Section, where it is determined whether or not they have gone through the formal labour migration system. All cases involving sex workers and children are immediately referred to the Police Attaché, but the discretion to decide how the vast majority of cases are handled rests with the Labour Attaché (Interview with Labour Attaché, 21 December 2009). The embassies in Hong Kong and Singapore have their own particular versions of this system.

Variance in these procedures is partly due to the fact that it is individual mission staff who ultimately decide how best to organize authority in the institution. Ambassadors and Consuls-General have a mandate to decide the role and responsibilities of all consular staff. Missions should avoid partisan behaviour when they do so, but institutional affiliations at home play an influential role in deciding whose interests are prioritized. A case in point is the assignment of jurisdiction over trafficking cases to a career policeman by the Ambassador to Malaysia. Tan Sri Da'i Bachtiar was partly motivated by the criminalization of trafficking in 2007, but equally influential was the fact that he is a former Chief of the National Police. As a result, the police in Indonesia have the final say on how the state responds to trafficking in Malaysia. In another example, the Ambassador supported the Labour Attaché's request for authority to perform functions that comprise part of the Ministry of Manpower's labour migration programme, such as evaluating local agents and endorsing job orders. Labour Attachés in other countries view the posting to Malaysia with envy because they have not had such success with their heads of mission. The missions in Hong Kong and Singapore are generally headed by officials from the Ministry of Foreign Affairs, who appoint fellow Foreign Affairs officials to perform those functions. In these locations, this particular division of labour has resulted in protracted conflicts between Manpower and Foreign Affairs officials as they compete with each other for authority to administer the programme, a situation Sim and Wee (2009: 180) observe can even arise between missions in different countries.

The effectiveness of embassies' responses to trafficking depends on the extent to which embassy staff are integrated into the bureaucracy at home. The Ministry of Foreign Affairs appoints bureaucrats from a range of departments to staff its embassies and consulates in order to ensure that the mission performs functions of the state, but also have someone who can 'speak the same language' as their home institutions (Interview with Consulate-General in Hong Kong, 24 February 2008). In some cases, the delegation of functions is related directly to expertise. In Singapore, for example, the Labour Attaché was required to develop a system for managing the accreditation of local agents and, for a period, to ensure that Indonesian agents' paperwork was in order before requests for endorsements were made to the Ministry of Foreign Affairs official with the authority to do so. She was given these tasks because she was assumed to be knowledgeable of the standards set by the Ministry of Manpower (Interview with Labour Attaché, 31 December 2009). But embassies also make use of the institutional ties that staff bring with them because their informal links with bureaucrats in Jakarta often expedite the processing of requests. For example, the Police Attaché in Kuala Lumpur claims to use his seniority in the National Police to put pressure on junior officers at home to prioritize the investigations of cases that he reports (Interview with Police Attaché in Kuala Lumpur, 23 June 2010).

The character of mission responses to trafficking can also depend on the choices of individual officials. The 2008–2010 Police Attaché in Malaysia spent most of his time investigating trafficking cases despite pressure from Jakarta to concentrate on narcotics and terrorism. He did so in part because of the prevalence of trafficking but also because of his belief that the crime should be his major priority, since it affects such a large number of Indonesian citizens in the country. The Police Section deals with 'walk-ins', but also monitors the media for reports of possible victims which typically involved children or women who claim to have been coerced into sex work.[9] The Police Attaché claims that these cases represent only a small fraction of trafficking. Invisible victims of trafficking, he says, are generally men employed on construction sites and plantations without work permits. Based on this belief, he began surveying building sites in the city as part of an embassy-wide effort to monitor the labour rights of irregular workers in response to reports that construction companies had started calling in Malaysian immigration authorities to arrest undocumented migrants in order to avoid paying their wages. However, undocumented workers have warned the Police Attaché not to interfere because the presence of embassy staff unsettles site managers, which they feared could compromise their employment opportunities (Interview with Police Attaché, 23 June 2010). This case demonstrates that institutional motivation to pursue human trafficking can depend on the personal interpretation and drive of the officials in charge. The discussion that follows shows how the Labour Attaché in another Indonesian embassy in the region uses discretion when handling cases of migrant workers and 'victims of trafficking'.

A Labour Attaché's dilemma

As in other countries with large populations of programme-deployed migrant labour, Indonesian domestic workers in Singapore must report to the Labour Section before applying for an extension of their travel documents. The applicant is required to sign a standard employment contract in an interview that must also be attended by her employer. The contract was designed by the Labour Attaché, who lobbied the Ambassador to include it as part of the process to extend passports for domestic workers because many of their labour rights are not regulated by host laws. Technical staff hired for the specific purpose to assist in the Labour Section are required to ensure that employers rather than agents attend the interview, and that they agree to the minimum wage set by the Indonesian Government. Migrant workers are also asked to confirm their names and dates of birth. These steps must be followed before the Immigration Section will accept an application for passport renewal. Most cases are handled by technical staff and are passed to the Labour Attaché for a signature. When irregularities arise, applicants are referred to the Labour Attaché, who then decides on the best way to deal with the case. In most instances where migrant workers are found to be using counterfeit or misappropriated passports, the Labour Attaché chooses not to report the case to law enforcement. Rather, the passports are confiscated and the bearers issued with limited validity travel documents which should force them to return to Indonesia where they can recommence the migration process.

The Labour Attaché claims that the interview process turns up at least two clear cases of trafficking each month, mostly involving females aged between 14 and 16 who have been recruited into employment as domestic workers on passports that overstate their ages. Identification of such cases is not always straightforward because underage migrants may look older than they really are and because they work hard to conceal their true age. During our interview, the Labour Attaché presented a binder full of such cases, pointing to the most recent one which involved an individual holding a passport stating that she was 23, but who was later found to be only 14 years and 9 months old. The discrepancy was uncovered when the Labour Attaché probed deeper into the girl's education history, asking when she started and finished primary school. Employers typically claim that they had no idea that their workers were children, and in private interviews argue that they are not responsible for recruitment and documentation processes carried out by local agents and their partners in Indonesia. Migrants themselves generally assert that they consented to the falsification of documents in Indonesia because they needed the work to support their families. Regardless, the Labour Attaché generally reports such cases to authorities in Indonesia, recognizing that it is often parents and not the children themselves who give consent.

The Labour Attaché has corresponded with the Ministry of Foreign Affairs, the Criminal Investigation Section of the National Police, the National Board for the Placement and Protection of Overseas Indonesian Workers, the Ministry of Women's Empowerment and the Ministry of Manpower in Jakarta about such cases. She provides information about the worker's identity, a brief description of her story, the articles of the national recruitment law which have been contravened and the name of the agent in Indonesia who coordinated the migration process. The Ministry of Manpower is the only state body which responds with any regularity to these reports partly because, unlike many of the other institutions, it can discipline recruiters. The responsiveness of the Ministry is also the outcome of formal and informal arrangements whereby the National Police defer authority to civil servant investigators within the Ministry in the first instance. These bureaucrats establish whether there is enough evidence to pursue legal sanctions or if the Ministry's administrative sanctions should be applied instead. The immediacy of the effect of these sanctions on the ability of agents to operate legally in Indonesia makes them more willing to comply with the rulings of the Ministry – and, by extension, with the Labour Attachés in Indonesia's embassies. For this reason, the Labour Attaché addresses all correspondence on illegality involving recruitment agents in Indonesia to the Ministry of Manpower, notifying other state institutions with a carbon copy.

But the Labour Attaché does not always report agents through official channels. In some cases, agents may be instructed to report directly to the Ministry of Manpower. In such cases, the Labour Attaché corresponds privately with colleagues in Indonesia to brief them on the case and thereby ensure that it is handled within the Ministry, a process which avoids involving the police. In her view, the police are not always best placed to address recruitment agents' illegal practices, as agents confess that police officers in the Criminal Investigation Section often accept bribes in exchange for dropping charges. Agents complain that they are often the target of extortion by police officers who threaten to push for formal investigations into their cases. Such investigations are acknowledged to lead to more extortion and possibly fines and imprisonment. Mistrusting the police, the Labour Attaché personally conducts preliminary investigations instead, taking note of the agents' version of events, and then making a decision about how best to report the case to colleagues in Indonesia for further action.

On some occasions, the Labour Attaché chooses not to respond to the inclusion of false data in migrant workers' travel documents at all. While she was much more consistent in the reporting of recruiters who transgressed the minimum age requirement for deployment when first posted, she started to make exceptions especially after agents complained that it was difficult to find suitable recruits. For example, she discovered that recruits sometimes cooperated with agents and commission-seeking fieldworkers to obtain state documents that overstated their age. Moreover, some migrants claimed to have approached agents with full sets of already modified papers, arguing that they chose to use those documents because barriers to overseas employment were too high. For the Labour Attaché, stories about the lack of employment opportunities at home eventually tipped the scale in favour of ignoring some transgressions. On the basis of these encounters, she decided to turn a blind eye to the overstating of migrants' ages when they were over the age of 18 and had the maturity to deal with the challenges of working in Singapore. She also instituted a 'two-strikes-and-you're-out' system for cases that involved women below the age of 18, giving agents a warning for the first transgression and reporting them for any subsequent violation.

The Labour Attaché also chooses to ignore evidence that passports did not contain true names. It is common for migrant workers who have formerly worked in Saudi Arabia to hold such documents because recruitment agents change the names of recruits in order to comply with Saudi immigration law, which requires visa applicants to have more than one name. Intending migrant workers with only one name tend to add their father's name as surnames joined by the Arabic *bin* (son of) or *binti* (daughter of). But agents may also change recruits' identities to avoid detection by authorities. The Labour Attaché claims to have reported a few instances that came to her attention. But after informal discussions with colleagues affiliated with the Directorate-General of Immigration about why it is difficult to guarantee the integrity of migrant workers' passports and interaction with the Police Attaché in another mission about the fact that the Criminal Investigation Section of the National Police prioritized inquests into other areas of illegality, she began to see her efforts to identify and report false names in passports to be an unwise use of her time.

The Labour Attaché found that a range of factors contribute to the prevalence of 'real but fake' documents held by Indonesian domestic workers (see also Ford and Lyons 2011). In her view, responding to every case that came to light would consume a sizeable proportion of already limited resources, although she notes that doctored identities can create problems for migrant workers in host settings. She also observed with irony that destination countries set high minimum age requirements but then set things 'right' for cases of manipulated data that come to their attention. The Labour Attaché explained that it was clear to all that when destination countries propose higher criteria that the end result would be greater demand for 'real but fake' documents in Indonesia because the policy did not address supply and demand issues in the labour market. In other words, she viewed the issue to be less a matter of individual cases and more that of systemic failure.

As these courses of action suggest, this particular Labour Attaché views the falsification of names and ages in state documents to be an administrative problem and not a form of human trafficking. She adopts a very different approach to cases of migrant workers who come to the embassy claiming that their husbands or fathers put pressure on them to register for overseas employment, and that their agents then ignored their requests to go home. Women recruits are denied the right to leave agents' training centres after they have begun the pre-departure process (Killias 2010; Lindquist 2010). In part, agents prevent them from doing so because they have given these women financial inducements in the form of 'pocket money' (*uang saku*) to sign up (Palmer 2010). The Labour Attaché argues that it is these kinds of practices that should be dealt with as trafficking because, unlike the falsification of identities, the intention to exploit is clear and the result-ant violation of human rights predictable.

The Labour Attaché's authority to handle cases involving migrant workers has not been consistent over the entire period of her posting to the embassy. At the outset, she was not permitted to inspect job orders but later succeeded in convinc-ing the relevant Foreign Affairs official to let her help ensure that the requests met government criteria before they were processed. In the process, she uncovered evidence that job orders she rejected had been subsequently endorsed. In response, she set up a shadow system to monitor the system's outcomes, and informally reported the data to the Director for Placements in the Ministry of Manpower in Jakarta so that officials there could vet defective paperwork. She also found, however, that the Ministry of Manpower sometimes issued recruitment permis-sion without a job order endorsed by the Embassy. After confronting both sets of officials with evidence, she was cut out of all processes that might bring her in contact with irregularities. The Ambassador chose to put exclusive control of those processes in the hands of a trusted Foreign Affairs official instead. Whatever the motivation for the reorganization of authority within the embassy, it is clear that the handling of migrant and trafficking cases will be subject to a new, highly personalized, discretionary regime.

Conclusion: discretion, illegality and trafficking

Lawmakers have the power to introduce a definition of trafficking into the state's legal framework for the purpose of identifying a crime, but bureaucrats decide the parameters of cases for which that definition is employed. Like this Labour Attaché, many government officials in Indonesia have reservations about treating migrant workers as victims of trafficking, even when they meet the legal require-ments of the anti-trafficking law. In their view, illegal acts under Indonesian law are indeed responsible for some of the trafficking-like conditions in which migrant workers find themselves when they cross international borders for work. However, this group of bureaucrats rejects the push to treat these conditions as evidence of trafficking because their institutional and personal knowledge indicates that they are a result of factors more varied and complex than coercion or the intention to exploit. Officials use this logic when deciding how to respond. The Singapore case highlights some of the considerations, demonstrating that this use of discre-tion can in fact lead to trafficking-like practices on the part of the state.

The actions of the Labour Attaché also demonstrate that government officials may ignore illegality for reasons other than corruption. In the case of age limits on migration, she believed that the law sets standards for what type of migration *should* take place while ignoring the reality of who actually *wants* to migrate. The official logic that informs the push for higher age and education limits is that older and more educated migrants are more mature and therefore more capable of dealing with issues such as the non-payment of wages and abuse. Initially, Indonesian law required citizens wanting to work in the informal sector overseas to be at least 21 years of age and to have attained at least a junior high school education. These requirements were challenged in the Constitutional Court, where returned migrant workers and an association of recruitment agents argued that the high limits were unconstitutional. The article that stipulated the minimum level of education was declared void because it had no 'justifying ground (*rechtsvaardingsgrond*)'.[10] But the age limit remained at 21 years because the Ministry of Manpower 'objectively and reasonably justified' the law with statistics that showed a decrease in the proportion of sexual harassment cases involving migrant workers returning from the Middle East since it had been implemented.[11] In the development of these standards, however, lawmakers and policy-makers did not sufficiently recognize the ease with which 'real but fake' documents can be obtained or the fact that the presence of fake documents can be actively ignored, as in the case of this particular Labour Attaché, where their bearers had successful migration experiences.

It is clear, too, from this example that government officials apply the law unevenly, ignoring regulations which they believe to be flawed.[12] In some cases, bureaucrats may view some forms of illegality to be a low priority. The legal concept used to describe such decisions is *de minimis non curat praetor*, meaning that government officials are not required to concern themselves with trifles. A parallel concept exists in regard to law enforcement (*de minimis non curat lex*) to protect the legal system from being overloaded with cases that involve trivial transgressions of the law.[13] These two concepts provide the legal basis on which employees of the state make decisions about whether to respond to – or disregard – illegality. Typically, they are invoked in relation to technical violations of the law for which consequences are considered insufficient cause for action. In the case of passports that contain false data, the Labour Attaché decided that there was no need for action where the data had not resulted in negative consequences for the document bearers. Instead, she prioritized the signing of employment contracts as part of the passport extension process to improve the quality of labour rights for Indonesian domestic workers.

Officials may also disregard instances of illegality that they consider to be systemic. The sheer number of workers who have migrated through the state programme with passports containing false names and dates of birth is evidence that Indonesian systems and processes for detecting irregularities in applications for travel documents are ineffective. Labour Attachés are only too aware of this problem. One described his response as being like a pendulum that swings from frustration at one extreme to apathy at the other. On the one hand, he was concerned that the systems and processes which guarantee the integrity of state documents were corrupted. On the other hand, he was reluctant to act on an inaccurate passport because doing so almost always disadvantaged migrants but resulted in little change in the way things are done in Indonesia (Interview with Labour Attaché in Kuala Lumpur, 4 August 2009). In short, he questioned whether it was fair that citizens should have to pay the price for the state's inability to manage its affairs.

On a day-to-day basis, these considerations inform the decision-making processes of Labour Attachés confronted with false data in passports. They clearly have the authority to initiate legal proceedings. However, they may choose not to do so. Labour Attachés ignore some forms of illegality partly because their location overseas means that they lack access to the full range of law enforcement mechanisms available in Indonesia. They are also swayed by their personal understandings of the complexities involved in establishing guilt. Another major consideration is the fact that the passport bearer is within the borders of another country, which has issued documents such as work permits and identity cards based on the data recorded in migrants' travel documents. If the embassy were to issue passports containing new data, migrants would have to undergo complicated processes to change their identity or might even lose the right to work. Confiscating documents and forcing migrants to return home poses another dilemma because it deprives citizens of much-needed work. It also raises ethical questions about whether it is fair to do so when it is well known that the migration process can be lengthy and costly. These pragmatic and well-meaning approaches represent at least one way in which the state becomes implicated in what at least look like trafficking-like practices. At the same time, as demonstrated here, ignoring evidence of illegality may be the best possible decision for all.

Notes

1 Between 2008 and 2011, I interviewed Labour Attachés in Hong Kong, Kuala Lumpur and Singapore. A Consul-General, an Immigration Attaché and a Police Attaché also participated in the research project. In Indonesia, senior officials from the Ministry of Manpower, National Board for the Placement and Protection of Overseas Indonesian Workers, Ministry of Internal Affairs, Ministry for Women's Empowerment, and bureaucrats in provincial and district level state institutions shared opinions and data. Some officials asked for their anonymity to be guaranteed. I treat such data by referring to state body affiliations without specifying positions, and to positions without providing information about the location.

2 Other international organizations also played a role in this process. See Ford and Lyons in this volume.

3 Mietzner (2008: 246) notes that senior bureaucrats also make payments to lawmakers to 'avoid long-winded negotiations with parliament'.

4 An IOM employee privately expressed astonishment at this assertion because membership dues are very low. IOM staff are more inclined to believe that the resistance of the state was partly in protest against the organization's reintegration activities concerning Free Aceh Movement fighters, which although sanctioned by a cooperation agreement, were deemed to be partisan.

5 The draft defined trafficking as a process that is carried out 'for the purpose to exploit or which results in a person being exploited' (Dewan Perwakilan Rakyat 2005b: Article 30), whereas Article 1 of Law No. 21/2007 defines trafficking as a process that is carried out 'for the purpose of exploitation or which causes a person to be exploited'.

6 For example, the Immigration Office in Entikong refused a passport application after establishing that only a few weeks earlier the applicant was issued with a passport in a different name. In response, officials in the District Civil Administration Office which issued the applicant's new identity threatened to burn down the immigration office for interfering in what is understood to be a locally accepted practice. The District Chief intervened by compelling the Immigration Office to repair relations in line with customary law which in this case was by providing a gift of pigs to officials in the District Civil Administration Office (Dewan Perwakilan Rakyat 2006b: 647).

7 See Ford and Lyons in this volume for a detailed discussion of this issue.

8 See Lindsey and Butt (2011) for an account of the 'judicial mafia' in Indonesia.

9 The list of trafficked persons who were registered with the Police Attaché in 2009 is on file with the author.

10 See Constitutional Court Decision 019/PUU-III/2005 of 28 March 2006: 40.

11 See the Hearing Minutes 028/PUU-IV/2006, 029/PUU-IV/2006 of 15 February 2007: 23–27 and the Constitutional Court Decision for 028/PUU-IV/2006 and 029/PUU-IV/2006 of 11 April 2007: 25.

12 Lindsey and Butt (2011) have commented on this issue more broadly.

13 See Veech and Moon (1947) for an extended discussion of these legal maxims.

References

Amnesty International (2010) *A Blow to Humanity: Torture by Judicial Caning in Malaysia*, London: Amnesty International.

Anechiarico, F. and Jacobs, J. (1996) *The Pursuit of Absolute Integrity: How Corruption Control Makes Government Ineffective*, Chicago, IL: University of Chicago Press.

Badan Nasional Penempatan dan Perlindungan Tenaga Kerja Indonesia (2008) 'Pemberitahuan', 16 June, Jakarta: Govenment of Indonesia.

Danuri, B. H. (2008) *Akselerasi Transformasi Polisi Menuju Polri yang Mandiri, Profesional dan Dipercaya Rakyat*, 22 September, Jakarta: Komisi Kepolisian Indonesia.

Departemen Luar Negeri (2005) 'Pernyataan pers tahunan', 19 January, Jakarta: Government of Indonesia.

—— (2009) *Kebijakan dan Program Departemen Luar Negeri dalam Pencegahan dan Penanggulangan TPPO*, 16–17 October, Jakarta: Government of Indonesia.

Departemen Tenaga Kerja dan Transmigrasi and Kepolisian Negara Republik Indonesia (2007) *Penegakan Hukum dalam Rangka Penempatan dan Perlindungan Tenaga Kerja Indonesia di Luar Negeri*, KEP.103/Men/II/2007 and B/306/II/2007, Jakarta: Government of Indonesia.

Dewan Perwakilan Rakyat (2005a) *Penyampaan [sic] Usul Inisiatif Rancangan Undang-Undang tentang Pemberantasan Tindak Pidana Orang. Pimpinan Komisi VII DPR-RI (Wakil Ketua)*, addressed to Pimpinan Dewan Perwakilan Rakyat Republik Indonesia. TU.OO/153/KOM.VIM/2005. Jakarta, 6 July.

—— (2005b) *Rancangan Undang-Undang Republik Indonesia Nomor . . . . Tahun . . . . . tentang Pemberantasan Tindak Pidana Perdagangan Orang*, Jakarta: Government of Indonesia.

—— (2006a) *Risalah Rapat Panitia Khusus Rancangan Undang-Undang tentang Pemberantasan Tindak Pidana Perdagangan Orang: Rapat Dengar Pendapat Umum*, 1 February, Jakarta: Government of Indonesia.

—— (2006b) *Risalah Rapat Panitia Khusus Rancangan Undang-Undang tentang Pemberantasan Tindak Pidana Perdagangan Orang: Rapat Dengar Pendapat Umum*, 8 March, Jakarta: Government of Indonesia.

—— (2006c) *Risalah Rapat Panitia Khusus Rancangan Undang-Undang tentang Pember-antasan Tindak Pidana Perdagangan Orang: Rapat Dengar Pendapat Umum*, 9 February, Jakarta: Government of Indonesia.

—— (2006d) *Usul DPR mengenai Rancangan Undang-Undang Republik Indonesia tentang Pemberantasan Tindak Pidana Perdagangan Orang. Kepala Dewan Perwakilan Rakyat*, addressed to Presiden Republik Indonesia. RU.02/6063/DPR-RT/2006. Jakarta, 28 July.

Ford, M. and Lyons, L. (2011) 'Travelling the *aspal* route: "Grey" labour migration through an Indonesian border town', in Aspinall, E. and Klinken, G. van (eds) *The State and Illegality in Indonesia*, Leiden: KILTV, pp. 107–22.

Ford, M. and Piper, N. (2007) 'Southern sites of female agency: Informal regimes and female migrant labour resistance in East and Southeast Asia', in Hobson, J. M. and Seabrooke, L. (eds) *Everyday Politics of the World Economy*, Cambridge and New York: Cambridge University Press, pp. 63–79.

Heyman, J. and Smart, A. (1999) 'States and illegal practices: An overview', in Heyman, J. (ed.) *States and Illegal Practices*, Oxford and New York: Berg, pp. 1–24.

IOM (2009) *Guidelines for Law Enforcement and the Protection of Victims of Trafficking in Handling of Trafficking in Persons Cases*, Jakarta: International Organization for Migration Mission in Indonesia with support from the United States Department of State Office to Monitor and Combat Trafficking in Persons.

—— (2010) *Consequences of Trafficking and Policy Responses*, Geneva: International Organization for Migration.

Kementerian Koordinator Bidang Kesejahteraan Rakyat (2007) *Kinerja Tim Koordinasi Pemulangan Tenaga Kerja Indonesia Bermasalah dan Keluarga dari Malaysia (TK-PTKB) Tahun 2007*, December, Jakarta: Government of Indonesia.

—— (2008) *Kinerja Tim Koordinasi Pemulangan Tenaga Kerja Indonesia Bermasalah dan Keluarga dari Malaysia (TK-PTKB) Tahun 2008*, December, Jakarta: Government of Indonesia.

Kementerian Pemberdayaan Perempuan dan Perlindungan Anak (2009) *Tentang Kami*, Jakarta: Government of Indonesia.

Kepolisian Negara Republik Indonesia (2009) *Kikis Percaloan*, Surabaya: Government of Indonesia.

Killias, O. (2010) '"Illegal" migration as resistance: Legality, morality and coercion in Indonesian domestic worker migration to Malaysia', *Asian Journal of Social Science*, 38 (6): 897–914.

Klinken, G. van and Barker, J. (2009) 'Introduction: State in society in Indonesia', in Klinken, G. van and Barker, J. (eds) *State of Authority: The State in Society in Indonesia*, New York: Southeast Asia Program Publications, pp. 1–16.

Lindquist, J. (2010) 'Labour recruitment, circuits of capital and gendered mobility: Reconceptualizing the Indonesian migration industry', *Pacific Affairs*, 83 (1): 115–32.

Lindquist, J. and Piper, N. (2007) 'From HIV prevention to counter-trafficking: Discursive shifts and institutional continuities in South-East Asia', in Lee, M. (ed.) *Human Trafficking*, Cullompton, Devon: Willan Publishing, pp. 138–58.

Lindsey, T. and Butt, S. (2011) 'Judicial mafia: The courts and state illegality in Indonesia', in Aspinall, E. and Klinken, G. van (eds) *The State and Illegality in Indonesia*, Leiden: KILTV, pp. 189–213.

Lyons, L. and Ford, M. (2010) 'Where are your victims?', *International Feminist Journal of Politics*, 12 (2): 255–64.

Mietzner, M. (2008) 'Soldiers, parties and bureaucrats: Illicit fund-raising in contemporary Indonesia', *South East Asia Research*, 16 (2): 225–54.

Naovalitha, T. (2007) *Kompleksitas Mekanisme Penempatan BMP ke Luar Negeri: Beberapa Permasalahan dan Alternatif Solusinya*, Jakarta: World Bank.

Palmer, W. (2010) 'Costly inducements', *Inside Indonesia* 100. Online. Available at http://www.insideindonesia.org (accessed 10 January 2011).

Piper, N. (2005) 'A problem by a different name? A review of research on trafficking in South-East Asia and Oceania', *International Migration*, 43 (1/2): 203–33.

Rose-Ackerman, S. (1999) *Corruption and Government: Causes, Consequences, and Reform*, New York: Cambridge University Press.

Scott, P. G. (1997) 'Assessing determinants of bureaucratic discretion: An experiment in street-level decision making', *Journal of Public Administration Research and Theory*, 7 (1): 35–58.

Sim, A. and Wee, V. (2009) 'Undocumented Indonesian workers in Macau: The outcomes of colluding interests', *Critical Asian Studies*, 41 (1): 165–88.

Swasono, M. H. (2006) 'Menteri Pemberdayaan Perempuan', in Kementerian Koordinator Bidang Kesejahteraan Rakyat and World Bank (eds) *Prosiding: Seminar dan Lokakarya Perlindungan Sosial untuk Buruh Migran Perempuan*, Jakarta: Government of Indonesia and World Bank.

Tremblay, V. J. (1993) 'Consistency between law and its enforcement: The case of mergers', *Antitrust Bulletin*, 38 (Summer): 327–48.

US Department of State (2001) *Trafficking in Persons Report*, Washington, DC: Government of the United States.

—— (2002) *Trafficking in Persons Report*, Washington, DC: Government of the United States.

—— (2003) *Trafficking in Persons Report*, Washington, DC: Government of the United States.

—— (2005) *Trafficking in Persons Report*, Washington, DC: Government of the United States.

—— (2006) *Trafficking in Persons Report*, Washington, DC: Government of the United States.

—— (2007) *Trafficking in Persons Report*, Washington, DC: Government of the United States.

—— (2009) *Trafficking in Persons Report*, Washington, DC: Government of the United States.

Veech, M. L. and Moon, C. L. (1947) 'De minimis non curat lex', *Michigan Law Review*, 45 (5): 537–70.

Index

Printed in Great Britain
by Amazon